MW00625657

DAVID

The Strange Case of Jonathan Pollard
and The Two Decade Battle to Win His Freedom

ELLIOT GOLDENBERG

13-digit ISBN 978-1-939521-18-7

10-digit ISBN 1-9395211-8-1

Elliot Goldenberg is an extraordinarily brilliant writer who has taken a highly controversial topic – the Pollard spy case – and made it once again pertinent while breathing new life into an incredible and compelling story…A page turner, Spy of David is as riveting as the best spy novel as it explores the worlds of government cover-ups, Hollywood deals gone awry, and the ongoing threat of radical Islamic terror. It's a book you won't be able to put down.

Brigitte Gabriel,
Author of Because They Hate; President, ACT for America.org

A remarkably thorough collection of behind-the-scenes information, and a riveting, historically accurate, and up-to-date portrayal of events surrounding what is called "The Pollard Affair," what's presented in this book is first-rate. Goldenberg has done his homework: he's connected all the dots, identified the players, and kept my attention throughout – and I've lived this story. This extraordinary book is a "must read" for anyone interested in the Jonathan Pollard case. Well done!

Carol Pollard, sister of Jonathan Pollard

Elliot Goldenberg has done it again with his masterful retelling and updating of one of the most appalling injustices in American history. Spy of David is a must read for anyone who is concerned about the fate of an American Jew who was unjustly sentenced to life imprisonment after cooperating with the government and being promised a considerably lower sentence. It is also a must read for anyone who cares about the American system of justice which was hijacked in this case by zealots who were prepared to lie and cheat in the name of our government in order to deny basic fairness and due process to Jonathan Pollard. The ends do not justify the means, as this book brilliantly demonstrates.

Alan Dershowitz,
Author of Taking the Stand: My Life in the Law, October 2013

Almost anything you do will be insignificant,
but it is very important that you do it.

Mohandas K. Gandhi

Nice try kid, but it looks like you brought
a knife to a gunfight.

Indiana Jones

CONTENTS

This book is dedicated to my parents, Pearl and Abe Goldenberg, who were far better people than I will ever be.

ACKNOWLEDGEMENTS

Many have contributed to making this book a reality, but I'd like to especially thank Suzanne Migdall; William Northrop; Strategic Media Books publisher Ron Chepesiuk, for daring to take on such a controversial subject; the magnanimous Alan Dershowitz; my literary agent, Eunice Murray; the fearless Brigitte Gabriel; Allen Migdall; Carol Pollard; Dr. Morris Pollard; Dr. Wayne Dyer; my graduate adviser years ago and a lifelong inspiration; staff and volunteers, past and present, at the Jewish Federation of Broward County for all the good work they do; Marie Judd; Dr. Herb Nagasawa; and the late Dr. Robert Keller, who, along with Dr. Nagasawa, should get the Nobel Prize for their medical research.

Spy of David: The Strange Case of Jonathan Pollard and the Two Decade Battle to Win His Freedom is an attempt to shed a bright light over a dark stain on both the American judicial system and our intelligence community, while, at the same time, solve a decades-old puzzle—knowing that, for way too long, the truth surrounding this most gut-wrenching of spy cases has remained hidden, blurred, and obscured.

Among the book's revelations:

- Dennis Ross, the chief American negotiator at the Wye River Accords chaired by President Bill Clinton, admitted that Pollard's freedom was on the table during the talks but that he advised Clinton this was only to be used as a bargaining chip in final negotiations for a Palestinian state—even though Ross personally believed Pollard should have been let out of prison.

- John Daly, the British-born producer of thirteen Oscar-winning movies, including *Platoon*, and box office hits like *Terminator*, wanted to make a feature film based on Elliot Goldenberg's book, *The Hunting Horse*—but Daly claimed his investors were warned to "stand down" by Washington lobbyist and convicted felon Jack Abramoff, who also allegedly conspired to defraud SunCruz casino owner Gus Boulis who was later found murdered in Fort Lauderdale.

- Nevada U.S. Senator Chic Hecht, sitting on a flight to the Bahamas next to motion picture producer Suzanne Migdall—who for years tried to sell a feature film based on the Pollard case—told her that Pollard had done something "so horrible that it could never be made public," and that this was why Pollard remained in prison. Hecht, and many other

Washington policy-makers, erroneously believed that Pollard's spy operation had cost the lives of U.S. moles behind the Iron Curtain.

- Admiral Bobby Inman and Defense Secretary Caspar Weinberger were so angered by Israel's destruction of Iraq's nuclear reactor at Osirak, in 1981, that they decided to cut off much of the intelligence flow to Israel—which set the stage for Pollard's espionage activities. The first information Pollard ever gave the Israelis in fact dealt with satellite overheads of the Osirak raid. Ironically, Israel's first astronaut, Col. Ilan Ramon—one of seven astronauts who perished when the space shuttle Columbia burst into flames—was the youngest of the ten Israeli pilots in that Osirak mission.

- Janet Burrows-Tapia, an executive at the David Wolper Company at Warner Brothers—and the person who was pushing the hardest to get a feature film made on *The Hunting Horse*—was murdered in her Los Angeles home on the day she was scheduled to pitch the project to the Turner Company, also a Warner Brothers affiliate. The killer has never been found.

T WAS A drizzly early evening—torrential rains would come down a few hours later—when I arrived at the building in North Miami where CNN had its local studio. It was Labor Day, September 1, 2003, and Miami was unusually quiet.

Still, national holiday or not, the news had to go on. As for me, I was about to become a small part of a big story.

I had made the nearly hour long ride from my home in Tamarac, a western suburb of Fort Lauderdale, to CNN's Miami office, because I was one of two people booked by the network to do a live interview about the Jonathan Pollard spy case. It was a subject I had already written two books about, and was well into a third. The other guest would be CNN host Wolf Blitzer, who had also written his own book on the case, the well-researched *Territory of Lies*. While I would be speaking via satellite to host Soledad O'Brien from Miami, Wolf would be in studio in New York.

Pollard was once again a hot topic. The following day he was going to be seen in public for the first time in sixteen years, and was scheduled to appear in Washington, D.C., in front of U.S. District Court Judge Thomas Hogan. Pollard's very able attorneys, Eliot Lauer and Jacques Semmelman, were finally going to have the chance to argue the legal merits of continuing with their client's appeal. The two lawyers knew that the session would be procedural in nature, however, and would in no way settle the issue of whether Pollard should be re-sentenced.

But at least the case was again being talked about.

Although buried behind bars, unlike Alexandre Dumas' fictional *Man in the Iron Mask*, Pollard's name, in truth, had never been entirely forgotten. Back in March of 1987, the controversial spy had been convicted on one count of passing classified information to the State of Israel. To many, that made him a Jewish hero. Many more thought of him as a traitor. When it came to Pollard, there was rarely a gray area.

For me, what had always been especially troubling was that Pollard—a former GS-12 level civilian U.S. Naval Intelligence analyst—was the only person in the history of the United States to ever receive a life sentence in prison for committing "friendly espionage" for an American ally. Pollard's supporters demanded to know why.

So did Pollard's attorneys. Among the points they would make was that their client's sentence was not only way too harsh; it also violated the original plea bargain agreement he made with his prosecutors. Another point Lauer and Semmelman would argue was that Pollard's original lead attorney, Richard Hibey, failed to file the paperwork in time that would allow for an appeal. Was that just an oversight? Or was there something more sinister involved?

In addition, Pollard's lawyers wanted to see what was in the secret documents the government filed—redacted portions of the forty-six-page damage assessment report, followed by the so-called "Weinberger Memorandum—that were handed to District Court Judge Aubrey Robinson, in March of 1987, prior to Pollard's sentencing.

One thing was clear: Something about this case was, at the very least, troubling.

As noted attorney Alan Dershowitz wrote in his Foreword to my second book on the Pollard case, *The Hunting Horse*: "As a loyal American I am deeply ashamed of the way my government has handled the Jonathan Pollard spy case. To begin with, our government has broken the plea agreement it made with Pollard. Pollard pleaded guilty, thereby giving up his constitutional right to a trial at which he might well have been acquitted, in exchange for a promise by our government that it would not seek life imprisonment. Then, the government arranged for the secretary of defense, Caspar Weinberger, to submit an affidavit which, in effect, demanded life imprisonment."

Dershowitz called the introduction of that Weinberger memorandum "one of the sneakiest moves I have ever observed in nearly forty years of law practice."

A question I was often asked after *The Hunting Horse* was published was why that title. Actually, Pollard had the epithet "Hunting Horse" given to him by Israeli Military Intelligence (AMAN) officers in 1984. Very few knew the Hunting Horse's true identity; however they did know such a man (or woman) existed. Upon hearing this I felt *The Hunting Horse* would be a good name for my book, mainly because I thought it would be catchy. The idea seemed to work, since, once I had that title, I was also able to get a quality publisher, Prometheus Books. (The official publication date of *The Hunting Horse* was September 2000.)

"Hunting Horse" was in fact a transliteration from the Hebrew, and loosely meant Pollard would "hunt" up information on request and that he was a "horse" for his handlers—an exceptional agent on whose back his handlers rode up the promotional ladder.

He was certainly that and more. Indeed, Winston Churchill's description of Russia in 1939 easily could have been said of Pollard, too: that he was a "riddle, wrapped in a mystery, inside an enigma."

Less than twenty hours before the so-called "Hunting Horse" was scheduled to have his day in court, my own evening got off to a less than auspicious start. It seemed that the television gods were against me when I got to the building where CNN had its office on the first floor, and I found the front door to be locked. When I then tried to use the code to call CNN's office, I got no answer. I began banging on the door, but, still, no one responded. Then, I had a stroke of luck. A Hispanic woman with a young boy, who appeared to be her son, approached me. I asked the woman if she could get me into the building and she said she could. She took out a card—the kind of card you would use to get into a hotel room—and slid it by the doorknob to open the door. Relieved, I thanked her and went inside. A few seconds later, when I turned around, she was gone.

Perhaps, I thought, she was my guardian angel. Then again, perhaps she was the cleaning lady. Whoever she was, if my interview with CNN in any way helped advance Pollard's cause, helped advance my own good fortune, and helped make the case for the State of Israel in the eyes of the world, then this cleaning lady, like some angel, may indeed have been part of a grand cosmic plan.

The day following my appearance on CNN, Pollard appeared before Judge Hogan. The Associated Press reported that Pollard wore a *yarmulke* (skull cap) and a green shirt stamped Arlington County Jail. The AP also reported that he looked both heavier and grayer than the man who stood in the same courthouse, and admitted committing espionage, in 1987.

"Pollard, who stopped cutting his hair in protest over his sentence in the late 1990s, now has a gray-brown beard and shoulder length curly brown hair," reported Carol D. Leonnig in *The Washington Post*. "It was his first appearance in federal court since his conviction."

Pollard nodded hello to his wife, Esther, in the courtroom's front row, then sat with his hands folded. He didn't speak as his lawyers argued that the government should be forced to turn over the secret files that could help his request for clemency. Jewish religious leaders, such as Mordechai Elianu, Israel's former chief rabbi, and other supporters, such as U.S. Rep. Anthony D. Weiner (D-NY), filled several rows in the courtroom, while Pollard's eighty-nine-year-old father, Dr. Morris Pollard, from whom he was estranged, sat in the back.

"Jonathan Pollard is sitting here in court today, and asks only for justice and a fair sentencing, as guaranteed by our Constitution," his attorney Jacques Semmelman said. "He has not had that."

"The government agreed that they would not seek a life sentence, and that's exactly what they did," added his other attorney, Eliot Lauer. "Jonathan Pollard has repeatedly been denied justice."

The *Washington Post* reported that prosecutors nevertheless opposed letting Pollard's attorneys review the government documents, saying the defense team had "brought forward no new information or central flaw in Pollard's conviction or sentencing."

In the past, Pollard's prior attorneys—including Theodore Olson, a former attorney for two presidents: Ronald Reagan and George W. Bush—were also denied access to the secret government documents on Pollard. At the same time, three former presidents—Reagan, George H.W. Bush and Bill Clinton—denied giving Pollard a presidential pardon before leaving office.

I also never got to see the documents in question. As a journalist, I felt I had that right. At the same time, I steadfastly refused to see myself as an "advocate" for this controversial spy, and was certainly not blind to everything he had done, or at least was accused of doing. Still, I wanted this man released from prison. I was convinced that he had suffered enough and that the severity of his punishment was not only unwarranted, but was a classic injustice. His attorney Eliot Lauer described it as "a stain on the American legal process." I agreed.

The bottom line was that a life sentence for an American spying for Israel just didn't make any sense. And if there was more to this, then I wanted to see the fire, not just the smoke.

The late Miami Dolphin and South Florida sports talk show host Jim "Mad Dog" Mandich liked to say about those who incessantly try to pull the wool over our collective eyes: "I put it to my nosy, and it don't smell so rosy."

When it came to the Pollard case, there was a real stench in the air, no doubt in my mind. My purpose, I felt, was to clear the air. Since I was sitting on top of what may have been the story of a lifetime, I also felt that I had a real shot of getting the story on the "silver screen." All I needed, I thought, was a little bit of luck.

So keep your eye on the prize, I continued to tell myself. I knew that a lot of people were counting on me. No matter what—and I repeated the words like a mantra—don't trip up.

Just don't blow it.

CHAPTER ONE

PRELUDE TO WAR

TO PARAPHRASE WINSTON Churchill, a storm was gathering on the horizon. It was January 19, 2003, two days before the birthday of Martin Luther King Jr., the great civil rights leader who preached non-violent protest, and more than thirty-thousand people were marching in Washington D.C. in protest of the war between the United States and Iraq—a war that everyone knew was now sure to come.

The Rev. Jessie Jackson, who as a young man marched beside King, and, on this day was one of the speakers, exhorted the crowd that America should "choose minds over missiles and negotiations over confrontation." It was classic Jessie Jackson: a person who was controversial to say the least, but most would agree never missed an opportunity to espouse his own clear-cut vision of what America should be, and where its priorities should lie. President George W. Bush, who was getting ready for the State of The Union Address he would deliver on January 28, also had a clear-cut vision, one that was quite different. Did the president know something that the so-called "peaceniks" didn't?

While there was some difference of opinion on Capitol Hill over what to do about Iraq, the administration was united in the belief that Iraqi leader Saddam Hussein had to disarm—or had to be forced to disarm. There were the so-called "hawks"—people like Defense Secretary Donald Rumsfeld, Vice President Dick Cheney, Deputy Secretary of Defense Paul Wolfowitz, National Security Advisor Condoleezza Rice (who would later become secretary of state), and advisors like Richard Perle. And there were those portrayed as slightly more "moderate," most notably Secretary of State Colin Powell. On the so-called "Arab street," as *New York Times* columnist Tom Friedman liked to call it, it perhaps all played out like some "good cop, bad cop" routine.

For the president, however, there were no illusions about the potential danger of Iraq, a nation governed by a madman with nuclear aspirations, whose role model was Josef Stalin, and who, allegedly, had a hidden stash of bio-chemical weapons. It was a situation, Bush felt, that couldn't be allowed to fester like an open wound.

George W. Bush, whether right or wrong, was a person steeled by his beliefs. The hyper-smart Bill Clinton was an extremely competent commander-in-chief, but his friend, President Bush, appeared to be a rock-solid man of principle. George W. was in many ways like his father, and those I spoke to, especially those who knew him or worked with him, also admired the first President Bush, or "forty-one" as he liked being called. Among the attributes that made George W. different from his father, though, was that the younger Bush was an unwavering supporter of the State of Israel, something that was not always said about any of the presidents who preceded him—including "forty-one."

Israel, in fact, may have factored into the White House Iraqi policy more than we were being told. While the spin of much of

the world media was that the acquisition of Iraqi oil, the bran-
dishing of American power, and even a "crusade" against Islam,
were the "real" reasons Saddam had been targeted, I suspected
something else. I wondered if it was the fear of Iraq someday
using its bio-chemical weapons against Israel—and a resulting
Israeli nuclear response—that was, behind closed doors at least, a
worst case scenario that was always on the minds of those closest
to the president.

That being said, everyone outside of the most radical in the
Muslim world, and those misguided Arabs who envisioned
Saddam as some kind of modern day Saladin, saw Saddam as
a menace. As for other Arab leaders, Marc Ginsberg, appointed
by Clinton as U.S. ambassador to Morocco, personally told me
he didn't know of any of these men who wanted to see Saddam
remain in power. Notwithstanding, many believed the American
president still hadn't made a strong enough case about the "clear
and present" danger of Saddam—at least to the satisfaction of
the American public, and most of Europe.

So during his 2003 State of the Union address the poker-
playing George W. Bush showed some of his cards. Iraq, he said,
could not account for more than twenty-five thousand liters of
anthrax, more than thirty-eight thousand liters of botulinum
toxin and perhaps as much as five hundred tons of sarin and other chemical agents. All told, what Saddam still hadn't revealed
to U.N. and American inspectors could allegedly kill millions of
people. According to Bush, U.S. intelligence reports stated, also,
that Saddam had "upwards of thirty thousand munitions capable
of delivering chemical agents," not to mention his attempt to
acquire "significant quantities of uranium from Africa" to be used
for nuclear weapons—an erroneous point that would later come
back to haunt the president.

"Our intelligence sources tell us that he has also attempted to purchase high-strength aluminum tubes suitable for nuclear weapons production," Bush said bluntly. "Saddam Hussein has not credibly explained these activities." To the president, whatever Saddam was making, whatever he was hiding, one day he would be using.

Defense Secretary Rumsfeld, reacting to the growing anti-war backlash, had already set the stage for the president, arguing that, in word and deed, Iraq had shown it was willing to strike both the U.S. and its allies—including Israel. "No living dictator has shown the deadly combination of capability and intent," Rumsfeld said two weeks earlier, during a January 2003 address to the Reserve Officers Association. Rumsfeld, at the time, spoke matter-of-factly about Iraq's aggression against its neighbors, its pursuit of weapons of mass destruction, its use of WMDs, and its support of terrorism.

Then, on February 5, 2003, Colin Powell, following up Bush's State of the Union with his own address to the United Nations, made his well-received case against Saddam Hussein. The articulate Powell masterfully revealed what he termed "an accumulation of facts and disturbing patterns of behavior" by the Iraqi regime, indicating Iraq's failure to comply with the U.N. resolution that Baghdad disarm. Tape recordings, satellite photographs, and informant statements were shown, one after another, constituting what the secretary of state called "irrefutable and undeniable evidence" that the Iraqi leader was concealing his weapons of mass destruction.

At the same time, however, there were rumblings in the media about how, two decades earlier, the United States may have helped create this monster in the first place. Did we know the extent of Saddam's bio-chemical weapons programs because *we* were the ones who, initially, had armed him? If so, was this done with the goal in mind of halting the spread of Islamic fundamentalism by having a person in place, even more ruthless than the mullahs, to do our bidding for us while keeping the fundamentalists at bay?

Then, as American troops were massing in the Persian Gulf and Saddam was being given his "last chance" by the president to disarm, a story officially broke that had long been rumored to be true. According to declassified U.S. documents that had just been published by the National Security Archives at George Washington University, the Reagan White House was well aware of Iraq's willingness to use chemical weapons when then-special envoy Donald Rumsfeld met with Saddam, in 1984, with the idea of re-establishing diplomatic ties. As Rafael Lorente noted in the *Ft. Lauderdale Sun-Sentinel*: "Even after complaining to the Iraqis about chemical weapons attacks, the United States embraced Baghdad, and helped Iraq in its war against Iran."

It was the threat of Saddam that also led to the exploits of spy Jonathan Pollard, who, according to his copious notes that were passed on to me, exposed to the Israelis our ill-advised arming of the Iraqis with the technologies to create biological and chemical weapons, if not giving them the actual weapons themselves.

Back in 1981, just one year before then-CIA director William Casey went to Iraq, arguably to begin our secret relationship with Saddam Hussein—and three years before Rumsfeld was sent there—Israeli pilots, in a daring raid, demolished Iraq's Osirak nuclear facility near Baghdad. It was an act that drew a condemnation from some members of the Reagan administration, including Defense Secretary Caspar Weinberger, and the Deputy Director of the CIA, Adm. Bobby Inman, but silent approval from others, including Casey and President Reagan himself.

As for Pollard, the first information he ever gave the Israelis dealt with satellite overheads of the Osirak raid. The person he handed those overheads to was Israeli Col. Avi Sella, the man who helped plan that operation, and would become Pollard's de-facto "handler." Ironically, Israel's first astronaut, forty-eight year old Col. Ilan Ramon—one of seven astronauts who perished when the space shuttle Columbia burst into flames just four days after President Bush delivered his State of the Union Address—was the youngest of the ten Israeli pilots in that Osirak mission.

***

Before he left his hotel room to go to Temple Beth Israel, in Sunrise, Florida, for a February 2, 2003 press conference—to be followed by a reception and speaking engagement co-hosted by the synagogue and the Jewish Federation of Broward County—former Israeli Prime Minister Ehud Barak had a difficult phone call to make.

"Just an hour ago I spoke to Col. Ramon's father," Barak would later tell the assembled media, his voice slightly cracking. "I personally offered my condolences."

It was Barak, when he was Israel's Army Chief of Staff, who had personally made his friend, Ramon, a colonel. Barak referred to Ramon as an air force "top gun" and a "highly impressive, intelligent individual." He also mentioned that Ramon was one of the Israeli pilots who flew their F-16s in extremely close formation, so as to appear on radar to be a single passenger jet, before bombing and leveling the Osirak nuclear reactor.

"The whole world, including the Reagan administration, condemned Israel at the time," Barak said, as the TV cameras rolled and the reporters and journalists who were there took notes. "If we were not ready to execute this operation, it is probable that by 1991, during the first Gulf War, we would have been dealing with a nuclear Iraq."

Barak, who fully backed President George W. Bush in his resolve to rid Iraq, and the world, of Saddam Hussein, added:

"Israelis understand how deeply intertwined are the activities of rogue dictators and world terror."

The former prime minister then referred to the upcoming war as "the first world war of the twenty-first century," and felt the American-led forces would have little trouble with any Iraqi resistance. "The American force is so superior [to Iraq's] that the war will be decidedly won," Barak said. "And it won't take months, but weeks."

Barak finished his remarks by speculating on what would happen if Israel was drawn into the conflict and was attacked by the Iraqis with bio-chemical weapons. He left little doubt that Saddam Hussein would be making a grave tactical error.

"We will have to respond," the former prime minister said with strong emphasis, "very severely."

I was standing perhaps a foot or two away from Barak after he finished speaking in front of the TV cameras. I was among a small group of journalists who still had some additional questions we wanted to ask him. I specifically wanted to know what Barak meant by Israel responding "very severely." I was also going to ask him if during the first Gulf War—as I had been led to believe—Israel's nuclear-armed Jericho missiles were in their launch mode, ready to be used at a moment's notice if the Scuds that landed in Tel Aviv were loaded with poison gas.

I had already been told the answer to that question by a high-level source in Israeli intelligence, but I wanted to hear it from a former prime minister who had been an army chief of staff.

Just before I could ask him, Ehud Barak was whisked out of the room.

CHAPTER TWO

WINKS AND NODS

MANY SHARED PRESIDENT George W. Bush's belief that Saddam Hussein, his sons Odai and Qusai, and the whole rotten regime in Iraq that had murdered tens of thousands of people, had to be eliminated. Many others were asking, though, "At what price?"

One thing I was sure of: Iraq *did* have weapons of mass destruction. At the very least, Saddam's regime had possessed these weapons in the past. But, in the final analysis, it wouldn't have mattered. During the war, the "shock and awe" of the American air and land campaign so completely overwhelmed whatever resistance Saddam and his advisors might have been planning, there may never have been an opportunity to use those outlawed weapons, if, in fact, Saddam still had them. After the war with the Iraqi military—which, as Ehud Barak had predicted, would end quickly—people were then asking: "If the weapons of mass destruction existed, where are they?"

During a post-war joint press conference with Bush in Washington, British Prime Minister Tony Blair addressed the issue.

Using seemingly faultless logic, Blair stated that when Saddam first kicked the inspectors out of his country, he had to have weapons of mass destruction "or else why kick the inspectors out?" And once the inspectors were gone, Blair opined, "would Saddam Hussein then get rid of the weapons of mass destruction on his own, without having to worry about the inspectors even being there? I think not."

Still, after stepping down as the U.S. special advisor who led the hunt for weapons of mass destruction in Iraq, David Kaye made headlines in January of 2004 when he said about Saddam still having those weapons: "I don't think they existed."

Questions were being raised, especially by Democrats. Did the president lie about Saddam's weapons of mass destruction to the American public? Was the intelligence faulty, or was this a deliberate deception?

Of course, if Bush was himself duped about the extent of Saddam's weapons program, so were others—including former President Bill Clinton.

"One way or the other, we are determined to deny Iraq the capability to develop weapons of mass destruction and the missiles to deliver them," said Clinton on February 4, 1998. Two weeks later, Clinton said: "If Saddam rejects peace and we have to use force, our purpose is clear. We want to seriously diminish the threat posed by Iraq's weapons of mass destruction program."

A day later, Secretary of State Madeline Albright added: "Iraq is a long way from [the United States], but what happens there matters a great deal here. For the risks that leaders of a rogue state will use nuclear, chemical or biological weapons against our allies is the greatest security threat we face."

Then, on December 5, 2001—less than two months following the terrorist attacks of September 11—a letter to President Bush stated: "There is no doubt that Saddam Hussein has invigorated his weapons programs. Reports indicate that biological, chemical and nuclear programs continue apace and may be back to pre-Gulf War status. In addition, Saddam continues to redefine delivery systems and is doubtless using the cover of a licit missile program to develop long range missiles that will threaten the United States and our allies." Among the signatories of that letter was Sen. Bob Graham (D-FL), who, at the time, was the chair of the Senate Intelligence Committee and would later make a run for the Democratic nomination for the presidency.

On September 23, 2002, former vice president and Democratic presidential nominee Al Gore had this to say: "We know [Saddam Hussein] has stored secret supplies of biological and chemical weapons throughout his country."

Four days later, Sen. Ted Kennedy (D-MA) stated: "We have known for many years that Saddam Hussein is seeking and developing weapons of mass destruction."

Fellow Massachusetts Senator John F. Kerry said, on October 9, 2002, that he would vote to give the president "the authority to use force, if necessary, to disarm Saddam Hussein because I believe that a deadly arsenal of weapons of mass destruction in his hands is a real and grave threat to our security."

The following day, Sen. Jay Rockefeller (D-WV) was quoted as saying: "There is unmistakable evidence that Saddam Hussein is working aggressively to develop nuclear weapons and will likely have nuclear weapons within the next five years. We also should remember we have always underestimated the progress Saddam has made in development of weapons of mass destruction."

That same day, Sen. Hillary Clinton (D-NY) was also quoted on Saddam's fixation with these weapons. "In the four years since the inspectors left, the intelligence reports show that Saddam

Hussein has worked to rebuild his chemical and biological weapons stock, his missile delivery capability, and his nuclear program," Sen. Clinton said. "He also has given aid, comfort and sanctuary to terrorists, including al Qaeda members. It is clear, however, that, if left unchecked, Saddam Hussein will continue to increase his capacity to wage biological and chemical warfare and will keep trying to develop these weapons."

On January 23, 2003, Sen. John F. Kerry reaffirmed his commitment to ending the "oppressive regime" of the despotic Iraqi ruler. "Without question, we need to disarm Saddam Hussein," Kerry said. "He is a brutal, murderous dictator. He presents a particularly grievous threat because he is so consistently prone to miscalculation. And now he is miscalculating America's response to his continued deceit—and his consistent grasp for weapons of mass destruction."

One year later, John F. Kerry had locked up the Democratic nomination for the presidency. Saddam, a pathetic shell of what he once was, was an American prisoner awaiting payment for his horrendous crimes against humanity.

***

"For months now," began Ted Koppel in a *Nightline* segment aired on September 13, 1991, "we've been producing and broadcasting a series of reports setting forth how Iraq, during much of the 1980s and into the '90s, was able to acquire sophisticated U.S. technology, intelligence material, ingredients for chemical weapons, indeed, entire weapon-producing plants, with the knowledge, acquiescence and sometimes even the assistance of the U.S. government. Sometimes, I should add, in violation of U.S. law."

A few days before that program aired, Koppel spoke to Caspar Weinberger, who served admirably as secretary of defense during the Reagan administration. It was Weinberger, who, in March of 1987, wrote a secret memo to District Court Judge Aubrey Robinson ensuring that spy Jonathan Pollard would receive a life sentence for passing classified information to the Israelis.

"I told [Weinberger] that we had learned of the shipment of U.S. artillery in the early 1980s from Jordan to Iraq and that the U.S. was aware of the transfer," Koppel recalled.

Weinberger denied any such shipment ever occurred. "The idea of any re-transfer from Jordan was strictly forbidden, completely forbidden, and had it happened, we would have had every possible sanction we could use to prevent it from happening again," Weinberger said on camera.

Howard Teicher, a former National Security Council official in the Reagan administration, had a different recollection. "In the Defense Department and the State Department I began to hear unconfirmed reports that transfers had taken place," Teicher said. "Jordan denied it formally and vigorously, and the U.S. didn't press the case. This is a good example of a way that communications can be established, and approvals can be given, with winks and nods, without documentation, and with plausible deniability."

Koppel told Weinberger that *Nightline* had also learned of the transfer of U.S. satellite intelligence to Iraq, as early as 1982.

"Well, they're quite wrong about that," Weinberger said bluntly. "There was no assistance given to Iraq, and no intelligence that I know of given to Iraq, nothing that I can recall in the way of any affirmative support, technology, weapons, or anything of that kind given to Iraq."

However, in 1987, when he testified before the House Committee on Foreign Affairs—the same year he wrote the memo on Pollard to Judge Robinson—Weinberger said something entirely different.

A Foreign Affairs Committee member asked: "Mr. Secretary, could you tell us about Iraq, what help did we give Iraq?"

"Iraq?" Weinberger asked.

"That's right," the committee member replied.

"Well," said Weinberger, "we've given very substantial help to ..."

"Also intelligence," the committee member interrupted.

"To Iraq, yes sir," Weinberger said.

Iraq's arsenal of weapons of mass destruction in the 1980s—and the role America might have played in the initial arming of Iraq with those weapons of mass destruction—may have been an important component of what the Jonathan Pollard spy case was all about. That's because Pollard, quite possibly, could have connected at least some of the dots. As is noted in *The Hunting Horse*, Pollard's testimony before a court of law may have served to help open up the Pandora's box that Iraq was not only attempting to produce its own chemical and biological weapons, but was apparently doing so with American help.

Perhaps it was Pollard's knowledge of the White House's duplicity concerning Iraqi efforts to further develop and refine these outlawed weapons that was among a growing list of reasons why his enemies—in the White House as well as the intelligence community—considered him such a threat. Pollard, under oath, may have been able to link Iraq to the German chemical company Imhausen-Chemie; he could have then linked Imhausen-Chemie to the late Dr. Ishan Barbouti (who helped build the chemical weapons plant at Rabta, Libya); and he perhaps could have linked Barbouti to the CIA.

As one of my intelligence sources explained to me: "Pollard was the first person to actually identify Imhausen-Chemie as being the prime supplier of the chemical weapons plant at Rabta. And he identified Barbouti, as well. Actually, something like ninety or ninety-five German companies were in some way involved in the mass production of chemical and biological weapons. The Germans looked at this as a very positive cash flow."

One thing was certain: Pollard's continued incarceration certainly wasn't about treason; it wasn't about the revealing of our sources and methods; and it wasn't about the deaths of CIA moles, then working behind the Iron Curtain—men who were exposed and executed, purportedly because of information Pollard gave the Israelis in 1984 and 1985.

That should have all gone out the window with the February 22, 1994 arrest of Aldrich Ames, the CIA's onetime director of Soviet and Eastern Bloc Counterintelligence. Ames, following his arrest, revealed it was he, and not Pollard or anyone else, who caused these valuable double agents to be "rolled up."

According to a report on CNN, Ames began selling U.S. secrets to the KGB in 1985, and, within a decade, had exposed more than one hundred covert operations and betrayed at least thirty agents, ten of whom were later executed by the Soviets. In a March 1998 interview with CNN Ames frankly admitted: "I knew quite well, when I gave the names of our agents in the Soviet Union, that I was exposing them to the full machinery of counterespionage and the law, and then prosecution and capital punishment."

The February 18, 2001 arrest of the FBI's Robert Hanssen, another spy for the Soviets, confirmed much of what Ames had alleged.

Still, the CIA, and others, seemingly had it in for Pollard, who had already served far more years in prison than anyone who had ever passed U.S. secrets to an ally.

The bottom line was that, because of all the questions it raised, the Pollard saga made for an extraordinary story—the kind of story that reporters live for. When I wrote my two books on the Pollard case—*The Spy Who Knew Too Much* and, later, *The Hunting Horse*—I also knew they could one day be the basis for a made-for-TV movie, or even a feature film.

Not surprisingly, people whose opinions I trusted, and, like me, were intrigued by the idea of a motion picture—and wanted to get involved in the process of putting one together—were convinced that a surefire way to get Pollard released from prison was, in fact, to tell the inside story of his case, mainly from his point of view. Warts and all, the cinematic product we envisioned would be an uncompromising tale of an enigmatic and brilliant civilian U.S. Naval Intelligence analyst who passed on classified U.S. information to his handlers in Israel, not for financial gain, as many had alleged, but to help ensure Israel's survival. Pollard was a flawed individual to be sure. Nevertheless, we saw him more as an ideologue than an opportunist.

Not everyone agreed. Others saw Pollard in a far less flattering light, and would take issue with what we were doing. That was fine with us; they were entitled to their opinions. But we were determined to make our motion picture, and to do it our way. As for those who didn't like what we were doing, who thought we were wrong about Pollard, and who, like his prosecutor, U.S. Attorney Joseph diGenova, believed Pollard should never again see the light of day, well, it's a free country.

They could go make their own movie.

CHAPTER THREE

BAD KARMA

IN THE QUEST to bring the Pollard story to either the small screen or the big screen I had help. The impetus (and chutzpah) to turn this dream into a reality was provided, mainly, by motion picture and television producer Suzanne Migdall, who lives in Fort Lauderdale and became my longtime partner in the project. Well aware of the challenges of producing a film based on such a controversial subject, Suzanne knew, from day one, that a made-for-TV movie, or a motion picture deal, would be difficult to finance. But she knew, also, that we were sitting on top of a great story—a story that, both of us felt, had to be told.

Suzanne, more than anything, is a "people person" who knows how to pitch a movie project—and how to talk to filmmakers once she made contact. A confident business woman who today also chairs the Broward Public Library Foundation in Fort Lauderdale, she honed her professional skills as an entrepreneur and successful concert promoter working with music executives and top-flight agents and celebrities during the golden era of Fort Lauderdale's legendary "spring break."

During the 1980s, Suzanne and her husband, Allan, an attorney, were in fact the owners of the popular "Summers on the Beach," featured on MTV and one of Fort Lauderdale's most successful night clubs. Among the nearly seven hundred acts that appeared on the stage at Summers—which was known as "South Florida's Home of Rock 'N Roll"—were such popular attractions as David Crosby, The Bangles, Flock of Seagulls, Edgar and Johnny Winter, Joan Jett, Steppenwolf, Leon Russell, Kris Kristofferson, and The Supremes.

Using contacts she made in those years, Suzanne also began producing a number of low-budget made-for cable films. With South Florida themes and locales, they were shown on HBO, Cinemax and Showtime. Those films included *Can it be Love* (1992) and *South Beach Academy* (1996), which had an eclectic cast including young Corey Feldman and old Al Lewis—better known as Fred Gwynne's friend, "Grandpa Munster."

Not surprisingly, Suzanne began working with celebrities and talented actors outside the music world: mega-stars like "Sly" Stallone, who she met through her business partner, Jackie Stallone, Sly's mom. Sly and Jackie enjoyed many dinners in LA with Suzanne and another business partner of Suzanne's, Hal Stone, at places like Nicky Blair's on Sunset Boulevard.

Yet while she had produced successful TV cable movies, Suzanne wasn't satisfied. She wanted to a produce a motion picture that was "weighty" and dealt with more serious subject matter— subject matter like the case of Jonathan Pollard.

I can't remember the exact date that Suzanne and I met, although I do remember the circumstances. It was during the late spring or early summer of 1993 and I was going to a networking function at a Fort Lauderdale hotel. I parked my car nearby, and a woman, who got out of her own car the same time I did, engaged me in conversation. I told her I was a writer; she told me she was a real estate broker who had just moved back to town from Los Angeles and that she "dabbled" in the motion picture business.

My interest piqued, I mentioned that I happened to have a book coming out (*The Spy Who Knew Too Much*) and, like so many writers, was hoping to have it turned into a feature film. The real estate broker—her name was Leah Novrad—admitted that while she never produced a movie herself, she did know someone who might not only have an interest in such a project; this person might even have the wherewithal to make it work.

A few days later, I met that person: Suzanne.

Totally unpretentious—probably because she lived in Fort Lauderdale, not Beverly Hills—Suzanne immediately put me in a comfort zone. I showed her my book's galleys (a "printer's proof" of the book before it went to print). I then signed a contract with her company, Summers Productions.

Within a few months of my signing the contract, *The Spy Who Knew Too Much* hit the bookstands and my new partner began to package the project for Hollywood's elite. It wasn't long before she received a personal letter from Stirling Silliphant, one of filmdom's most honored and respected screenwriters.

The initial contact with Silliphant was actually set up by Suzanne's close friend and mentor, casting director Beverly McDermott. The South Florida-based McDermott, whose credits included *Lenny*, *Black Sunday*, *Cocoon*, and a number of Burt Reynolds films, saw Silliphant as a good fit. Suzanne agreed.

An Oscar winner for his 1967 script for the motion picture *In the Heat of the Night*, and a Golden Globe Award winner for his screenplay for *Charley*, Silliphant was also the creator of the TV series *Naked City*, and the creative force behind an equally successful 1950's TV series, *Route 66*. A once prolific writer, Silliphant was semi-retired and living in Thailand when a business associate of McDermott's, Paul Saltzman, sent Silliphant a copy of my new book.

After reading it, Silliphant both faxed and mailed a letter to Saltzman, CEO of Sunrise Films in Toronto. Silliphant told Saltzman he would like his name to come up for consideration as the possible screenwriter for the story, should it go into development. Silliphant then sent a separate letter to Suzanne. "I wanted to congratulate you on your acumen in having acquired so visceral and vital a property," he wrote. "That fact, in itself, is a tribute to you as a human being."

"Not since *Judgment at Nuremberg* or since *All the President's Men*," the Academy Award-winning screenwriter added, "have I known a project which so deserves production as *The Spy Who Knew Too Much*. The central issue of responsibility of the individual finding his highest moral principles in conflict with the edicts of the state, when those edicts violate such principles, is an issue which cannot be told too often. It needs to be drummed into the consciousness of every human being so that injustice, despite its legal trappings and its pretending to be in the national interest, cannot destroy honest individuals…"

Silliphant, who obviously wanted to get paid for his services, was willing to work with Hollywood producers on the project, but, because of the project's political nature, felt it would be a tough sell. Nevertheless, still confident that it could get done, he asked for an upfront fee of fifty thousand dollars from us to write our screenplay.

Suddenly, we were in a high-stakes poker game—and we needed the chips to sit with the big boys at the table.

Looking for financing, Suzanne immediately flew to the West Coast to meet with Nick Grillo, the development person at

Neufeld/Rehme. The company partnered by Mace Neufeld and Robert Rehme, Neufeld/Rehme had produced *All The President's Men*—a motion picture Silliphant had mentioned in his letter to Suzanne—as well as other profitable films. Suzanne was hoping to get Grillo to package our project with a bankable writer, and she obviously had one in mind: Silliphant. Unfortunately, Grillo wasn't willing to place his bets on an "out of the loop" Oscar winner.

"Nick took a meeting with me, and took future meetings with me as well," said Suzanne, who connected with Grillo in LA. "But Nick felt that Silliphant, sadly for us, wasn't in demand. The way Nick put it was that Silliphant was no longer on the 'A-list'."

"Pollard's just not that compassionate a character, anyway," Grillo also told Suzanne. Referring to the fictional hero of *The Hunt for Red October*, *Clear and Present Danger* and *Patriot Games*, Grillo flatly added, "Too bad he can't be more like Jack Ryan."

We never did get to work with Stirling Silliphant. A man with true passion for just causes, on April 26, 1996, he passed away from prostate cancer at his home in Thailand. He was seventy-eight.

Suzanne, though, was just getting started. And it wasn't long before another industry heavyweight appeared on her radar screen: a top-flight film producer who, in his own way, was every bit as passionate as Silliphant. His name was Marvin Worth, and he had helped finance a number of wonderful motion pictures such as *Lenny* (based on the life of heroin-addicted comedian *Lenny Bruce)* and *Malcolm X* (the Spike Lee directed motion picture starring Denzel Washington). It was obvious that Worth had a propensity for tackling controversial subjects. Just as important, he was a childhood pal of Allan Migdall's father.

Suzanne wasn't aware of this when she first wrote a letter introducing herself to Worth after learning that her friend, Beverly McDermott, had worked with Worth on *Lenny*. It was McDermott who suggested that Suzanne contact him. When Suzanne's letter arrived, Worth immediately called her. "I see that your name is Migdall," Worth said. "Do you have any relatives in New York?"

"When Marvin found out who Allan was, and who Allan's father was, I think that he kind of felt like we were family," Suzanne recalled. "He remembered Allan's dad very well. He said about him, 'When we were both young, I thought he was the best dancer in New York.'"

Worth, who was notoriously difficult to even schedule a phone meeting with, scheduled a face-to-face meeting with Suzanne. Suzanne flew to Los Angeles, "pitched" our project to Worth, and, according to Suzanne, was very interested—even though, like both Silliphant and Grillo, he believed Pollard would probably be a tough sell.

During her fruitful meeting with Worth, Suzanne also asked him about the Malcolm X film, which was critically acclaimed and was perhaps Spike Lee's best work. Interestingly, Worth said they lost money on it. "However, we made a lot of money on the sale of the baseball caps with the 'Xs' on them," Worth said.

Knowing how controversial the Malcolm X film was, Suzanne felt compelled, also, to ask Worth if her life could somehow be in danger because of the Pollard project.

"See how high my hand is," Worth replied, lifting his arm nearly straight up. "That's how high my file with the FBI is because of *Malcolm X*. But since you're a filmmaker, you're fine. I really don't think you have anything to worry about."

"HBO really wanted to work with Marvin," Suzanne later said. "But he was involved at the time with a movie he wanted to do about James Dean and talked about an amazing newcomer he wanted to play him—Leonardo DiCaprio."

Like so many deals in Hollywood, that one never material-
ized. And before any deal between Suzanne and Worth could be
brought to fruition, the seventy-two year old motion picture producer died at the UCLA medical center of lung cancer—almost
two years to the day following the death of Stirling Silliphant.
Perhaps, I thought, the universe was trying to send us a message.

When they met in LA, prior to the decline in Worth's health,
Worth had suggested to Suzanne an iconic movie director who
might also be "intrigued" by the Pollard project. As a result, Suzanne
spoke by phone to Alan J. Pakula, whose list of credits, including
Klute and *Sophie's Choice*, was every bit as impressive as Worth's.

Prior to speaking with Pakula, Suzanne had purposely sent
him a copy of Stirling Silliphant's letter in which Silliphant
compared the importance of *The Spy Who Knew Too Much* to that
of *Judgment at Nuremberg* and *All the President's Men*. Pakula, after all, was the director of *All the President's Men*—and won an
Academy Award for his efforts.

Pakula, like Silliphant and Worth, said he had a "serious interest" in the Pollard material. Before anything ever came of it,
however, the seventy-year-old filmmaker's life came to a tragic
end while driving on the Long Island Expressway. Eight months
following the death of Marvin Worth, a car driving in front of
Pakula's apparently kicked up a metal pipe lying on the highway,
thirty-five miles east of New York City. The pipe was turned into
a projectile that went crashing through Pakula's windshield. Losing control of his car, he crashed into a fence. He was taken to
North Shore Hospital in Plainview, Long Island, where he was
pronounced dead.

Suzanne was left shaken, but undaunted. If anything, she was
now more determined than ever. Using her people's skills, dog-

gedness, and moxie, she would eventually hook up with yet another industry insider, Mark Wolper, son of David Wolper, the producer of *Roots* and *The Thorn Birds*. The Wolper Company was part of the giant Warner Brothers and could easily package a deal.

As always, Suzanne exuded optimism. Of course, what neither Suzanne nor I could have counted on was the inexplicable bad karma that would continue to follow our project, as well as those who had gone out of their way to try to help us.

It was as if we had all been cursed for eternity by a band of gypsies.

***

On March 12, 1999, Janet Burrows, an executive with the Wolper Company, sent Suzanne a letter. "Per your request," she wrote, "I am writing you to confirm our interest in your project THE HUNTING HORSE.

"From our vantage point, although this is a highly controversial project, we feel it could be a tremendous film, and would like to negotiate a deal for book rights and producing services, and a paid option for the book The Hunting Horse …We are fighting the good fight at Warner TV in order to get upfront monies, but have been delayed by the recent regime change. The only definitive information we have received from Warner TV is that they would not be interested in acquiring the Pollard family rights. We will try to expedite the process, and promise to keep in touch with our internal status."

The story, which was only three paragraphs long, appeared on Saturday, July 26, 1999, in the *Los Angeles Times*. It began: "HIGHLAND PARK—Police on Friday were seeking the killer of a woman who was shot to death in her home." The story continued: "Janet Burrows-Tapia, 39, who was four months pregnant, was found about 11 a.m., Thursday at her home in the 900 block of North Avenue 65, said Los Angeles Police Officer Donald Cox. A neighbor was asked to check on her welfare after the victim failed to show up for work.

"Responding paramedics pronounced Burrows-Tapia dead at the scene, Cox said. Although there were signs of a forced entry, the motive for the slaying is unknown."

The murder victim's full name was Janet Burrows-Tapia, but I knew her only by her maiden name, Janet Burrows. She and I had never met, nor do I recollect that we ever spoke on the telephone. But Suzanne had gotten to know Janet quite well and genuinely liked and respected her.

While our Pollard project was with Warner Brothers, I was told it was Janet, the development director at the Wolper Company, who was really championing our project and was the driving force behind getting our project off the ground. With Janet's energy, and the Wolper name behind us, we seemingly had a good shot to finally get our movie made. After all, in addition to producing *Roots* and *The Thorn Birds*—two of the most successful and highly acclaimed miniseries' in television history—David Wolper, a Hollywood institution, had also been the executive producer of the multi-Academy Award nominated film *LA Confidential* starring a then unknown Australian actor named Guy Pearce and another virtually unknown Australian named Russell Crowe.

The three-paragraph article on Janet Burrows-Tapia that appeared in the *Los Angeles Times* was apparently the end of the story, at least as far as the local police were concerned. What was not said in the *LA Times* news piece was that Janet's body was found after she failed to appear at a meeting she had with ex-

ecutives at the Turner Company. The Turner Company, founded
by media mogul Ted Turner, was a division of Warner Brothers,
which, in turn, was tied to the Wolper Company.

Suzanne recalled being told by Kevin Nicklaus—who would
eventually take over for Janet—that Janet had been shot once in
the head, "execution" style. Was the murder a professional "hit?"
Was the killer a neighborhood drug dealer, since there were more
than a few in the area where Janet lived? Was it a domestic crime?
Or was it someone who wanted to stop *us*? And since Janet was a
fairly high profile person, with a high profile company, in a high
profile industry, why didn't her homicide get any more attention
in the press?

In the months that followed, Suzanne would occasionally look
up the name of Janet Burrows-Tapia in the *Los Angeles Times'*
archives to see if anything else had been written in the paper
about Janet's murder. Nothing had: just that one story that came
out two days after Janet's death. There was also no update from
the police. All we knew was that there was an "ongoing investigation." As for Janet, her tragic end was one of those "unsolved
homicides"—with a trail that, every day, seemed to grow colder.

Among her many attributes, Janet was one of those people
who apparently didn't scare easily. And she seemed to be especially attracted to controversial subjects. At the same time that
she was working with us she had also been working on a project
about "Ruby Ridge," detailing the story of heavily armed Aryan
Nation sympathizer and "survivalist" Randy Weaver, and his
family's deadly run-in with the U.S. government.

What happened at Ruby Ridge—especially the killing of
Weaver's wife, Vicki, by an FBI sharpshooter—was an event that
supposedly shaped the thinking of an impressionable young man

who shared with the Weavers a distrust and contempt for the U.S. government.

The name of that young man was Timothy McVeigh.

Stirling Silliphant, Marvin Worth, Alan J. Pakula, and Janet Burrows-Tapia were all linked, in one way or another, to our Pollard project. It was a little like TV's *The X-Files*, in which all those who got caught up in Special Agent Fox Mulder's near fanatical search for "the truth" about an "alien conspiracy" often fell victim to forces that didn't want the truth revealed.

As we thought about those whose paths we crossed, and who were seriously considering getting involved with us, Suzanne remembered a conversation she once had with Janet.

"You know, there have been some unusual occurrences," Suzanne told the ill-fated film executive, almost reluctantly. "It seems that a lot of people we've done business with in Hollywood have died suddenly."

"Well," Janet said, "I know nothing like that will happen to me."

They both laughed.

CHAPTER FOUR

AT WAR WITH A BEAST

I **HAD MET JOHN** Loftus a number of times and admired him for all he had accomplished. A former federal prosecutor, and the author of *Unholy Trinity: The Vatican, the Nazis and the Swiss Banks* and *The Secret War Against the Jews*, Loftus fancied himself not only a gadfly, of sorts, but a champion of Jewish causes. To a large extent, he was. A great story teller with a supple brain, he was also a wonderful speaker, as humorous as he was controversial, who knew how to enthrall and charm his audience, usually at the same time. As I heard him say during one of his many lectures in either synagogues or Jewish community centers, "Once again we have an Irish-Catholic talking to Jews about the history of Israel." The audience would laugh as Jewish audiences almost always did when Loftus spoke.

My first book on the Pollard case, *The Spy Who Knew Too Much*, had hit the bookstores in November of 1993, and I met Loftus for the first time, a few months later, at a lecture he was giving in the Fort Lauderdale area in late winter, or early spring of 1994. Before that meeting I had never heard of Loftus. After his lecture, we spoke for a few minutes and I told him I'd have my publisher send him a copy of *The Spy Who Knew Too Much*. He said he would reciprocate by having his publisher send me a copy of *The Secret War Against the Jews*, which he did.

I bumped into Loftus a number of times after that, but it wasn't until a few years later—on January 15, 1998 to be exact—that I approached him again, this time to ask if he would consider the possibility of us working on a book on the Pollard case together. Loftus was the special guest speaker that evening at the Woodmont Country Club in Tamarac, Florida.

Back in the spring of 1994, after months of rumors, I learned that my publisher, Shapolsky Publishing, or S.P.I. as it was also known in the publishing trade, had officially filed for bankruptcy. *The Spy Who Knew Too Much* was selling well, but I knew I wouldn't be getting any royalty checks from a publisher who had gone "belly-up." So I made a deal with S.P.I.'s publisher Ian Shaplosky. Ian would owe me no royalty checks, and, in return, I would have the sole rights to republish material from my book with another house. He agreed.

Then, in the summer of 1994, I began writing a spin-off book about the Pollard case that I hoped would uncover the "real" reasons why this man, who received a life sentence for spying for *Israel*—after all he didn't spy for the former Soviet Union, North Korea, Iran or Iraq—had been handed a punishment that seemed so out of proportion to his crime.

By the time of my January 1998 meeting with Loftus most of my still untitled second book on the Pollard case was finished. The problem I was having was selling it. That's where Loftus came in. Like two pirates who have separate pieces of a map that, together, can lead them to some buried treasure or untold riches, I believed that Loftus and I —since he said he was also writing his *own* book on the Pollard case—each had something the other needed. While I couldn't find a quality publisher who was interested in my book, Loftus had the entree to a major publishing house, St. Martin's Press. However, I was convinced he lacked what I could in turn give him: a "smoking gun."

After we chitchatted for a few minutes Loftus suggested we step outside the lecture hall where we could talk some more and he could light up a cigarette. I didn't want to tell him exactly what I believed my smoking gun was—that Pollard had exposed to the Israelis the secret arming of Iraq with chemical and biological weapons from the United States—but I certainly hinted at it. I told him, "One reason I believe Pollard is in prison for life has to do with Iraq."

Loftus dismissed it. I don't recall exactly what he said, but he seemed to feel that the key to Pollard's harsh sentence could be found in "Iran-contra," and some connection this all had to the first President Bush. Since Loftus didn't buy what I was selling, he wasn't about to work with me on another book. Evidently he believed he had all the smoke in his gun that he needed.

I wasn't surprised when Loftus said that, while he wasn't willing to work with me on my new book (later to be titled *The Hunting Horse*), he would be happy to help get me a top draw agent or publisher if I passed my manuscript along to him. I was sure he was being above-board. Nevertheless, as much as I trusted Loftus, I felt somewhat reluctant to hand over my manuscript to someone who had his own project that dealt with essentially the same subject.

Jonathan Pollard, at the time of my January 1998 meeting with Loftus, had given only two interviews to reporters. One of those interviews was with Wolf Blitzer, now a host on CNN, but then with the *Jerusalem Post*. That interview took place before Pollard was officially sentenced and became a foundation for much of Blitzer's well-researched book, *Territory of Lies*. The other was by Mike Wallace for the TV news show *60 Minutes*. Both interviews were later used by the government as "proof" that Pollard had violated his plea bargain agreement which basically forbid him to speak to the press.

As Blitzer noted in *Territory of Lies*, in the government's presentencing memorandum prosecutors cited his interview with Pollard as a reason to justify Pollard receiving a harsh sentence.

"Pollard, the government said, 'had violated an express provision of the written plea agreement'," Blitzer recalled in his book. "Unwittingly, and unhappily, I found myself part of the story. Yet I did not sneak into the prison. I signed U.S. Department of Justice forms on both occasions—clearly stating my purpose for meeting with Pollard—and of course identified myself as a reporter with the *Jerusalem Post*. If those interviews were not approved, why was I allowed into the prison?"

While I, myself, never interviewed Pollard in prison, I did use, as the basis for much of *The Spy Who Knew Too Much*, an eighty page hand-written "letter" Pollard wrote, originally sent to a "Rabbi Werb," in which Pollard explained why he felt he had little choice but to spy for Israel. That letter was sent out by Pollard, or members of his family, to a number of journalists. The hope, I assumed, was that one of us would tell Pollard's side of the story in a book, which is exactly what I did. Pollard (or his family) picked me because I had already written a number of published articles about the case. Subsequently, I received hundreds of other personal letters from Pollard.

It's important to stress that the material Pollard released, in what has come to be known as the "Werb letter," was ostensibly cleared by Naval Intelligence sensors before I ever read any of it. Still, there's a good chance this material was never supposed to see the light of day, because, one month after the *Spy Who Knew Too Much* hit the bookstores in November of 1993, a story on the "Pollard leak" made the front page of the *New York Times*.

The person interviewed for that story, then-Secretary of Defense Les Aspin, was literally enraged that Pollard had released "classified information" from prison in the form of letters, although he didn't say what was in those "letters," or who they went to. Notwithstanding, I had a sneaking suspicion that what really infuriated Aspin was the publication of my book.

To find out for sure, I immediately called Carol Pollard, Jonathan Pollard's sister, who then called Pollard's high profile attorney, Theodore Olson. Olson, a top insider in Washington, D.C., was President Ronald Reagan's, and, later, George W. Bush's, personal attorney. After Bush won the 2000 presidential election, it was Olson who would be appointed by the new president as Solicitor General of the United States. (Tragically, Olson's wife, Barbara, happened to be aboard one of the airliners hijacked during 9-11.)

Olson quickly responded to Carol Pollard's phone call. Carol then called me.

"You're right, Elliot," Carol said. "It is about your book."

In a subsequent letter to Carol Pollard, meanwhile, for protection against any possible lawsuits pertaining to movie rights, I included a chronology of my direct connection to her brother's case. The chronology began with the first article I ever wrote on the case, which appeared in print on September 26, 1990.

Nine months later, in June of 1991, I was introduced to Carol Pollard when she appeared as a special guest speaker at Temple Anshei Emuna, an Orthodox synagogue in Delray Beach, Florida. On June 13, 1991, I published an article based on Carol's lecture at Anshei Emuna, and on her appeal to the Jewish community to help get her brother released from prison.

A year later, in June of 1992, I read an article by intelligence operative William Northrop, titled "The Ghost of the Sealed Rooms," which explained, in detail, how, in the mid 1980s, Israel had altered its defense policy to protect its citizens from an Iraqi poison gas attack after Pollard's information helped reveal the scope of Saddam Hussein's bio-chemical weapons program.

It was on July 1, 1993, that Suzanne Migdall acquired the movie rights to my soon-to-be book, *The Spy Who Knew Too Much*.

By November of 1993, *The Spy Who Knew Too Much* was in bookstores across America.

On December 27, 1993, Carol Pollard met actor Jon Voight and his associate, Hank Paul at a Pollard rally in Los Angeles.

On February 6, 1994, I introduced Carol to Suzanne at a rally in Ft. Lauderdale.

On February 17, 1994, Suzanne contacted Hank Paul, who said he doubted anyone in Hollywood would touch this project.

As for Pollard, he remained a salmon trying to swim upstream. Over time, according to a high level Israeli source, the case environment in regards to Pollard apparently became even further polluted by the possibly misguided tactics of Esther Zeitz-Pollard, who "married" Pollard in prison (his first wife, Anne, had since divorced him); and the competent attorney Larry Dub, who Zeitz hired to be Pollard's lawyer. As a result, a widening schism existed between Pollard's sister, and parents, and the Zeitz camp. Pollard, for his part, always sided with Zeitz whom he believed to be his most trusted ally, and the best hope for his release.

Pollard's beliefs notwithstanding, his sister and father had pulled some strings just to keep him alive—something Zeitz might not have been able to do in the early years following Pollard's arrest. Before Zeitz entered the picture, the Pollards also hired one of the top lawyers in Washington—Ted Olson—to defend Jonathan through the appeal process. And the Pollards used their influence, and some diplomacy, to get Jonathan transferred out of Illinois' maximum security Marion Penitentiary—perhaps the toughest prison in America—to Butner, a medium security prison in North Carolina. As well-intentioned as she may have been, all Zeitz apparently seemed to accomplish was to make enemies.

"[Zeitz and Dub] are currently attacking the government of Israel in general and [Prime Minister] Ehud Barak in particular in the Israeli courts and press," one of my Israeli sources said in a letter he wrote to Carol Pollard. "As we see it, the battle is not about Jonathan, but rather about Zeitz and Dub being the 'sole and legitimate representatives.' They are not considered 'serious' and are being ignored. It is my understanding that the PM will not even grant them an audience."

Getting a motion picture made on the case which would tell the story as we saw it—and the story that the *Israelis* purportedly wanted told—would hopefully have the by-product of getting Pollard released from prison. At the same time, with powerful enemies lurking around virtually every corner, not to mention the usual roadblocks one encounters while trying to make a Hollywood movie, bringing this project to fruition was proving to be a monumental challenge.

"Carol, I do not need to tell you that, in the fight for your brother, we are at war with a very large and formidable adversary," my intelligence source concluded in his letter to Pollard's sister. "We are at war with a beast."

CHAPTER FIVE

POGO MEETS POLLARD

IN THE LONG running TV series *Magnum P.I.*, starring Tom Selleck, the role of the prissy British "caretaker," Higgins, eventually won critical praise for John Hillerman, who in real life was a Texan. One of the story lines in the Emmy Award-winning show dealt with whether Higgins was really the best-selling author Robin Masters, who only masqueraded as the caretaker of the huge Hawaiian estate shared by his nemesis Magnum, a part-time private investigator and former Naval Intelligence operative who lived in the guest house and drove around "paradise" in Robin's Ferrari.

Before *The Hunting Horse* was published I had a good color photo of Jonathan and Esther Zeitz-Pollard that I wanted to use in the book. To get permission to use the photo, I called Zeitz-Pollard at her office in Toronto, since the photo originally came from that office. A woman who said her name was "Nomi" answered the phone, and said she would give Esther the message. A few days later, when I called again, Nomi said Esther "absolutely forbids me" to use it.

Knowing how the overly protective Zeitz-Pollard operated, I was hardly surprised. What did surprise me was that no matter how many times I called her office, Zeitz-Pollard was never available. For some reason Nomi always answered the phone. It was as if she was the secretary in some Fortune 500 company. I wondered: Like Higgins and Robin Masters were Esther and Nomi possibly one in the same?

When my book finally did come out, Zeitz-Pollard hardly gave it her stamp of approval. That was in spite of the fact that, if successful, the publicity from the book would have done nothing but help her husband's cause.

A news release, dated February 4, 2001, appeared on the Zeitz-Pollard website, Justice 4JP, which Esther called the "official" Pollard website. The release dealt specifically with my book. It stated, "In response to inquiries about *The Hunting Horse* by Elliott (sic) Goldenberg, Justice4JP would like readers to be aware that this book is not recommended. Like the previous works on the Pollard case by the same author, *The Hunting Horse* combines a little fact with a lot of highly questionable and factually flawed speculation. Justice4JP does not endorse the factual accuracy of *The Hunting Horse* or other material by the same author and does not recommend it as reliable source material on the case."

Then the caveat: "For reliable source material, visit the Justice 4JP website at http://www.jonathanpollard.org. The Justice4JP website is the only source of information authorized by Jonathan and Esther Pollard."

It seemed that Esther was not about to offer me any of her support. Truth be told, that put me in some fairly good company.

On January 7, 1994, an opinion piece written by Israeli cabinet secretary Elyakim Rubinstein appeared in the *Jerusalem Post.*

"The whole [Pollard] affair was a very serious mistake, something that never should have happened," stated Rubinstein, who had been deputy chief of the Israeli Embassy in Washington, D.C. when Pollard was arrested, outside that embassy, on the morning of November 21, 1985. Rubinstein was in charge of the embassy that day because Meir Rosenne, Israel's ambassador to the United States, was attending a conference in Paris.

It was Rubinstein who "gave Pollard up" into the waiting hands of the FBI. Did the deputy chief of the Israeli embassy make a mistake? Should he, instead, have brought Pollard "in from the cold?" And what would Meir Rosenne have done? These and other questions have always weighed heavily on Rubinstein's conscience.

"Pollard and his former wife (Anne Pollard, who also spent time in prison) have paid a very heavy price for his mistakes and the mistakes of his handlers," Rubinstein noted. "These people were employed by the government of Israel and presented themselves to Pollard as such. This being the case, it is the government's moral duty, if not its formal obligation, to help bring about Pollard's release.

"It is true that Israel has no formal judicial standing in the matter vis-à-vis the U.S. government. But just as the U.S. has turned to us not infrequently on humanitarian issues, so do we now turn to them. Our U.S. colleagues understand this."

As is noted in *The Hunting Horse*, contrary to popular belief Israeli leaders did, in fact, have a plan in place to "bring Pollard in" prior to his arrest in November of 1985. As an Israeli intelligence source told me: "Back in the Kirya (Israel's Pentagon), in Tel Aviv, word had gotten out that there was trouble concerning an operative in the United States. Col. Avi Sella (Pollard's original handler) informed his air force boss, who in turn informed

Gen. Ehud Barak (the same Ehud Barak who would eventually be elected Israel's prime minister) at AMAN (Israeli Military Intelligence). Officers in AMAN's Unit 504 had begun to talk about a rescue contingency.

"As AMAN hoped, although few in Israeli intelligence knew the true identity of their 'Hunting Horse', Pollard called the Israeli Embassy in Washington. The problem was: no one in Unit 504 informed the Foreign Ministry that the embassy should take Pollard in. So [Elyakim] Rubinstein, who knew nothing about the rescue effort, ordered the Pollards expelled from the embassy. Rubinstein has never forgiven himself for Pollard's capture, and has long been one of the most vocal voices in Israel demanding Pollard's release."

That was all true. Then, on February 11, 1998, four years after his op-ed on Pollard appeared in the *Jerusalem Post*, the Associated Press reported that Rubinstein, then serving as Israel's attorney general, resigned from a "Free Pollard" committee in Israel after "being accused of responsibility for Pollard's arrest."

"Elyakim Rubinstein was the most senior diplomat present when the FBI arrested Pollard outside the Israeli Embassy in Washington in 1985," the Associated Press story stated. "Pollard had attempted to escape into the compound, but its iron gates were ordered shut. In a recent letter to Prime Minister Benjamin Netanyahu, Pollard wrote: 'Elyakim Rubinstein is not a disinterested party. He bears direct responsibility for the events that led to my bitter fate.'"

According to the Associated Press story it had not been established whether or not Rubinstein actually ordered security guards to close the embassy gate. Nevertheless, Yitzhak Feller, an aid to Israel's Immigrant Absorption Minister, Yuli Edelstein, said it was in response to Pollard's letter to Netanyahu that Rubinstein resigned from a ministerial committee trying to secure Pollard's release.

Certainly, Pollard's role in forcing Israel's attorney general, of all people, to resign from a panel working to secure his freedom made little sense on the surface. Not surprisingly, though, the story appeared prominently on the Justice4JP website—a website apparently controlled by Esther Zeitz-Pollard.

While Pollard and his new "supporters" wrote numerous letters on his behalf to Netanyahu, the prime minister reportedly tried to broker a deal for Pollard's release, with President Bill Clinton, during the Israel-Palestinian peace talks taking place at Maryland's Wye River Conference Center in October of 1998. According to numerous sources, Pollard's freedom was "on the table" during the talks, but Clinton, allegedly on advise from the CIA, apparently reneged on any promises he may have made to Netanyahu to pardon the Jewish spy.

Zeitz-Pollard then began to publicly attack the prime minister, just as she would later attack his successors, Ehud Barak and Ariel Sharon.

On October 21, 1999, Zeitz-Pollard, through Jonathan Pollard's attorney, Larry Dub, filed a legal demand with the Israeli Supreme Court that then-Prime Minister Barak produce specific documents "in order to clarify Barak's involvement in the Pollard affair."

The filing with the Israeli Supreme Court—which appeared on the Justice4JP website—stated: "As a result of new documents that have just been obtained from the U.S. government through the Freedom of Information Act, the petitioner (Pollard) has learned that, late in November 1985, the respondent, who was then the head of AMAN, IDF (Israel Defense Force) General

Ehud Barak, met with his American counterpart in the American Defense Intelligence Agency, regarding the petitioner's case.

"The petitioner maintains that most of the tasking orders that he received from the State of Israel originated in AMAN and were relayed to the petitioner via LAKAM (the branch of Israeli intelligence that ran Pollard).

"As head of AMAN at that time, the respondent would have been fully aware of the petitioner's actions and of the involvement of officials in the Ministry of Defense and other officials at the highest levels of the government.

"According to the documents, at that early date, the Americans still did not have a clear picture of exactly who in Israel was involved in running the petitioner in the U.S., and to what extent the government of Israel was involved in the operation.

"The initial contacts between the two countries set official Israeli government policy concerning the petitioner—a policy that was rooted in the dissemination of false information, such as the claim that the petitioner did not work for the State of Israel, that he was a mercenary, and that the operation itself was a rogue operation, not recognized or authorized by the State of Israel."

The points made by Zeitz-Pollard and Dub were accurate. As head of AMAN in 1985, Barak had been one of only a handful of people in Israel who, prior to Pollard's arrest, knew the "Hunting Horse's" true identity. But did it really make sense to try to embarrass the prime minister of Israel on a website available to the public? Didn't it make more sense to try to work with Barak, and not against him, behind the scenes?

On March 26, 2001, after Sharon had replaced Barak as prime minister, another article appeared in the Justice4JP website, blasting Sharon, as well, for not doing more for Pollard. "Sharon's indifference to the plight of Jonathan Pollard, in spite of the fact that he (Sharon) was a witness to the American pledge to release Pollard as an integral part of the Wye accords, is stunning," the article stated. "His apathy to the plight of an Israeli agent ... is morally reprehensible."

A year after Zeitz-Pollard declined to endorse *The Hunting Horse* book another press release appeared on the Justice4JP website warning buyers to beware. "In order to adhere to the highest standard of accuracy and truth, Justice for Jonathan Pollard will not endorse any book on the Pollard case which was not submitted to Jonathan Pollard and his attorneys to be vetted for factual accuracy prior to its publication," the release stated. "For this reason, Justice for Jonathan Pollard has not endorsed and does not recommend any of the books on the Pollard case currently on the market."

That latest "warning" was directed at a new book titled, *Miscarriage of Justice: The Jonathan Pollard Story*, which apparently also drew Zeitz-Pollard's ire. The book, which broke no new ground but stressed the legal aspects of the case, was written by Mark Shaw, an affable Indianapolis-based writer and attorney who physically resembled singer John Denver and once wrote a book on basketball's Larry Bird.

In the months that followed, yet another stern warning appeared on the Justice4JP website: this one regarding two Israelis who were attempting to raise money for a documentary on Pollard.

"Through well-intentioned but misinformed efforts," the warning began, "funds are being solicited to aid the efforts of would-be filmmakers Ami Amitai and Eran Preis to produce a documentary on the Jonathan Pollard case. Please be advised that Jonathan Pollard does not endorse this effort, and his attorneys regard this particular initiative as injurious to his case.

"The 'documentary' is rooted in subjective perspective, not hard fact. It is misinformed and not credible. Jonathan Pollard has distanced himself from the filmmakers and will not consent to be interviewed by them. Their efforts are fruitless and in vain. If you are approached and asked to donate funds, be aware that the project does not have the endorsement of Jonathan Pollard, or his attorneys."

I saw the completed documentary at the Ft. Lauderdale Film Festival in November of 2002. In fact, I was booked to lecture on the Pollard case after the documentary, which I thought was excellent piece of work: comprehensive, well balanced and thought provoking. Among the many people interviewed in the documentary was my old friend Roberta "Bobbi" Dzubow, a Pennsylvania woman who had worked tirelessly on Pollard's behalf; Anne Pollard, Jonathan's ex-wife; Jerry Agee, Pollard's boss at Naval Intelligence, and a person who came off as far more likable than I expected; and even Joseph diGenova, who prosecuted the Pollard case.

In total, five books (two by me, one by Bernard Henderson, one by Mark Shaw and one by Wolf Blitzer), as well as a documentary on Pollard, had so far hit the marketplace, and none of these ambitious projects were given Esther Zeitz-Pollard's stamp of approval. For Zeitz-Pollard—who apparently had little use for many former Pollard allies, not to mention at least three Israeli prime ministers—it had to be increasingly frustrating.

Although raised in Indiana, Jonathan Pollard was actually born in Galveston, Texas, on August 7, 1954. On August 6, 2003, Esther Zeitz-Pollard put a letter on her website that she wrote to her husband. In it she proclaimed that a march she organized for Pollard in Jerusalem, meant to correspond with his birthday, was a rousing success.

"My Beloved Yehonatan," Esther began, "I am so glad that you called last night so that you could hear the excitement in my voice and the sheer delight when I returned home from the protest march and demonstration in honor of your birthday! This event was a runaway success, the like of which we have never seen before! More than ten thousand poured through the streets of Jerusalem today, singing, clapping, shouting, chanting and calling your name! The energy was electric!

"I was carrying the Pollard Bear mascot—a large white plush bear, outfitted like a patriot in a blue and white *kipa* (skullcap) and sweater decorated with a menorah, and holding a large Israeli flag. I held the Pollard Bear high and the flag waved proudly as we marched.

"The crowd was so massive it overflowed the streets of Jerusalem and the police had to shut the roads down for us. Every now and then I would turn around to look at the crowd following behind us and I just stared in delight and disbelief. Wave after wave of people kept thronging forward. I could not see the end of the mass of people; it ran for city blocks and it looked like there was no end. I kept thinking, 'If only Jonathan could see this! He would never believe it!'"

Well, actually he would have believed it. Because the march wasn't in support of Pollard, although some Pollard supporters surely took part. Instead, what took place was the annual Tisha B'Av march to Jerusalem's famed "Western Wall," which commemorated the first such march, held in 1929, in which thousands of Jews demonstrated against the British occupation of Jerusalem.

Zeitz-Pollard apparently just linked the two things together. It reminded me of that famous line uttered by the legendary screenwriter Ben Hecht: "Never let the facts get in the way of a good story."

***

Around the same time that my book *The Hunting Horse* was bashed on the Justice4JP website, syndicated columnist Douglas M. Bloomfield wrote an article entitled "Pogo Meets Pollard." Bloomfield, who favored Pollard being set free, but was never a Pollard apologist, took his catchy headline, not from the witty Ben Hecht, but from a wily cartoon possum. "We have met the enemy," Pogo said, "and he is us."

In the book *Friends in Deed: Inside the U.S. - Israel Alliance*, authors Dan Raviv and Yossi Melman (who also wrote *Every Spy a Prince*), describe Bloomfield as "AIPAC's chief lobbyist for most of the 1980s." Bloomfield, they said, "made friends with other Jews concerned for Israel's welfare," and found Capitol Hill to be "fertile and familiar territory."

Bloomfield, a believer in building coalitions, not in tearing down alliances, began his January 2001 opinion piece with commentary on lame duck President Bill Clinton's refusal to commute Pollard's sentence before leaving office—which resulted, Bloomfield wrote, in "yet another vitriolic outburst from the convicted spy's supporters."

"Their disappointment is understandable, but their reaction is what has made that disappointment virtually inevitable," Bloomfield argued, referring to what he believed were the self-defeating tactics of Zeitz-Pollard and those closest to her. "Pollard is spending his sixteenth year in federal prison on a life sentence with little prospect for release, thanks to a conspiracy of his worst enemies. If he wants to identify them, he can start by looking in a mirror and then at his wife and some of his so-called friends and lawyers, many of whom have used him shamelessly for their own ideological purposes."

Bloomfield wasn't finished.

"The self-destructive tirades against those Pollard and company feel have 'done him wrong' are doing nothing to win friends or influence people," Bloomfield wrote. "Neither is the self-aggrandizing exploitation of his case by some who call themselves his friends and advisors."

Noted Bloomfield, one target of the Pollard camp's "vituperative denunciations" was Sen. Joe Lieberman (D-CT), a 2000 vice presidential nominee who would later plan a 2004 run at the White House. It was well documented that, after reviewing classified material on the case prior to his being picked as Al Gore's running mate in 2000, Lieberman, a self-described Orthodox Jew, decided to oppose Pollard's release from prison—or, at least, not support it.

According to Bloomfield, Zeitz-Pollard denounced Lieberman "for attempting to prove to the Gentiles that he is 'more Catholic than the pope'."

"[Lieberman's] office was bombarded with hate mail, and one right-wing rabbi called him 'evil and a traitor' and suggested there is cause to assassinate him," Bloomfield wrote. "And Pollard's supporters wonder why their campaign to release Jonathan has been so ineffective."

Bloomfield made many other points, not all of which I agreed with. Bloomfield, for whatever reason, may have had a bit of an ax to grind with Pollard. What I wholeheartedly did agree with, however, was that rather than build an impressive coalition of supporters, as Jonathan's sister, Carol; and father, Dr. Morris Pollard, had so adroitly done—both in their grass roots efforts and in alliances with political leaders—Zeitz-Pollard seemed content at making enemies, even out of one time allies.

Zeitz-Pollard immediately reacted to the Bloomfield article, calling the syndicated columnist "the odd fearful Jewish journalist who continues to attack Jonathan. The shrillness of Bloomfield's rhetoric makes one wonder what he is so afraid of."

A beltway insider, Bloomfield was a wonderful resource with a keen mind; exactly the kind of person Esther Zeitz-Pollard should have been cultivating. Instead, all Esther apparently succeeded in doing was to place one of America's most respected syndicated columnists, who could have been an invaluable ally of her husband, on the wrong side of the ledger.

When I saw Zeitz-Pollard's attack on Bloomfield on the Justice4JP website, I emailed Bloomfield a note telling him about my own "problems" with Esther. I also told him what I believed was at least one of the reasons the CIA, especially, was so reluctant to support Pollard being released. I wrote: "It was Pollard who exposed the conduit in the CIA's bizarre relationship with Iraq when we armed Saddam and his little friends with the technologies to produce bio-chemical weapons—weapons that were later possibly turned against American troops during the Gulf War."

That same day, February 9, 2001, Bloomfield emailed me back. "Thanks for your note," he began. "I've had calls from Pollard's family members also telling me they agree with my analysis."

He added that he wasn't entirely convinced that the Iraqi angle had anything to do with Pollard's continued incarceration, however. He said he wasn't even sure that Pollard was an "ideologue," as Pollard and his supporters claimed, instead of just "a mercenary traveling under the false colors of an ideologue." In his note to me, Bloomfield also referred to the "Tunis operation," which included classified information Pollard gave the Israelis that was later used by the IDF when Israeli jets raided Yasser Arafat's then-secret headquarters in Tunis in October of 1985.

"Forget Iraq, forget the Tunis operation, forget those other revisionist excuses," Bloomfield wrote. "Two things I've learned in over thirty years in Washington are: most wounds are self-inflicted, and if you have a choice between a simple explanation and a complex conspiracy, go for the simple one—and you'll be right 93.75 % of the time."

CHAPTER SIX

TATTOO OF A SNAKE

DOUG BLOOMFIELD HAD an interesting perspective on conspiracies. Considering how hard it is to keep a secret in Washington—and, at the same time, to keep that secret out of the media—he had a point. Certainly, alleged conspiracies, of the "Hillary Clinton had Vince Foster murdered" variety, can rarely be proven.

Still, there are those occasional conspiracies that may indeed be based on fact. Such a conspiracy, I believe, surrounded the Oklahoma City bombing.

It was a story I had become very familiar with. While doing my research for *The Hunting Horse*, I read a great deal about the events in Oklahoma City, and, as a person who closely followed the Pollard spy case, I saw linkages to the threat of militant Islamic terrorism everywhere, as did Pollard. Inexplicably, while some conspiracy theories take on a life of their own, others, like the possible Islamic terrorist link to the Oklahoma City bombing, simply wither on the vine and die. It was perplexing to me,

especially since I was becoming increasingly aware of the im-
minent dangers from Islamic terrorism that all Americans faced.

The "conspiracy" story first surfaced on April 20, 1995—the
day following the bombing of the Alfred P. Murrah Federal
Building in Oklahoma City which took the lives of one hundred
and sixty-eight men, women and children. The Israeli newspaper
Yediot Ahranot reported that day that the FBI had already begun
conducting a search for three men who may have been involved
in the attack "and appeared to be Arabs."

"Evidence is increasing that the act was perpetrated by a cell
of a Middle East Moslem terror organization," the story began,
shocking none of us who knew what Islamic terrorists were capable of. "The FBI yesterday launched a widespread search for
three young men, aged about twenty-five, two of them described
as wearing beards and being of Middle Eastern appearance…"

The story stated, also, that, according to eyewitness reports, the
three men were seen "fleeing the attack in a brown commercial
Chevrolet vehicle." According to *Yediot Ahranot*, the pick-up truck
would later be found abandoned at the Dallas-Fort Worth airport.

What was written at the end of this story was especially troubling: "Yesterday, it was made known that, over the last few days,
U.S. law enforcement agencies had received intelligence information, originating in the Middle East, warning of a large Islamic terrorist attack on U.S. soil. No alert was sounded as a result of this information."

Admittedly, there are few people, if any, who know more
about Islamic terrorism than Steven Emerson, and the youthful-
looking, red-haired Emerson had no reason to believe that the
bombing of the Murrah Federal Building was anything more

than a case of "homegrown" terrorism, as was widely reported in the U.S. media. In fact, in his popular book, *American Jihad: The Terrorists Living Among Us*, Emerson recalled how *Newsweek* had once offered him $10,000 to help write a cover story on the bombing in the hope that he could link the act to militant Muslims. He told *Newsweek* at the time to "save your money—they didn't do it."

In spite of his stance with *Newsweek*, Emerson, a doggedly determined investigator when it came to exposing Islamic terrorist cells, was thoroughly despised by Muslim extremists and dismissed by the likes of Palestinian talking heads such as the eye-catching Raghida Dergham and the flatulent Hussein Ibish. Prior to September 11, 2001, Emerson was readily dismissed by most of the politically correct members of America's liberal press as well.

After 9-11 that all changed, of course, and Emerson became a household name.

It was a warm November night and Steven Emerson, the evening's guest speaker, who could often be seen on both CNBC and FOX News, had just finished his 2002 Jewish Book Month presentation at the David Posnack Jewish Community Center, in Davie, Florida, when someone sitting behind me in the audience asked him about a possible Middle Eastern connection to the Oklahoma City bombing. My ears perked up. Emerson hesitated for just a second, then replied that he couldn't be sure whether there was an Islamic terrorist angle to the bombing, or not. But he emphasized, if there was one, he hadn't seen any hard evidence of it. "As far as I'm aware, there isn't any [connection]," he said.

Emerson and I had already met on a number of occasions. I had even sent him a copy of my book, *The Hunting Horse*, and he sent me a copy of his award-winning tape, *Jihad in America*.

When I later approached him, as he sat in another room signing copies of his book, *American Jihad*, he may have guessed what was coming next. Before I said anything, he glanced up at me and a thin smile crossed his face.

"Steve, you know I have material I can get to you that may change your mind about Oklahoma City," I said, knowing we had gone down that road before. He looked at me askance. "Please, don't send me any more on this," he said, grinning and shaking his head. "I know about (Oklahoma City television reporter) Jayna Davis, and all that. I just don't see anything there."

I honestly wouldn't have expected him to say anything else. All of us, after all, are only as good as our sources, and Steve Emerson had his and I had mine. Certainly, most investigative journalists think alike. If we can't touch it, feel it, or see it with our own eyes, we don't necessarily accept it. We don't deny what someone else says or believes; we just remain healthy skeptics if the information hasn't come up on our own radar screens.

When it came to the Oklahoma City bombing, therefore, while Emerson remained skeptical about what I was telling him, as he should have been, and as I would have been had I been in his shoes, at the same time I maintained a healthy skepticism about everything the media had been telling me. For one thing, the day after the bombing there were those stories about "three Middle Easterners" and a warning about a major Islamic terrorist attack. Then that story suddenly died. Why?

To me, personally, it all smelled like week old halibut.

***

Feral House, which was going to publish a book on the Oklahoma City bombing, *The Oklahoma City Bombing and the Politics of Terror* by David Hoffman, is a small publishing house that puts out books by conspiracy theorists. Hoffman's controversial book was scheduled for release by Feral House when Adam Parfrey, Feral House's publisher, was forced to pull the plug on it following a lawsuit by former FBI official (and a Steve Emerson source) Oliver "Buck" Revell who claimed the book contained "false and inaccurate statements" about him.

Hoffman, whose book instead appeared on the Internet, was proud that it nevertheless was proclaimed by Gore Vidal, in *Vanity Fair*, as the "best and most complete book on the Oklahoma City bombing."

When I looked at the acknowledgements in Hoffman's book, I was quite familiar with a number of the names. In addition to an Israeli source of mine who seemed to have inside information on the Oklahoma City bombing, others Hoffman named included former DEA agent Mike Levine, whose radio show I once appeared on; Bob Bickel, whose radio show I also appeared on; television reporter Jayna Davis, who I had a lengthy telephone conversation with; and Louis Champon and Moshe Tal, who were both quoted in *The Hunting Horse*, although I never personally spoke to or met with either of them.

Sometimes you don't need to go fishing for a good story. Sometimes, if you're fortunate enough to be a journalist who gets to know a good "spook"—especially a spook who like to shake the tree a little bit to see what falls off—a good story may instead find you.

Indeed, one of my Israeli sources got involved in a separate investigation of the Murrah Federal Building bombing, as opposed to the "official" investigation that was getting all the media ink. According to my source, that "other" investigation didn't only lead to homegrown psychopaths Timothy McVeigh and Terry

Nichols; it apparently also led to Arab extremists as well a young officer in Iraq's Republican Guard.

Perhaps it even led to Iraqi leader Saddam Hussein himself. David Hoffman had noted in his book a report by the *London Sunday Times* which, according to Hoffman, indicated that "President Saddam Hussein of Iraq may have been involved in both the (first) World Trade Center and the Oklahoma City bombings."

Here is what we do know for sure. In the days immediately following the bombing the media bombarded us with images of the composite drawings of possible suspects. At the time, those possible suspects were given the names "John Doe 1" and "John Doe 2."

There was never any disputing that John Doe 1 existed. And no one denied that John Doe 1 was Tim McVeigh, not even McVeigh himself. But, according to my Israeli source and others who were closely following the investigation, John Doe 2 existed, as well, and was hardly a figment of the imagination of overworked police or overzealous reporters.

After sources of mine involved in the investigation were fairly sure that the investigation was on the right track, I was given access to the dossier and surveillance shots of the man this team of investigators suspected of being the real John Doe 2—a person who allegedly had been seen in the company of the well-publicized John Doe 1, and may, or may not, have been a co-conspirator. According to these sources, this so-called John Doe 2 was likely an ex-Iraqi soldier. His name, I was told, was Hussein al-Hussaini.

Born on September 9, 1965, this would-be co-conspirator was relatively handsome, clean-shaven, and had a tattoo of a snake on his upper left arm. When I saw surveillance shots of him jogging in a tree-lined area he looked, to me at least, like a dead ringer of the artist's rendering of the John Doe 2 that millions of Americans had seen on the airwaves.

I also saw a copy of a confidential investigative report that was written a year after the Federal Building bombing. The report named a number of Arabs suspected of being terrorists, and included some more information on al-Hussaini, noting he had been an officer in the Hammurabi Division of Saddam Hussein's Republican Guard. According to the report, al-Hussaini had been "wounded, captured and medically treated" in Saudi Arabia. I presumed this happened during the Gulf War, although the report didn't specifically state this.

After sifting through all the material, I then put together an op-ed piece that raised questions, not only about McVeigh, but also about who might have been helping him. To give myself some added credibility, I included a tagline stating I was the author of *The Hunting Horse* and that Harvard's Alan Dershowitz had written the Foreword to that book.

As I quickly learned, none of this mattered.

Some smaller newspapers did pick my story up, but none of the major outlets would go near it. Of course, I had questions of my own about the case so I could understand the reluctance some of the editors must have been feeling. For instance, if McVeigh had co-conspirators besides Nichols, why didn't he name them? Also, if our intelligence community believed Iraq was involved—and it's hard to imagine an Iraqi soldier having committing such an act, in 1995, without being ordered to by Saddam Hussein—why didn't the Clinton administration simply come clean?

True, it didn't all make sense. But it also didn't make sense that O.J. Simpson could have slaughtered two people in front of his ex-wife's home, at 10 o'clock at night, and no one heard anything. Nevertheless, all the evidence, including DNA and blood, pointed to Simpson. Even if it wasn't Simpson—a billion to one shot—*someone* had to kill those people. No one moved the bodies from another location. Yet, no one heard anything, and no one saw anything.

The bottom line was that, while there were certainly holes in the story linking the Oklahoma City bombing to Iraq, there was enough "meat" there that there *was* a story. And the American people, I firmly believed, had the right to judge the veracity of that story for themselves.

CHAPTER SEVEN

DEAD MAN WALKING

AFTER THE HORRIFIC events of September 11, 2001, shocked our nation, I took my op-ed on the Oklahoma City bombing out of mothballs, re-worked it a bit, and once again submitted it, thinking this time the timing would be right.

The result was basically the same, however. Among the major media outlets, at least, there were no takers.

My piece did get published in a few smaller newspapers, and James Patterson, a gritty reporter at the *Indianapolis Star Times*, took the idea and ran with it, writing a series of hard-hitting articles in which he used me as a source. But the media giants like the *New York Times* and the *Washington Post*—the newspapers that have the greatest impact all over the country—apparently had little interest.

Basically, this is what I said in an article entitled "Did Missing McVeigh Documents Reveal a Middle Eastern Connection?" I argued that terrorist attacks against the United States, planned by Osama bin Laden—including the attack on the Pentagon and the destruction of the World Trade Center towers—were possibly not the first Islamic terrorist attacks directed at targets in the U.S. that succeeded in killing hundreds (or even thousands) of Americans. According to Israeli intelligence sources, I noted, Tim McVeigh may actually have been part of a broad conspiracy involving Islamic terrorists. And while a besieged Israel was attempting to deal with Hamas and Islamic Jihad suicide bombers, few Americans realized that Middle Eastern terrorists, with possible ties to McVeigh, had their sights set on targets here as well.

Simply put, while America remained in bin Laden's crosshairs, another story involving Islamic terrorism directed against the U.S. may have been buried.

Then I repeated something that one of my Israeli sources once told me. "It's more than a coincidence," I wrote, "that a number of Israeli agents were dispatched to Oklahoma City three days *prior* to the bombing of the Alfred P. Murrah Federal Building. Then, five days after the bombing, Israeli bombing experts determined that the bomb had some of the unique characteristics of those used by Arab terrorists." I was told that Israeli bombing experts gave the information they collected to the Bureau of Alcohol, Tobacco and Firearms before the FBI took over.

In his book, David Hoffman said a source told him that the Israelis were in Oklahoma City to "keep an eye on things." According to Hoffman, one of those Israelis was that source, himself; the other was Avi Lipkin, a former Israeli defense intelligence specialist on the Israeli prime minister's staff.

As was widely reported on May 10, 2001—just days before Tim McVeigh was first scheduled to die by lethal injection prior to his execution being delayed—the FBI, for some reason, failed to give McVeigh's lawyers all the information agents had gathered during the investigation of the bombing. While admitting that some evidence was withheld, the Justice Department stressed that this material still "did not cast any doubt" as to McVeigh's guilt. According to the Justice Department, the more than three-thousand documents included interviews and tips about potential suspects as well as photographs and other forms of evidence. It also included interviews with people who bore a resemblance to an artist's sketches of the possible bombing suspects.

I wondered: Was there a conspiracy to hide the truth? Or was all this material really superfluous, just as the FBI was telling us?

Perhaps no one can say for sure. But what I do know is that, back in May of 1998, I read a copy of a three-year old intelligence memo written the day of the bombing. What was disclosed in that memo—it had been passed on to the Washington Metropolitan Field Office of the FBI by Vincent Cannistrano, former chief of counter-terrorism operations at the CIA—was an apparent Islamic terrorist plot to blow up one of three "targets." Those would-be targets were located in Oklahoma City, Los Angeles, and, possibly, Houston.

Specifically, Cannistrano said he received a phone call on April 19, 1995, from an unidentified Saudi citizen who worked as a counter-terrorism official for the Saudi Royal Family. That source, calling from Jiddah, Saudi Arabia, was a person responsible for developing intelligence to prevent the Royal Family from becoming victims of terrorists. The source told Cannistrano he had solid information that there was a "squad" of people in the U.S. that had been tasked with carrying out terrorist attacks in Oklahoma City, Los Angeles, or Houston. At the time, Cannistrano could not comment on the reliability of the information, nor could he corroborate it.

Steven Jones, McVeigh's onetime lead lawyer, also mentioned this in his book *Others Unknown: Timothy McVeigh and the Okla-*

homa City Bombing Conspiracy. According to Jones, Cannistrano told him that he didn't know if the Saudi caller was credible or not. However, while Cannistrano may have had doubts about the information, I seriously doubt he had reservations about the source. It stands to reason that a source who deals with security for the Saudi royal family would be an extremely credible one.

According to David Hoffman, in March of 1995, Shin Bet (Israel's equivalent of the FBI) arrested approximately ten Hamas terrorists in Jerusalem, some of whom had recently returned from a trip to Fort Lauderdale. Hoffman noted that, according to an Israeli source, "the interrogation of those suspects was thought to have revealed information concerning the plot to bomb the Murrah Building."

Recalled Hoffman, an Israeli source also told him that that the German Bundesnachrichtendienst (BND, Germany's equivalent of the CIA) had also sent a warning to the U.S. State Department. That warning was followed by the April 19, 1995 memo from the Saudis to Cannistrano.

Two years after the Oklahoma City bombing, at the demand of Rep. Charles Key of the Oklahoma State Legislature, a grand jury was convened to look more closely into the tragedy. In September 1997, the Oklahoma State Grand Jury subpoenaed Jayna Davis, a former television reporter for KFOR, Channel 4, in Oklahoma City. In reports aired on KFOR, Davis had been the first person to publicly identify the never-before exposed "John Doe Number Two." Without yet naming him, she alleged he was a former Iraqi soldier who may have entered the U.S. as a student at the University of South Florida.

It was through a source in Oklahoma City that I actually learned this former Iraqi soldier's name. I was also told that the former Iraqi soldier had been seen in Oklahoma City, in the company of McVeigh, only days before the bombing.

In my op-ed, however, I purposely left out al-Hussaini's name. I did so because, even though Jayna Davis had not revealed his name at the time, al-Hussaini—who vehemently denied any association with the bombing—had sued both Davis and KFOR-TV for libel and defamation of character. The last thing I wanted to do was sabotage any chance of my op-ed being picked up because of the fear of lawsuits after I revealed this man's identity.

In November of 1997, three and a half years before Tim McVeigh's life would be taken by the state of Oklahoma, a county grand jury in Oklahoma City reported that an eighteen-month investigation of the bombing had found no evidence of any more co-conspirators. Wrote Arnold Hamilton in the *Dallas Morning News*: "The panel also said that it found no credible evidence that federal agents had prior knowledge that the Alfred P. Murrah Federal Building was targeted for attack. It rejected several other conspiracy theories offered by various people ..."

But Rep. Key maintained that the private investigative committee he formed to look into the attack would produce its own report, which it eventually did. "It will read quite different from this report," Key predicted at the time, obviously sensing a cover-up. "The only thing this report lacked," Key tersely added, "was the words on it, 'signed by the FBI'."

As for Jayna Davis, the Oklahoma State Grand Jury recalled her for two days of testimony in January of 1998. While her testimony was kept secret, bits and pieces seeped out: In addition to the warning by the Saudi Arabian source, Israeli intelligence had also issued two warnings prior to the bombings; Israeli intelligence had agents in place in Oklahoma City prior to the bombings, while, after the bombings, two other Israelis were sent there to help with the investigation; and although the American public was told that the bombings were the result of "homegrown" terrorism, there was an investigation centering on a group of Arabs who were in Oklahoma City at the time—Arabs who had strong connections in the Tampa area, and had been identified by eyewitnesses as spending a great deal of time in both Miami and Fort Lauderdale.

When I asked one of my Israeli sources whether al-Hussaini was a co-conspirator, he admitted that he couldn't be certain. But he doubted the conspiracy ended with Tim McVeigh and his partner in crime, Terry Nichols. "Put it this way," the source told me, "some of us still like to refer to McVeigh as 'Lee Harvey' McVeigh."

Casey Barrett, a producer at the TV show *Inside Edition*, called me soon after my second op-ed on the Oklahoma City bombing was published. He said he read my piece with great interest, and told me he was researching a story of his own concerning possible connections McVeigh may have had with Islamic terrorists. He said he was also researching a "broader piece" that could have linked McVeigh to white supremacists and neo-Nazis.

I spent probably an hour on the phone with Barrett. After checking with my source in Oklahoma City, to see if it would be okay for me to do the interview, my source then called Barrett himself. He spoke to Barrett at length; then gave the TV producer the names and phone numbers of other people Barrett might want to speak to. I also faxed Barrett a copy of the Cannistrano memo.

That was as far as it got. *Inside Edition* decided not to go with the story.

When I had sent my second op-ed on the Oklahoma City bombing to the *Wall Street Journal*, as was the case with the *New York Times* and the *Washington Post*, they declined to print it. A year later, however, the *Journal's* senior editor, Micah Morrison, wrote his own piece, appearing on September 5, 2002, and entitled "The Iraq Connection: Was Saddam involved in Oklahoma City and the first WTC bombing?"

With war clouds forming over Iraq, with Saddam Hussein about to lose his country, and with the one-year anniversary of 9-11 just a week away, the *Journal* editor called it an appropriate time "to look at two investigators who connect Baghdad to two notorious incidents of domestic terrorism."

One of those investigators, Morrison said, was Jayna Davis, the former Oklahoma City TV reporter. Morrison also brought up the name of Laurie Mylroie, who linked Iraq to the first bombing of the World Trade Center, in 1993, and wrote a book on the subject.

Morrison noted that former CIA Director James Woolsey had told the *Journal*: "When the full stories of these two incidents are told, those who permitted the investigations to stop short will owe big explanations to these two brave women. And the nation will owe them a debt of gratitude."

I wasn't too concerned with what Mylroie had to say, since I had never investigated the first World Trade Center bombing, although it wouldn't shock me if al Qaeda and Osama bin Laden were involved, just as they were with the second World Trade Center attack. As for what Jayna Davis had to say, however, I had a personal interest, since she and I had actually compared notes. Not only had we spoken at length about the Murrah Federal Building bombing over the telephone; we even had the same source in Oklahoma City for much of our information.

For many, however, Tim McVeigh's death officially closed the Oklahoma City bombing case. In truth, from the minute he was arrested McVeigh had been a "dead man walking." He was finally executed in June of 2001, while Terry Nichols—who was still facing murder charges—was sentenced to life in prison for conspiracy and manslaughter.

Yet, from the information I had been privy to, I felt there may have been more to this tragic story than just McVeigh and Nichols. In his *Journal* article, I felt Micah Morrison did a good job of laying out certain heretofore-unpublished facts in the case. (At least they were unpublished in the major print outlets.) Surely, those "facts" had never seen the light of day when the bombing was being called an act of "homegrown" terrorism: a spin the media seemed strangely satisfied with.

Morrison wrote, for instance, that Jayna Davis had obtained a copy of a bulletin put out by the Oklahoma Highway Patrol immediately after the Federal Building bombing. Stated Morrison: "It specifies a brown car occupied by a Middle Eastern male subject, or subjects." According to a transcript of police radio communications at the time, also obtained by Davis, a search was on for "a brown Chevrolet pick-up occupied by Middle Eastern subjects." That description was similar to the one in the Israeli newspaper *Yediot Ahranot*.

"When an officer radioed in asking if this was 'good' information, a dispatcher responded 'authorization FBI'," Morrison noted in his article. Mysteriously, that FBI bulletin was lost.

What we do know is this: There were widely publicized sketches of two men seen together—the infamous John Does 1 and 2. Number 1 turned out to be Tim McVeigh: no argument there. But after the arrest of Terry Nichols, the justice department quickly changed its tune about John Doe 2. Government spokespeople said there had been "some confusion."

However, when she covered the case for KFOR-TV, Davis, convinced John Doe 2 did indeed exist, identified him as an unnamed Iraqi soldier (who turned out to be Hussein al-Hussaini). The original warrant described John Doe 2 as a man of average height—about 5'10"—and average weight. The warrant said he also had brown hair and a tattoo on his left arm. Davis said more than twenty witnesses placed this Iraqi soldier (al-Hussaini) in the vicinity of the Murrah building on the day of the bombing.

As Micah Morrison reported in the *Wall Street Journal*, it was about seven weeks after the Oklahoma City bombing that KFOR-TV in Oklahoma City began broadcasting a series of reports on a possible Middle Eastern connection to the tragedy. And while al-Hussaini wasn't yet named, the reports did include photos of him that digitally obscured his face. After al-Hussaini sued for libel and defamation, that particular suit was dismissed in November 1999 by U.S. District Court Judge Tim Leonard. The judge ruled that al-Hussaini bore "a strong resemblance to the composite sketch of John Doe 2, that he was born and raised in Iraq, and that he served in the Iraqi army." According to Morrison, al-Hussaini's Oklahoma City employer allegedly also had connections with the PLO. Al-Hussaini, meanwhile, appealed Judge Leonard's decision to the 10th Circuit Court.

Patrick Lang, former director of the Defense Intelligence Agency's human intelligence collection section, at the same time sent a memo to Davis telling her that al-Hussaini was likely a member of Unit 999 of the Iraqi Military Intelligence Service. That unit, Lang wrote, was headquartered in Salman Pak, southeast of Baghdad. Said Lang, the unit dealt with "clandestine operations at home and abroad."

On June 21, 2002, three months before Morrison's story appeared in the *Wall Street Journal*, the Associated Press reported that U.S. authorities were "warned several times before Timothy McVeigh struck Oklahoma City, in 1995, that Islamic-backed terrorists were planning to bomb a government building."

Noted reporter John Solomon: "The information prompted the Clinton administration to urge stepped-up security patrols and screening at federal buildings nationwide, including those in Oklahoma."

According to Solomon, documents obtained by the Associated Press showed that the U.S. Marshall's Service issued an alert on March 15, 1995, to federal courthouses the Marshall's Service protects, including the one in Oklahoma City. According to the documents, the Marshall's Service also warned that a *fatwa*—a religious edict—had been issued to suicide bomb a federal building where U.S. marshals work. "Allegedly, the *fatwa* is being disseminated to persons in the United States who have the capability to carry it out," the document warned.

As for Hussein al-Hussaini, after the reports of his alleged possible involvement in the Oklahoma City bombing aired, he reportedly moved back to Boston, where he had first entered the United States. According to Morrison, al-Hussaini was haunted by the publicity surrounding his libel suit and was even admitted to a psychiatric clinic. According to notes taken by a nurse at the clinic, Morrison said al-Hussaini quit his job as a cook at Logan Airport in November 1997 because "if anything happens here, I'll be a suspect."

Perhaps al-Hussaini was prophetic.

It was from Logan Airport, four years later, that hijacked planes were used during the terrorist attacks on both the World Trade Center and the Pentagon.

CHAPTER EIGHT

A BLIND SQUIRREL

AS THE OLD saying goes, even a blind squirrel finds an acorn every now and then. Esther Zeitz-Pollard found such an acorn when she was connected to two well-respected lawyers, Eliot Lauer and Jacques Semmelman, of the Park Avenue law firm of Curtis, Mallet-Prevost, Colt & Mosle LLP. In May of 2000, both Lauer and Semmelman agreed to represent Jonathan Pollard pro bono.

Lauer, with nearly three decades of experience as a civil and criminal litigator, and Semmelman, who had served as a federal prosecutor in New York, knew how to navigate the treacherous legal waters that Pollard was apparently drowning in and would make a formidable team. They summarized the Pollard case in an Executive Summary of the Current Legal Initiatives for Jonathan Pollard, prepared in December 2001 and updated in May of 2002.

The two lawyers noted in their brief that Pollard, a civilian Naval Intelligence GS-12 analyst when arrested, was incarcerated in the federal prison in Butner, North Carolina, and was serving a life sentence. After being arrested in 1985, his sentence was imposed in 1987 as a result of his delivering classified information to the State of Israel. Six of his years behind bars were spent in solitary confinement at Marion Penitentiary in Marion, Illinois. The lawyers noted that Pollard admitted his guilt and acknowledged that what he did was wrong. "Mr. Pollard never intended, and was not charged with intending, to harm the United States," Lauer and Semmelman stated.

The lawyers stressed that, in return for Pollard's guilty plea and cooperation, the government made several promises, the most significant of which was that it agreed not to ask the court to impose a sentence of life in prison. Life in prison was the maximum sentence for Mr. Pollard's offense, the lawyers explained, and it was the maximum sentence that could have been imposed, even if Pollard had invoked his right to remain silent, had refused to cooperate, and had insisted on his right to a public trial.

He did none of those things.

Claimed Lauer and Semmelman, Pollard's life sentence was instead the direct result of "ineffective representation" by his then-counsel (Richard Hibey) who "repeatedly failed to act while the government violated its plea agreement."

Lauer and Semmelman argued that the government did this by asking for a life sentence for Pollard after promising not to do so; by failing to advise the sentencing judge (U.S. District Court Judge Aubrey Robinson), in good faith, of the nature and extent of Pollard's cooperation (which it had promised to do); and by going beyond the facts and circumstances of the offenses in its sentencing presentation to the court.

In addition to the defense counsel's failure to deal effectively with any of the government's breaches of the plea agreement, what was perhaps even more significant, Lauer and Semmelman noted, was that, after Pollard's sentencing, the defense counsel never filed the one-page Notice of Appeal. In addition, the defense counsel, allegedly without telling Pollard, allowed the 10-day statutory appeal period to lapse. "As a result," Lauer and Semmelman wrote, "there has never been any direct appellate review of Mr. Pollard's life sentence."

In March of 1992, two Circuit Court justices for the District of Columbia Court of Appeals—justices Lawrence Silberman and Ruth Bader Ginsburg—used the technicality that Pollard never filed for an appeal in their arguments against vacating Pollard's sentence. In a dissenting opinion, Judge Stephen Williams wrote that the sentence nevertheless *should* have been vacated "because the government's breach of the plea agreement was a fundamental miscarriage of justice requiring relief."

Pollard's two new attorneys also took issue with former Secretary of Defense Caspar Weinberger's 46-page pre-sentencing declaration, in addition to the four-page supplemental declaration that he handed to Judge Robinson, on March 3, 1987, just before the U.S district court judge sealed Pollard's fate.

Argued Lauer and Semmelman: The four-page declaration, in which Weinberger accused Pollard of having caused as much or greater harm to national security than any other spy in the "Year of the Spy," was a well understood reference to the espionage cases of John Walker (head of the infamous Walker spy ring), Jerry Whitworth (a member of the Walker spy ring), and Ronald Pelton. Each of these men had spied for the Soviet Union, and each had been sentenced to life in prison just a few months earlier.

According to the attorneys, the government's message in the Weinberger Supplemental Declaration was unmistakable: Pollard had caused no less harm than had Walker, Whitworth or

Pelton. Pollard should therefore not receive a lesser sentence than they did—meaning life in prison.

Yet, in spite of Weinberger's assertions, the government's allegations about Pollard were false, Lauer and Semmelman insisted. In addition, the attorneys said, the Weinberger Supplemental Declaration "falsely accused Mr. Pollard of 'treason,' a crime for which he had not been charged, and which he had not committed."

The attorneys argued that another example of ineffective representation occurred several months prior to his sentencing when Pollard applied, in writing, for permission from the government to allow journalist Wolf Blitzer to enter his jail cell and do an interview. "The government approved Mr. Pollard's application," Lauer and Semmelman noted, "and two interviews took place inside the prison with government approval."

As the lawyers correctly stated, under the plea agreement any interviews had to be authorized by the Director of Naval Intelligence. Pollard had apparently been led to believe that his written requests for authorization had received all necessary approvals. "It would not have been possible," the attorneys stressed, "for Mr. Blitzer to enter the prison at all, much less equipped with his tape recorder and camera, without government approval."

Nevertheless, at sentencing, the government claimed that the interviews were "unauthorized," and, by giving the interviews, Pollard had violated his plea agreement.

"In response, Mr. Pollard's defense counsel completely mishandled the situation," Lauer and Semmelman said. "Counsel failed to tell the sentencing judge that Mr. Pollard had sought and obtained the government's permission to give the interviews. Counsel also failed to demand an evidentiary hearing to determine who, within the government, had known and approved of the interviews.

"Given such ineffective representation, the government ran roughshod over Mr. Pollard's valuable rights bargained for in the plea agreement. The government received the benefits of the plea agreement—full cooperation and no need for a trial in an espionage case—then violated its obligations under that agreement. With no effective advocate for Mr. Pollard, the court accepted the government's recommendation, and sentenced Mr. Pollard to life in prison."

Lauer and Semmelman added that "speculation, opinion and outright falsehoods" on the Pollard case had also been leaked to the press as if they were fact. "Rebutting such tactics," the lawyers said, "requires counsel to have access to the facts."

They used as an example a TV interview during which Tim Russert, host of NBC's *Meet the Press*, stated he had been informed by Joseph diGenova, the chief prosecutor in the Pollard case, that Pollard had "disclosed the identities of U.S. agents in the field." Lauer and Semmelman immediately wrote to Russert and diGenova challenging diGenova's assertions and demanding proof.

Said Lauer and Semmelman, diGenova conceded that this assertion was merely his "opinion," and not, necessarily, a fact.

The lawyers noted that another tactic used by Pollard's detractors was the mantra, "I cannot tell you because the information is classified."

"These kinds of assertions say nothing," Lauer and Semmelman argued, "but are intended to convey the impression that the speaker speaks with authority, and that Mr. Pollard caused unspeakable harm."

Not surprisingly, Pollard had powerful detractors in the intelligence world, including CIA director George Tenet who purportedly once told then-President Bill Clinton that he would resign if Clinton gave a presidential pardon to Pollard, or commuted Pollard's sentence.

As is noted in *The Hunting Horse*, former CIA director James Woolsey was also against the idea of Pollard being set free (although years later he would have a change of heart). Woolsey told a National Press Club audience that he had recommended against a pardon for Pollard, in 1994, because, even though Pollard stole secrets for a friendly government, "what he stole was so massive and so highly classified that I thought a lengthy penalty was entirely justified."

It was also widely reported—when Pollard was used as a bargaining chip during the Israeli-Palestinian peace talks at the Wye River Conference Center between Clinton and Israeli Prime Minister Benjamin Netanyau—that the chairman of the Senate Intelligence Committee, Sen. Richard Shelby (R-Ala.), wrote a letter to Clinton stating how "deeply disturbed" he was that the release of Pollard was even being considered by the president. Shelby said in the letter that he had "the strongest objections, now or in the future," concerning the pardoning of Pollard.

Notwithstanding, one of those in the intelligence world who strongly disagreed with the assessment of Tenet, Woolsey, Shelby and others, concerning Pollard, was Angelo Codevilla, a former senior staff member of the Senate Intelligence Committee.

Codevilla had bluntly stated on the record: "I know as much as there is to know about the intelligence business. I've offered many times to talk to anybody who thinks Pollard has done great harm to U.S. intelligence."

Addressing the accusations that the information Pollard gave Israel cost the lives of American operatives in the former Soviet Union, the former Senate Intelligence Committee staffer, in an interview with *Washington Weekly* reporter Wesley Phalen, put it this way: "Those losses were later attributed to, and rightly so, to (CIA spy and traitor) Aldrich Ames. It's significant that the man who wrote the damage report on Pollard was none other than Aldrich Ames himself."

CIA spokesperson Anya Guilsher disputed Codevilla's claim, however. In an article he wrote in *The Forward*, reporter Seth Gittell said Guilsher told him that Ames played no role in the Pollard damage assessment.

Woolsey agreed with Guilsher. "I know the individual who did the [damage report], and it was not Aldrich Ames," the former DCI said, not elaborating on who that person was.

Told of the assertion by Guilsher and Woolsey, Codevilla said it struck him as "a bold-faced lie."

"If the assertion is made that Pollard had something to do with the compromise of agents in the former Soviet Union and Eastern Europe, why would the chief of counterintelligence in Eastern Europe and the Soviet Union not have a role?" Codevilla rhetorically asked.

Guilsher responded, "In theory, you would think that Ames had a role, but at the time the assessment was done, he didn't."

"The CIA is engaged in the Clintonization of language," Codevilla shot back. "The CIA is hiding the fact that Ames played a major role in convincing it that Pollard was responsible for agent compromises."

John Walker is a retired U.S. Navy Chief Warrant Officer who operated as a full-time agent for the Soviets, and masterminded, organized and recruited his own little spy ring that did extensive cold war damage to the United States. In his interview with Wesley Phelan, published in January 1999, Codevilla argued that Pollard—who spent six years in solitary confinement in Marion

Penitentiary, in Marion, Illinois—was treated worse than the likes of Walker and, even, Aldrich Ames.

"Ames and Walker are the people who, without a doubt, have done the greatest harm to the U.S.," Codevilla said, two years before the arrest of another infamous spy, the FBI's Robert Hanssen. "In the case of Walker, it is fair to say that if there had been a war between the U.S. and the Soviet Union in the 1970s or 1980s, the Soviet Union would have won it largely due to the efforts of John Walker. Walker gave them the capacity to read all our Navy generated messages, and, therefore, many of the other messages generated by U.S. code machines."

Asked what it was specifically that Ames did, Codevilla explained that Ames was "the man in charge of validating all the information from the U.S.S.R., and the man in charge of safeguarding our own agents in the U.S.S.R." As Codevilla recalled, Ames handed the Soviets the names of every one of America's moles working in the former Soviet Union.

"That allowed the Soviets to capture or turn those agents," Codevilla said. "That means all of the intelligence—and I do mean all—coming from human sources in the U.S.S.R., from about 1985 to the collapse of the U.S.S.R., was manipulated entirely by the Soviets."

Phelan then asked Codevilla what was it, exactly, that Pollard gave to the Israelis?

"He gave them that part of the flow of U.S. intelligence they used to receive regularly, but which the U.S. cut off after 1981," Codevilla said.

Codevilla said the U.S. had a long-standing, mutually beneficial intelligence exchange agreement with Israel. In 1981, Codevilla explained, Israel used some of the information it got from American satellites to strike and destroy Iraq's nuclear reactor at Osirak. As is noted in *The Hunting Horse*, this angered Admiral Bobby Inman, at the time the deputy director of the CIA, who made the decision, along with Defense Secretary Weinberger, to—in the words of Codevilla—"cut off a good chunk of the information flow."

"Because of that strike?" asked Phelan.

"Yes," Codevilla said. "I was in the U.S. Intelligence Committee hearing room when Bobby Ray Inman came in and told us how outraged he was that Israel had destroyed Iraq's nuclear reactor. He told us that the U.S. was engaged in a 'sophisticated and very successful effort' to turn Saddam Hussein into a pillar of American foreign policy in the Middle East. The Israelis, in their blundering ways, as he put it, had misunderstood Saddam Hussein. They had figured this nuclear reactor posed a danger of Saddam building nuclear weapons. Our CIA 'knew better than that,' and was outraged that the Israelis had done this. As a result, Inman was unilaterally cutting off the flow of U.S. intelligence to the Israelis."

What was Weinberger's motive in presenting to the judge a false memorandum?" Phelan asked.

"It comes down to this," Codevilla replied, "the embarrassment over a dumb, failed policy, and, moreover, a policy in which Weinberger had a personal interest. The policy was building up Iraq, a policy to which Weinberger and much of the rest of the U.S. government sacrificed true American interests during the 1980s.

"And up until the very eve of the (first) Gulf War, the U.S. government was still incredulous that Saddam Hussein would play anything other than the role which the best, and the brightest, of the Reagan and Bush administrations had assigned him."

Exactly what was in the so-called "Weinberger memo," many believed, held the key to getting Pollard released. In a letter to the editor that appeared in the *New York Sun*, on February 19, 2003, lawyers Lauer and Semmelman told of their dilemma of getting to see exactly what was in that memo.

In that letter, the lawyers stressed that information Pollard passed on to the Israelis, nearly two decades earlier, included American-gathered information about Iraq's chemical warfare production capabilities, "such as satellite pictures and maps showing the location of production factories and storage facilities, some of which were apparently constructed by Bechtel, Inc., Caspar Weinberger's former company."

Lauer and Semmelman stressed that Weinberger, as secretary of defense, took the "unprecedented step" of personally intervening in Pollard's sentencing and urging the court to give Pollard a life sentence.

"Pollard provided Israel with information concerning Iraq's chemical weapons at a time when America was facilitating Iraq's acquisition of chemical and biological precursor agents, and supplying Iraq with intelligence information as part of its new pro-Iraq, anti-Iran policy—a policy spearheaded by Weinberger," the lawyers said.

They added that in May 2000, when they took on Pollard's case, pro-bono, they immediately applied for—and obtained—Top Secret security clearance so they could examine the more than forty pages that made up the pre-sentencing declaration, and the four-page supplemental declaration, signed by the defense secretary. "These pages were from Pollard's sentencing file, sealed pursuant to the government's request," Lauer and Semmelman stated. "No one—including Pollard and his lawyers—has seen these pages since the day of his sentencing on March 4, 1987. These documents consist of redacted portions of a declaration by Weinberger and related material."

Despite their security clearances, Lauer and Semmelman were denied access, as they put it, "stonewalling our efforts with un-yielding and thus far successful tactics before the federal court."

"We suspect," they concluded, "that the government's refusal to allow us access to the documents, cloaked in a purported concern for 'national security,' is, in truth, fueled by a desire to prevent its own embarrassment were the contents of the document to be reviewed."

Documents, no doubt, that could have held the very key to Jonathan Pollard's fate.

CHAPTER NINE

ELVIS HAS LEFT THE BUILDING

O N MARCH 5, 2003, Jonathan Pollard's wife, Esther Zeitz-Pollard, once again took aim at one of her favorite targets: Ariel Sharon.

Asked by interviewer Aaron Lerner to react to the swearing in of the new Israeli government a week earlier—when the prime minister stressed his government's commitment to the release of an Israeli political prisoner in Egypt, Azzam Azzam, but made no mention of Jonathan Pollard—Zeitz-Pollard said she was "shocked, but not surprised."

"Sharon's omission of Jonathan while the eyes of the world were upon him was calculated," Zeitz-Pollard said. "The message was not lost on the Americans—namely, that Pollard is a non-issue for Israel. For years, Sharon has been consistent in his antipathy toward Jonathan."

Zeitz-Pollard stressed that soon after Ariel Sharon first took office she met with the new prime minister, along with Israeli minister Rechavam Ze'evi, who "pleaded with Sharon not to abandon Jonathan."

Zeitz-Pollard said at the time they provided Sharon with what she called an "effective plan" to secure Pollard's release. "Sharon refused to act upon it, or any other initiative," Zeitz-Pollard said. "After the meeting, Sharon privately made it clear to Rechavam that the only way he is prepared to bring Pollard home is in a coffin. All of Sharon's actions since then have been consistently hostile."

Lerner then asked Zeitz-Pollard to respond to people who blame her for her husband's plight, and argue that if she would cooperate with the Israeli government, instead of criticizing it, "Jonathan would have been out long ago."

"Blaming the victim is a convenient excuse for inaction," Zeitz-Pollard said. "For more than a decade Jonathan cooperated fully with the government of Israel, and he remained silent while they subverted his case and buried him alive. I am Jonathan's voice in the outside world. By necessity, I speak for him when he is not permitted to do so for himself."

Zeitz-Pollard was a bit less caustic in her remarks about former Israeli Prime Minister Benjamin Netanyahu than she was about the other Israeli prime ministers with whom she had met. She called Netanyahu by his nickname, "Bibi," and said Netanyahu—who attempted to negotiate the release of Pollard when he met with President Bill Clinton during the ongoing Israeli-Palestinian peace talks at the Wye River Conference Center—"had the potential for greatness."

"He has a good heart and he means well," Zeitz-Pollard said. "But he fears man when he should fear only heaven. And that has repeatedly been his undoing."

***

On January 7, 2002, Netanyahu, no longer the Israeli prime minister, was ushered into a large room to meet with a prison inmate, not in Israel, but in North Carolina. The prisoner was being held at the Medium Security Facility known as the Federal Correctional Institution at Butner, and the number he wore on his shirt was 09185-016. Netanyahu had flown to Raleigh-Durham, then made the twenty minute drive to the prison, to talk to the inmate, Jonathan Jay Pollard, the infamous American Jewish spy who received a life term in prison for passing classified information to the State of Israel. Netanyahu felt it was the least he could do.

Edwin Black, author of the best-selling book *IBM and the Holocaust*, wrote a six thousand word article on the Pollard case. In his article Black recalled Netanyahu's visit that day with the Jewish spy. To get Netanyahu's impressions firsthand, Black spoke to the former prime minister, reaching him by telephone.

"For a few hours, within earshot of a National Security Agency monitor, Netanyahu and Pollard spoke about the anguish of his (Pollard's) imprisonment, and practical ideas to set him free," Black wrote.

Black recalled Netanyahu telling him: "Contrary to perfidious rumors about his manner, Pollard was absolutely clear and in control, both intellectually and emotionally. Remember, he did not work for anyone but Israel, yet he remains in jail after seventeen years. Others worked for other countries, and they were set free long ago. A great injustice has been perpetrated by keeping Pollard endlessly in jail."

The phone call woke me up from a Sunday nap. Groggily, I lifted up the receiver. "Hello," I said. For a moment I didn't hear anything. Then I heard the voice of a man who told me his name, but, since I was still half asleep, I couldn't understand what he was saying.

"Who is this?" I asked.

"Edwin Black," came the reply, as if his name should have meant something to me.

I could barely hear him. I thought he was phone solicitor trying to sell me a satellite dish or a new telephone service.

"Who is this?" I asked again. "Edwin Black," he repeated. "Are you the author of *The Hunting Horse?*"

My ears perked. "I am," I said.

Still only half awake, I listened as Edwin Black told me who he was, that he had written the book *IBM and the Holocaust*, that he had read my book *The Hunting Horse*, that he got my phone number from my publisher, and that he wanted to ask me a few questions for a story he was doing on the Pollard case.

"Sure," I said. It wasn't long before I became at least somewhat coherent and I tried to help him as much as I could.

It was perhaps a week or so later that Edwin Black emailed me to let me know what day his story would be coming out, and where I could find it. When the story appeared in a local newspaper, *The Miami Herald*, I read it. While disappointed that my quotes were nowhere to be found, the story was nevertheless the kind of comprehensive work I would have expected from someone with Edwin Black's sterling reputation.

In his article, Black stressed that while Pollard had a lot of powerful people in his corner who wanted to see him set free, he also had many enemies who wanted to keep him just where he was. "Virtually the entire U.S. intelligence and defense establishment, with CIA Director George Tenet acting as the point man, want Pollard to rot in jail, forever," Black stated. He noted there were many Jewish leaders, as well, who were "revolted" by Pollard's "misguided treachery."

He continued: "Opinion makers, columnists and journalists—many of them Jewish, such as syndicated Jewish media columnist

Doug Bloomfield—have filled the airwaves and printed pages with damnation for Pollard's betrayal."

Actually, I knew that Bloomfield—we later met at a Jewish Federation event after our back-and-forth emails—wasn't quite as harsh about Pollard as Black implied. From the conversation we had, and from his opinion pieces that I read, Bloomfield in fact seemed to be far more critical of Pollard's wife, Esther, and the problems she may have inadvertently caused for her husband, than he was about Pollard himself.

Black, who mentioned that four books had been written on the Pollard case, also referred to Wolf Blitzer's book as the "gold standard"—something I had to take issue with, as well, since, while I had great respect for Wolf, I unabashedly felt that *The Hunting Horse* was the real gold standard. Of course, I wasn't exactly unbiased.

In his expansive piece Black noted that Pollard, in 1987, was convicted of a single count of disclosing documents to an ally foreign government, and not to an enemy such as the former Soviet Union. As Black correctly stated, Pollard received, by far, the longest sentence in U.S. history given to anyone for spying for a friendly government.

The question all of us have asked was *why?*

Black hypothesized that, after an "an intense review" of thousands of pages of Pollard documents, dozens of interviews with prosecutors, senior intelligence officers, and current and former Israeli and American government officials, the answer seemed to focus on two men: attorney Richard Hibey, who was accused by Pollard and his new team of lawyers, Eliot Lauer and Jacques Semmelman, of bungling his defense; and Pollard, himself, whose "provocative conduct," in the words of Black, "sealed his own fate."

In a section of his article that he titled "The Crime," Black recalled an interview he had with former Defense Secretary Caspar Weinberger. Black stated that, according to Weinberger, it was Judge Aubrey Robinson who requested a damage assessment report from Weinberger, and not the other way around. A redacted copy of the sworn forty-six page declaration Weinberger gave Robinson alleged that Pollard "compromised the most sensitive aspect of American intelligence," Black said. "More than just intelligence substance, Pollard revealed the carefully guarded aspect of American intelligence known as 'sources and methods'."

Black noted that while three classifications—confidential, secret, and top secret—govern U.S. intelligence, there is a special designation, beyond top secret, called Sensitive Compartmented Information (SCI). "Beyond even the highest security clearance, SCI limits access to those with a demonstrated 'need to know'," Black said. "Adding a 'code word' to the top secret/SCI classification restricts access to those not only with a top secret clearance, but also codeword specific authority."

Based on what he said he was told by Weinberger and others, Black stated in his article that, as a "key analyst" in the office of Naval Intelligence, Pollard enjoyed SCI multi-codeword access. As a result, numerous messages, some of which were "codeword sensitive," reached Pollard's handlers in Israel. In addition, Black stressed, Pollard gave the Israelis more than eight hundred unredacted reports and publications.

Even more importantly, Black stated, Israel was suspected of re-editing and, then, trading the information with other intelligence services. Stated Black: "Washington resented that its secret information was no longer under U.S. control. It could theoretically end up anywhere, including Moscow, as a bargaining chip while Israel was trying to free Soviet Jews."

Black also levied some other charges. He stated that Pollard passed along to the Israelis a special "compendium" of intelligence community documents that outlined for the Israelis just how much Washington was withholding under a March 1982 Israel-American intelligence-sharing agreement.

On that point, Black and I agreed, because I knew that to be true.

Black also repeated the charges that numerous intelligence reports about Soviet missile systems, delivered by Pollard, exposed the way America analyzed Soviet weapons.

In addition, Black noted, Pollard photocopied the massive ten-volume RASIN Manual, an acronym for Radio and Signals Intercepts and Notations. Black described the manual as the "Bible" of the intelligence world, emphasizing its extraordinary importance. He stressed that the RASIN Manual details America's global listening profile, "frequency by frequency, source by source, geographic slice by geographic slice." RASIN, Black stated, was, in effect, a "complete roadmap to American signal intelligence."

An intelligence source of mine nevertheless strongly disagreed with Black's depiction of RASIN's actual importance.

"RASIN is simply a listing, country by country, of all their radio and signals, meaning radar and microwave, etc.," my source told me. "It is then easier for signals spooks to find the right frequency to listen to alien communications. It is eavesdropping, known in the intelligence world as 'coverage.' But it is by no means the 'Bible' of the intelligence world.

"As far as it being a 'complete roadmap,' I also fail to see the correlation. It is simply everyone else's signal frequencies, and, frankly, I believe that everyone else knows their own frequencies. It is highly classified because the National Security Agency (NSA) does not want everyone to know that the NSA knows their frequencies, and is listening in, which of course they do know. Besides that, the frequencies change daily, sometimes hourly, so the real value is questionable.

"Another point about RASIN is that it is so highly classified that people cleared to use it daily in their work are never allowed to use more than one volume at a time. So the very idea that that Jonathan Pollard, a GS-12 from Navy Intel in Suitland, could get his hands on a complete set of RASIN manuals is ludicrous. The NSA is located in Fort Meade, Maryland, and RASIN, unlike Elvis, never leaves the building."

Regardless, Black stressed that, according to "informed sources," Pollard's RASIN Manual disclosure was the crux of that secret courtroom exchange held just moments before the outraged judge finally pronounced a life sentence. "Some estimate the loss of the RASIN Manual cost America billions of dollars, and many years to completely restructure our worldwide eavesdropping operation," Black wrote.

But Angelo Codevilla, echoing the sentiments of my intelligence source, also took issue with the exaggerated claims of the damage Pollard caused.

"Pollard wrongly took it upon himself to provide to Israel that which had been cut off," acknowledged Codevilla, who, from 1978-1985 served as a senior staff member for the Senate Intelligence Committee. Still, as he had in past interviews, Codevilla argued that it was highly doubtful Pollard could have even gotten his hands on the kinds of intelligence flow that would fall under the heading of "Codeword." He noted that what Pollard gave Israel consisted of "satellite pictures, reports of all kinds, electronic directories, so on and so forth."

"But Pollard could not have provided codes, because he did not have access to codes," Codevilla said bluntly. "GS-12 analysts don't."

After reading Edwin Black's story, I sent him an email and congratulated him on a job well done. I then brought up some areas in which I disagreed with his conclusions.

"As for Jonathan Pollard's clearances, it's my understanding that he had across the board Top Secret, but not Codeword clearance," I said, "so I'm not sure how he betrayed our sources and methods, as was told to you by your sources. By the way, the exposing of our sources and methods, as I note in *The Hunting Horse*, is an all-encompassing Band-Aid that is always used by the intelligence community."

"You mention that Israel is suspected of re-editing and trading information to other intelligence sources," I continued. "As far as I know, there is no proof of this. These rumors probably took root after Pulitzer Prize-winning author Seymour Hersh wrote in his book, *The Samson Option*, that a sanitized version of some of Pollard's information was given to the Soviets by then-Prime Minister Yitzhak Shamir. We do know that information that reached the KGB resulted in the "rolling up" (and executions) of CIA moles operating behind the Iron Curtain. But while suspicion fell on Pollard, in actuality the man who fingered these people was Aldrich Ames—and that was later verified by Ames, himself, and FBI spy Robert Hanssen."

Former Defense Secretary Weinberger, who in the Second World War fought bravely in the Pacific under the command of Gen. Douglas MacArthur, later served in both the Nixon and Reagan administrations. In his comprehensive memoir, *In the Arena*, he seemingly pulled no punches, yet did not mention anything about the Pollard spy case. I found that extremely interesting, especially considering that Weinberger once said that, during his watch, Pollard did "substantial and irrevocable damage to this nation," and was the "worst spy in American history." Apparently, Ed Black was also puzzled about this. When he interviewed Weinberger, he asked him why the Pollard case wasn't mentioned in his book.

Weinberger told Black, "Because it was, in a sense, a very minor matter. It was made bigger than its actual importance."

Pressed by Black on why the case was made far bigger than its actual importance, Weinberger replied, "I don't know why. It just was."

CHAPTER TEN

THE AFFABLE IRISHMAN

WHILE **SUZANNE MIGDALL**—my partner in our motion picture project—was working day and night on developing a motion picture deal based on *The Hunting Horse*, I kept my "day job," which consisted of doing publicity and marketing for the Jewish Federation of Broward County, Florida—a charitable organization, similar to United Way, serving Fort Lauderdale and the surrounding areas.

Cooper City, one of those surrounding areas, was a growing, affluent community. Like much of Broward County, it received an influx of people after Hurricane Andrew struck in neighboring Dade County a decade earlier. Davie, which bordered Cooper City, was a place that was dotted with ranches and where you could find real, live cowboys. Cooper City was more like the town of Weston, also in Broward, and where Miami Dolphins football legend Dan Marino lived with his family in a multi-million dollar home. In Cooper City, as in Weston, there were no cattle, but plenty of Lexus', BMWs and SUVs.

The purpose of the Jewish Federation was a noble one: to help those in the Jewish community, such as the indigent elderly, who needed communal assistance. Therefore, those who lived in the well-healed enclaves like Cooper City and Weston were asked by Federation volunteers to give back to the less fortunate, which they often did. One way this was done was through Federation fundraising events featuring well-known guest speakers.

On October 24, 2002, Temple Beth Emet, a Cooper City synagogue, was scheduled to host such an event that was being sponsored by the Jewish Federation's Women's Division. The special guest speaker that evening was to be John Loftus, the Irish Catholic former federal prosecutor and author who championed Jewish causes.

Truth be told, I was looking forward to going to the event and hearing what Loftus had to say, since I knew how well informed, bright, articulate, and hilariously funny he was.

Before interviewing Loftus I wrote an article on him that I then sent out to various media in the hopes of publicizing our event. The article appeared in both the *South Florida Sun-Sentinel* and the *Miami Herald*.

I wrote in part:

John Loftus, the muckraking Irish-Catholic former federal prosecutor who has long been a champion of Jews and Israel—and is the author of several major books, including *The Secret War Against the Jews* and *Unholy Trinity: The Vatican, the Nazis and the Swiss Banks*—insists that the United States government has covered up evidence of a massive Saudi network to finance Islamic terrorists.

Currently president of the Florida Holocaust Museum in St. Petersburg, Loftus, who has filed a lawsuit to expose this network, claims it has used Florida charities to launder money to terrorist organizations.

Making a reputation for himself in the Justice Department as a hunter of Nazi war criminals in America, Loftus, for the past 20 years, has been a gadfly of the U.S. intelligence community, publishing books and articles based on information from whistleblower "spooks." A number of his sources have alleged that at least some members of America's intelligence-gathering agencies, perhaps because of political expediency, have also ignored intelligence vital to U.S. security.

In his lawsuit, however, it's a Kuwaiti national, Sami al-Arian, whom Loftus has directly in his crosshairs. Al-Arian is the controversial professor who has been suspended from the University of South Florida amid charges that he's been a liaison of the Iranian-sponsored terrorist group Islamic Jihad. Al-Arian, and his brother-in-law Mazen Al-Najjar, a fellow teacher at the University of South Florida (and who was himself deported in August), co-founded the World and Islam Studies Enterprises (WISE), a now defunct Islamic think tank at the USF that was the focus of an FBI raid in 1995. WISE's former head, Ramadan Abdulah Shallah, left that group the same year before resurfacing as the head of the terrorist organization Islamic Jihad.

Loftus charges that the Justice Department has refused to prosecute al Arian despite acquiring substantial evidence to show that he had committed numerous crimes, including mail and tax fraud. The reason for this hands-off approach, Loftus said, is that the prosecution of al Arian would disclose that he was a small, but significant part of a global money laundering network operated under the guise of purported American charities run by the government of Saudi Arabia. "In truth and in fact, the government of Saudi Arabia has used these charitable fronts in America to fund hate groups, racist organizations and terrorist operations," Loftus said.

Loftus, who cites "confidential client sources," said the State Department asked the Justice Department to terminate a 1995 criminal investigation of al Arian after the discovery of Saudi involvement. The pressure by the State Department on the FBI grew so great, states Loftus, that a key agent, John O'Neill, quit the bureau in protest.

"In the last year," Loftus said, "I have received highly classified information from several of my confidential clients concerning a Saudi covert operation. The Saudi relationship is so sensitive that, for more than a decade, federal prosecutors and counter-terrorist agents have been ordered to shut down their investigations for reasons of foreign policy."

The purpose of his filing his lawsuit in Hillsborough County Court, Loftus said, is to specifically expose the manner in which Florida charities were used as a money laundry for "tax-deductible terrorism."

"The complaint sites specific testimony, including highly-classified information which has never been released before," Loftus said. "Simply put, the Saudi government was laundering money through Florida charities run by University of South Florida professor Sami al Arian for the support of terrorist groups in the Middle East. And through the al Arian network, and others, the Saudi government secretly funded al Qaeda, Hamas and Islamic Jihad."

To Loftus—whose forthcoming book will be titled *Prophets of Terror: Jonathan Pollard and Peace in the Middle East*—the purpose of the Saudi backing of terrorists has basically been two-fold: it would hopefully lead to the destruction of the State of Israel, and it would prevent the formation of an independent Palestinian state. After all, explained Loftus, to the Saudis, a Palestinian nation that could conceivably become a democratic state would be a veritable "cancer" in the Arab world. "It would be a destabilizing example of freedom," he said, "that would threaten Arab dictators everywhere."

The tough-minded former prosecutor apparently believed not only in being proactive in fighting terrorists, but in taking the fight to those who financially support them. One way to do this, he felt, was by cutting off the flow of the money by choking off the source—in this case, the government of Saudi Arabia.

My interview was scheduled, and I called Loftus at his home in St. Petersburg, Florida. When he answered, I told him who I was—I wasn't sure if he remembered me—and that I represented the Jewish Federation. Since I was doing the interview for the Federation, I definitely wanted to include some kind of a Jewish angle.

"John," I asked, "what got you so involved in Jewish causes? Was it your background with the Justice Department prosecuting ex-Nazis?"

"My involvement really began when I was handling CIA cases and Nazi war crimes cases," he replied. "Then I got permission from the intelligence community to be a whistle-blower."

Now that I got that out of the way, I wanted to focus on the Saudis. I also wanted to pick Loftus' brain concerning the Oklahoma City bombing, which I still felt had a Middle East connection. Could there also have been Saudi terrorists involved?

"Have you ever found an al-Arian link to the Oklahoma City bombing, which some in the intelligence community have already linked Iraq to?" I asked.

"No," he said. "There may be an al Qaeda link, though, but it's still too early to tell."

"What is your opinion on our waging war with Iraq at this time?" I then asked. "Are we compelled to 'take out' Saddam Hussein before he becomes too powerful?"

"It's pretty clear that Saddam Hussein is rearming [Iraq] with chemical and biological weapons," Loftus told me. (I agreed wholeheartedly, in spite of the fact that those weapons were proving hard to find). "If Saddam Hussein gives up some of his bio-chemical weapons to terrorists, then the casualties to Israel, and America, could be very high. We're going to have to fight Saddam Hussein sooner or later. It might as well be sooner."

"Why is there so much opposition to our attacking him now?" I asked.

"People are always suspicious of a war that gets launched just before Election Day," he replied.

"How dangerous are the terrorist cells in the U.S.," I asked, "and what should the public know about these cells that we don't already know?"

"Really, there is a lot that we still don't know," he said, "and there are still so many leads that need to be followed up."

"Can we dry up the money sources of these terrorists?" I asked "How best to do that?"

"We can disrupt their financial operations," replied Loftus, "which is what we did with the Saudis, and we can disrupt the base of their operations, like we did in Afghanistan, which leaves them in chaos. The bulk of the money [supporting terrorism] was coming from the Saudis. In one of our lawsuits we're now going after the Saudis on behalf of the victims of September 11. It's a trillion dollar lawsuit—$300 million for each family."

"Do you think you can actually win this lawsuit?" I asked.

"I think so," he said. "We have a shot to win. I first ran it by forty of the top lawyers in America. Then, on August 15 [2002], our lawyers filed a lawsuit [against the Saudis] in the District of Columbia."

I finished up my questions with one that, by Loftus' reaction, would let me know if he remembered our meeting regarding my own Pollard book that I was trying to get off the ground. .

"Will your new book on the Pollard case, *Prophets of Terror: Jonathan Pollard and Peace in the Middle East*, be coming out soon?" I asked.

"Every time I think I have a chapter completed in this book," he said matter-of-factly, "something else new about the case comes up."

On the day of the event, I saw Loftus, we shook hands, he asked me how I was doing, I asked him about his health—since I knew he had survived a bout with colon cancer—and I wished him well. He nodded that he was fine, then walked away to hob-nob with the guests.

Minutes later, however, Charlotte Baker, a Federation volunteer who knew about my book *The Hunting Horse*, and knew about Loftus' interest in Pollard, intercepted Loftus, and told him that I had written a "wonderful" book about the Pollard case. At that instant, a light bulb appeared to go off in the affable Irishman's head.

Loftus turned toward me. He then smiled warmly, perhaps in recognition that I was able to get my book published, after all.

I felt like saying, "You bet your ass, I did."

CHAPTER ELEVEN

WINDOW INTO A COVERT WORLD

LESS THAN A year after John Loftus and I met at that fundraiser in Cooper City, Florida, Loftus wrote an article that appeared in *Moment Magazine* in which he gave his own spin on the Pollard case. Loftus argued that the reason Jewish leaders didn't rally to Pollard's side, early on, was because, just prior to Pollard's sentencing in March of 1987, Senator Chic Hecht (R-NV), a senior member of the Senate Intelligence Committee, urged them not to.

Hecht "telephoned the leaders of every major Jewish organization to warn them not to support Pollard in any way," Loftus said. According to Loftus, Hecht told the Jewish leaders that Pollard had done something "so horrible, that it could never be made public."

Considering that the senator had earned his stripes with Jews, he had to be taken seriously. In August 1985, three months before Pollard's arrest, Hecht and fellow Senator Jessie Helms (R-N.C.), had made a private trip to Israel and came back to Washington as staunch Israeli supporters. In an article that was picked up in a number of newspapers, reporter Dennis J. Wamsted wrote that Hecht was also the recipient of "$45,000 from pro-Israel PACs."

***

An extremely powerful and politically well-connected source, who wished to remain anonymous—and may have had something to do with Jessie Helms and Chic Hecht's trip to Israel—shared his personal insights with Suzanne Migdall upon learning that Suzanne was developing a motion picture based on the Pollard case. Considering whom he was, this source's conclusions were illuminating.

"You might want to consult with the Israeli consul general in Miami and ask how the State of Israel will feel about a movie on Pollard," Suzanne's source wrote her in a letter dated June 24, 1998. "I don't think the State of Israel will welcome such a picture. This matter has been very embarrassing to the Israelis. Jeb Bush—Florida's gubernatorial candidate—asked his father to release Pollard. His father would not. I thought President Clinton would release Pollard. He has not. I hate to say it, but there must be something awful in this matter to have the White House (both Republican and Democrat) resist entreaties and enormous pressure from their traditional Jewish friends on this issue.

"I really have no advice on this matter. I hope what I have written is food for thought."

John Loftus, meanwhile, stated that credible Washington insiders, like Chic Hecht, thought they knew a big, dark, secret: that there were secret documents confirming that Pollard's little spy operation had cost the lives of U.S. moles behind the Iron Curtain. It was believed, Loftus said, that Pollard had given Israel a list of "every American spy inside the Soviet Union."

I had come to a similar conclusion when I first heard about the deaths of those agents. Not that I believed that it was Pollard's information that caused these agents either to be "turned," or "rolled up," but that it was Pollard who was taking the rap.

On a *Nightline* segment that aired March 11, 1992, journalist Pat Buchanan echoed the sentiments of many in Washington when he told host Chris Wallace that Pollard "is a traitor and spy who stole our secrets and gave them to the Israeli government, and, according to Seymour Hersh, the Israeli government then gave them to the Soviet Union."

From the information he had at his disposal, I could understand Buchanan's painting of Pollard as a traitor. The problem was: none of that information was true.

In December of 1993, within weeks of the publication of my first book on the Pollard case, *The Spy Who Knew Too Much*, *Time* Magazine also reported that one of the documents Pollard allegedly slipped to the Israelis was a huge National Security Agency compendium of frequencies—used by foreign intelligence services—that may have found its way into Soviet hands. *Time* was obviously referring to the RASIN manuals, which, in actuality, Pollard could never have gotten his hands on.

In a December 10, 1993 letter to the magazine, Pollard's attorney, Theodore Olson, angrily retorted: "Five layers of innuendo, and no facts, equal a manifestly frivolous story. The 'officials' who are using you to sabotage the Pollard commutation effort obviously have no facts to back up their insinuations."

Nearly ten years later, John Loftus noted in his *Moment* Magazine article that, on several occasions before Pollard's arrest, Soviet agents in New York had posed as Israelis. Loftus reasoned that this same game was possibly being played in Israel, where it's likely the Mossad could have been infiltrated by Soviet spies.

One scenario was that it was those spies who passed Pollard's information on to the KGB, thereby "wiping out American human assets in the Soviet Union."

It was a classic case of "false flagging," where agents of one nation pose as agents of another. The question is: Could Pollard have even gotten hold of that information in the first place?

What we do know for sure is this: Those American assets were wiped out. While Loftus stated that more than forty agents were captured or killed, the figure I heard was closer to a dozen or more of our spies. Regardless, Loftus was probably correct in his assessment when he stated that American intelligence had, for all intent and purposes, "gone blind behind the Iron Curtain."

In that context, Defense Secretary Weinberger could hardly have been blamed for calling Pollard the "worst spy in American history." Perhaps that's why, at Pollard's sentencing hearing on March 5, 1987, Weinberger angrily said, "It is difficult for me, even in the so-called 'Year of the Spy,' to conceive of greater harm to national security than that caused by the defendant."

As is noted in *The Hunting Horse*, Pulitzer Prize-winning reporter Seymour Hersh alleged in his book, *The Samson Option*, that Israeli Prime Minister Yitzhak Shamir okayed giving Moscow U.S. intelligence on the Soviet Union obtained by Pollard, and that the prime minister—who had always wanted to improve relations with the Soviet Union anyway—eventually gave Moscow a sanitized version of what Pollard gave Israel.

In a letter to me Pollard admitted that the KGB did have an interest in knowing the degree to which its activities in the Middle East were being monitored by the CIA and other western intelligence organizations. But, he added, "considering the reams of information the Soviets had received from people like (Soviet spy) John Walker, the Russians had access to things that were completely off limits to myself as a Naval Intelligence analyst."

Loftus came to a similar conclusion, stating in his *Moment* Magazine article that Pollard didn't have "blue-stripe" clearance. "The list of our secret agents in Russia had been kept in a special safe in a special room with 'blue stripe' clearance needed for access," Loftus explained. "The lack of 'blue stripe' clearance was the final proof that Pollard could not possibly have betrayed our Russian agents."

Aldrich Hazen Ames, who did betray those agents, was a CIA Soviet counterintelligence expert, who, as a double agent, passed on reams of top-secret data to his benefactors in Moscow. He and his Columbian-born wife, Maria, were accused of raking in more than $1.5 million for feeding classified information to Russian agents during the nine years Ames was on the Kremlin's payroll. Two weeks after his arrest, *Newsweek* revealed that sources told the magazine that the KGB used information supplied by Ames to "roll up" more than twenty CIA operations, and that at least ten agents—working for the CIA within the Soviet Union—died as a result.

In 1985, the year Pollard was arrested, Valery Martynov and Sergei Mortorin, two KGB officers recruited by U.S. intelligence, were among those reportedly executed. We know now that it was Ames, and not Pollard, who exposed those CIA assets. Was Pollard, in essence, paying the price for Ames' crimes?

As Ames, himself, told the *New York Times*: "In 1985 and 1986, as a result of the information I sold the Soviets, it was as if neon lights and search lights lit up all the way to the Kremlin saying: 'There is penetration.' No reasonable counter-intelligence officer, FBI or the CIA, was under any doubt by the spring of '86 that a penetration of S/E (the CIA's Soviet/Eastern Europe Operations Division, headed by Ames) was the single, most logical reason for the disaster that had occurred."

In this type of atmosphere, and with the intelligence community in a literal panic over their inability to locate the source of the penetration, Pollard may have been the perfect foil.

Ames meanwhile admitted his role in the exposure of the agents in an interview that appeared in the *Washington Post*. "In the summer of 1984 (the time Pollard admits to have begun working for Israel), the CIA bureau in Moscow seemed on the verge of collapse," Ames recalled. "Not only the Moscow agents, but recruited Soviet officials in a handful of posts around the world were lost."

The CIA was obviously desperate to find the leak, while Ames would have had every reason to blame someone else for what was happening in the Moscow bureau. When Pollard was arrested in November of 1985, Ames was the man in charge of Soviet and Eastern Bloc counterintelligence within the CIA. It's logical to assume that before Weinberger sent his infamous "memo" to Judge Aubrey Robinson—recommending the harshest sentence allowable by law for Pollard—he (Weinberger) likely conferred with Ames, or, at the very least, would have read his report.

Notwithstanding, according to Loftus, some have blamed Pollard for the *other* agents—there were more than forty in all by Loftus' reckoning—who were turned or killed. However, states Loftus, those agents were betrayed, not by Pollard, but by FBI spy Robert Hanssen, arrested in February 2001. And Hanssen admitted as much once he was in custody.

So what about reporter Seymour Hersh? How did he get his information about Pollard, which was apparently disputed by both Ames and Hanssen? In *The Hunting Horse* I wrote that, as his main source, Hersh had used Ari Ben-Menashe, an Iraqi Jew and a former Israel intelligence operative. (Interestingly, John Loftus admitted it was he who was his longtime friend Hersh's "secret source" for Hersh's highly acclaimed book, *The Price of Power: Kissinger in Nixon's White House*.)

"Ben Menashe's account might seem almost too startling to be believed, had it not been subsequently amplified by a second Israeli, who cannot be named," Hersh wrote in *The Samson Option*. "The Israeli said the Pollard material was sanitized and dictated to a secretary before being turned over to the Soviets. Some material was directly provided to Yevgeni M. Primakov, the Soviet foreign ministry specialist on the Middle East who met publicly and privately with Shamir while he was prime minister."

Of course, as is noted in *The Hunting Horse*, there is no proof—only Ben Menashe's word, and that of an unidentified source—that any of this exchange with the Soviets ever took place. And anyone familiar with the Ben-Menashe's background would be just a bit skeptical.

In April 1989, two year's after Pollard's sentencing, Ben-Menashe was indicted—although he was eventually acquitted of the charges—following a U.S. Customs sting operation during which he allegedly attempted to sell three C-130 Hercules Transport planes to Iran without the necessary State Department approval. As author Joel Bainerman, who met and interviewed Ben-Menashe, said about him in his book, *Crimes of a President: New Revelations on Conspiracy and Cover-ups in the Bush and Reagan Administrations*: "He was simply a mouthpiece, a window into a covert world. It is up to investigative journalists and congressional committees to verify [what he says]."

An Israeli source of mine also disputed what Hersh and his source, Ben-Menashe, alleged. Before Hersh ran his story on the Pollard connection to the Soviets, Hersh called my source and asked him for a confirmation regarding Pollard's information winding up in the Kremlin.

"I told him," said my source, "that it never happened."

CHAPTER TWELVE

MEET BRAD PITT

ON **FEBRUARY 28**, 2003, it was revealed that manager/ producer Brad Grey and actor Brad Pitt were going into the movie production business together. Brad Pitt's wife, *Friend's* star Jennifer Aniston, would also be involved in the yet-to-be-named company as an equity partner.

According to a news release, playing up the theme that "two Brads are better than one," it was reported that Warner Brothers "has dangled a large carrot in a first-dollar gross deal for any films the Brads make, plus a fund for development, and an option for them to put together their own equity financing. Pitt said he and Aniston would also be hands-on in using their relationships to put films together, even the ones they won't star in." The article went on to say that, in the past, Pitt had been "pro-active and fee-flexible" to get movies from *Fight Club* to *Ocean's Eleven* made, but had yet to produce a film.

Grey's Brillstein-Grey management company, meanwhile, represented one hundred and fifty clients. Among the many projects attached to Brad Grey Pictures were *City by the Sea*, with

Robert De Niro; and *A View From the Top*, with Gwyneth Paltrow. Among the hits produced by Brad Grey Television were *Just Shoot Me* and a little show about a New Jersey mafia family called *The Sopranos*.

In the release, Pitt said one reason he was going into this new venture was that he and his wife had gotten started in a development capacity at the same time his friend, Brad Grey, was looking to expand his film company. Pitt was quoted as saying: "We want to let this venture define itself. It becomes harder to find things that spark your interest, and I've found there is a lot to be excited about in the development stage, being involved from conception to incarnation. It feels like the right vibe."

It was in March 2003 that Suzanne Migdall received a call on her cell-phone while she was at her son, Alexander's, Little League baseball game. "Are you sitting down?" asked an associate of Suzanne's who had contacts in the film industry.

"Go on," Suzanne said.

"You have a meeting with Brad Pitt," Suzanne's associate said.

Suzanne put her cell-phone closer to her ear. "Brad Pitt?" she said, not sure she heard him right.

"Yes, Brad Pitt," he repeated.

Within days, Suzanne flew out to LA.

Besides Brad Pitt, his wife, Jennifer Aniston, would be at the meeting, along with Brad Grey, Kristin Hahn, who worked for Pitt and Aniiston's production company under the umbrella of Brad Grey Management, and Brad Grey's lawyer, who was presumably there to protect his clients' interests, which meant there was a good chance that he could sabotage any deal. The meeting was held at in Brad Grey's office on Wilshire Boulevard.

When Suzanne began her pitch she felt extremely comfortable with Pitt. For one thing, he wasn't late for the meeting. For another, she felt that Pitt was down-to-earth, a regular guy, and very bright. He had a background in journalism and the Pollard story apparently intrigued him.

As Suzanne later recalled, "He was politically savvy—and had a serious side."

Suzanne had become very familiar with the case and Pitt could easily grasp what she was talking about. He would later tell Suzanne that he was "very, very interested" in *The Hunting Horse* project, and that he was soon flying off to Europe to begin shooting a movie he was starring in about the Trojan War. (The movie was *Troy* and Pitt would be playing the warrior Achilles.) We had no script, and therefore no shot list, but Pitt said he saw *The Hunting Horse* as around an "eighty to a hundred and twenty million dollar motion picture."

Aniston, on the other hand, seemed distracted and didn't get involved in any of the discussion. Apparently, our testosterone filled project did nothing to make her toes tingle. As for Brad Grey, he was apparently only lukewarm about the project, and Suzanne later told me he was tough to read.

The following day Pitt requested a second meeting with Suzanne. This time, neither Brad Grey nor Jennifer Aniston would be present. The meeting lasted more than two hours.

Recalls Suzanne: "We discussed writers and directors for the project, including Tony Scott, who Brad (Pitt) had worked with before, and Robert Redford." Scott, one of Hollywood's top action directors (*Crimson Tide*, *Man on Fire*, *Enemy of the State*), had directed both Pitt and Redford in *Spy Games*, while the legendary Redford also directed his friend, Pitt, in *A River Runs*

Though It. Years later, Scott would tragically take his own life after learning that he had an inoperable brain tumor.

"Brad said he wanted to work with Robert Redford again," Suzanne said. "Brad also told me during our meeting that he was 'obsessed' with the material and that he 'couldn't sleep because it was so compelling.' He said the treatment I gave him to read was the 'best treatment he had ever read.' He asked, also, if he could keep our *60 Minutes* tape of the interview Pollard did with Mike Wallace. I said he could. I then contacted Kristin Hahn who wanted to know how my meeting with Brad went."

After that meeting Suzanne left a message on my answering machine as well. "I just got out of the meeting with Brad Pitt and it looks positive," she said, "but it's hard to tell exactly. I was told there will be a final decision after the weekend."

The weekend passed and no decision was made. Pitt left the country to begin filming *Troy* and it was months before we heard anything.

In the meantime I officially became a "talking head" on September 1, 2003, when I appeared as a guest on CNN. I had done television before, a number of times in fact, but never live TV. There is a difference. On live TV you don't get to do it over. You get one shot, and you better be good.

Three days earlier, on Friday, August 29, I received a phone call from CNN's Megan Hundahl. Megan contacted me to see if I would appear on Anderson Cooper's show, the following Monday, which was also Labor Day.

I was on CNN's "short list" of potential guests because of my book *The Hunting Horse*. On Tuesday, September 2, Jonathan Pollard—who had not been seen in public in sixteen years—was scheduled to appear in front of U.S. District Court Judge

Thomas Hogan, in Washington, D.C. Pollard, himself, was not going to be allowed to speak at the hearing, but his capable team of lawyers—Eliot Lauer and Jacques Semmelman—would have the chance to argue the legal merits of their client being allowed to continue with his appeal.

While this new story was being widely reported in the print media, network television and cable outlets—with the notable exception of CNN—were hardly mentioning it, if mentioning it at all. That meant if I fell on my face, or froze on camera like some deer in the headlights, there would probably be no "superstar" talking head, like the eloquent Alan Dershowitz, to make an appearance on Fox, or CNBC, or *Nightline*, to do damage control, and, more importantly, to do a better job of making Pollard's case in front of the American public.

Truth be told, before anyone contacted me CNN had actually tried to get Dershowitz, but September 1 was Alan's birthday— just as it was the birthday of Gloria Estefan, Keannu Reeves, Barry Gibb, Richard Farnsworth, Alan Ladd, Yvonne DeCarlo, and two of my favorite Miami Dolphins: Jason Taylor and Zack Thomas. The famed lawyer had other plans for his birthday, and simply wasn't available.

So it was my baby. When I told people I knew to tune in, I knew I would be under national scrutiny and, hopefully, I would react well under the pressure. "Just be tough and be prepared," I said to myself. "And think of George Forman."

Why Big George? I remembered reading an interview years ago—it might have been in *Playboy*—in which the former heavyweight champion and multimillionaire product spokesperson was asked if had had ever been afraid in the ring.

"Yes, once," the two-time champ said, "the first time I fought Joe Frazier."

Huh? I said. Forman pummeled Frazier that night in 1973, and his punches literally lifted Frazier off his feet. Who could forget the unforgettable voice of Howard Cosell as he ranted, "Down goes Frazier, down goes Frazier!"

Yet, Forman, a three-to-one underdog, was legitimately worried about going into the ring with such a devastating puncher as "Smoking Joe." How did Big George overcome his fear? "I was prepared," he said.

I knew when I entered that "ring," I, too, was going to be prepared. I had better be.

I wasn't at all familiar with Anderson Cooper's show. It was on weekdays from 7 to 8 p.m. and, if I watched TV at all at that time, I was usually watching something else, and, later, would watch the "No Spin Zone" on Fox with Bill O'Reilly. So, after agreeing to be his guest, I watched Cooper, for the first time, and was impressed. He reminded me of a younger Tom Brokaw.

It was early in the afternoon of September 1 when I received a phone call from Hanh Bowie, a producer at CNN. To set some parameters for my interview that evening, Hanh went over some questions with me so that the host for my segment—not Anderson Cooper but, guest host, Soledad O'Brien—would have a better familiarity with the case.

I'm sure this was done for another reason as well. News organizations like CNN have ratings to consider and therefore lots of money at stake. Some of the people there might have been familiar with my book, but they really didn't know me from a hole in the wall. At the same time, it's imperative that any guest who appears on CNN is glib enough to be seen on national television. Simply put, if you appear in the national spotlight, and you speak like Bug's Bunny's pal Porky Pig, it doesn't make for very good TV.

So Hanh asked me a number of pertinent questions. At the end of our conversation she then asked, "Mr. Goldenberg, when was the last time you did live television?"

"Not for a while," I said, "but I've done it."

That was a mistruth. Actually, I didn't understand Hanh's question. I thought she was asking me if I had ever *been* on TV before. And I had. I had been on a number of programs that were taped. But live TV was different. It's like if someone asked you, "Have you ever ridden a horse?" Being a small child sitting on a horse's back, as someone else holds the reins and walks the horse around a corral, is not the same thing as holding the reins yourself as the powerful animal starts to gallop. The horse immediately knows who's in control.

Being interviewed on live TV is a little like being on a horse. You better hold on tight, and hope you don't get thrown off.

After speaking to Hanh I relaxed myself by watching a ballgame on TV. The Florida Marlins had come out of nowhere to be in the thick of the race for the National League Wild Card, and a chance to play in the World Series. They had just lost arguably their best player, third baseman Mike Lowell, for the remainder of the regular season. Lowell was put on the shelf by an errant pitch that broke a bone in his left hand. That set the stage for the Marlins to make a trade with the Baltimore Orioles for one of their heroes of the past—Jeff Conine, also known as "Mr. Marlin"—which they did just minutes before the September 1 trading deadline.

For me, watching this drama unfold, seeing the return of "Mr. Marlin," and just taking in a good ballgame, was the perfect escape before I, myself, would be making my own appearance on center stage.

The ballgame was still on when I left for CNN's studio in Miami. I arrived there at around 7 p.m. Lucky for me that I left early because the directions I got weren't very accurate. Then, once I parked my car, I wasn't able to get into the building. The doors were all locked and no one picked up the intercom when I dialed the code to CNN's office. If not for a cleaning lady who happened to pass by with her son—at least I believe she was a cleaning lady—there would have been no one there to let me in.

Once the cleaning lady let me inside I saw someone in the hallway who I believed to be a sound engineer. He apologized for the inconvenience. He explained that, because it was Labor Day, there was only a skeleton crew working, and that he thought I wasn't going to arrive until a little bit later. I told him I understood.

Perhaps fifteen minutes before the Pollard segment was scheduled to go on the air, the sound engineer led me into a dark room and I was told to sit in a comfortable chair. In front of me was a cameraman and bright TV lights. I could also see the TV monitor—the cameraman was behind it—and watched an interview taking place on a split screen. Behind me was a blank wall. I was then hooked up for TV, and a little earpiece was put into my right ear.

I watched the comely Soledad O'Brien and her guest (an expert on al Qaeda), and, at the same time, I could hear Soledad, through my earpiece, doing her interview. But I couldn't hear her very well. Then, from CNN headquarters in New York a producer told me to count to ten. I did. He said he heard me clearly. Then he counted to ten. I heard him clearly. I told him I was still having trouble hearing Soledad, however. He said not to worry. "When you go on, it'll be fine," he said.

After a commercial break the Pollard segment began. "Convicted spy Jonathan Pollard will appear in court tomorrow, trying to win the right to appeal his life sentence," O'Brien said. "But as CNN national security correspondent David Ensor reports, even though this is Pollard's first public appearance in sixteen years, who he was spying for has kept his case in the spotlight."

On videotape Ensor then stated that Pollard had served eighteen years of a life sentence—he was arrested in November of 1985—for spying against the United States, and on behalf of a friendly nation, Israel.

Joseph deGenova, the U.S. Attorney for the District of Columbia who prosecuted the case, was seen, next, in film footage, uttering his famous quote after Pollard received his life sentence from District Court Judge Aubrey Robinson. Said deGenova: "Mr. Pollard, I believe, will never see the light of day."

Ensor re-appeared on the screen, saying that deGenova "welcomed the life sentence imposed" after then-Defense Secretary Caspar Weinberger told the court, "It was difficult to conceive of greater damage to national security." But Pollard's lawyers and supporters, Ensor added, "argue the punishment far exceeds the crime."

In a videotaped interview, Rep, Anthony Weiner (D-NY), a staunch Pollard supporter, agreed that Pollard should have not passed U.S. intelligence documents to Israel. "But it is certainly not something that rose to the level that Caspar Weinberger alleged that it did," Weiner said bluntly.

Many U.S. intelligence officials, however, saw Pollard in far a different light.

Former President Bill Clinton was also seen in film footage telling reporters: "With respect to Mr. Pollard, I have agreed to review this matter seriously."

Ensor then stated that when Israeli Prime Minister Benjamin Netanyahu "convinced" Clinton to consider a pardon, the story was leaked that CIA Director George Tenet privately told Clinton that he (Tenet) would "have to resign" if Pollard's sentence was changed.

In another videotaped interview, Richard Haver, a former U.S. intelligence official who worked on the case, called Pollard "a traitor to the United States."

"He also, as far as I'm concerned, would have compromised the Israelis in a heartbeat, too, if it had struck him as something that he wanted to do," Haver said, "because that was—that's the story of Pollard when you look at it. He is now reinventing himself as a great Jewish patriot, and tried to present that to the people."

I was just sitting there, watching all this, amused by it, waiting to go on live. I knew that Jonathan Pollard was certainly no angel, but I knew something else as well: I knew that everything Richard Haver was saying was total, unadulterated, horseshit. I would now have the opportunity to kick people like Richard in the rear end.

Some neat graphics appeared on the screen as David Ensor continued his piece. You could actually see computerized models of satellites in space beaming down signals as Ensor told CNN's huge audience of some other allegations concerning Pollard. "U.S. and law enforcement officials say there are indications that top secret satellite and signals intelligence Pollard gave to Israel ended up in the hands of the Soviet Union," Ensor said. "Pollard's motives, they say, was money, pure and simple. There is evidence, they say, that Pollard also approached Pakistan, South Africa, and others, offering classified materials for sale."

Weiner disagreed.

"There has never been anywhere in the court documents, or anywhere else, the allegation that he spied for anyone else," Weiner said in his videotaped interview. "But this is what Jonathan Pollard is up against. He's sitting in a jail cell in maximum security while members of the intelligence community, some of which are only tangentially connected to this, are essentially free to say whatever they want."

Ensor once again appeared on camera. "Some U.S. officials say that if Israel was ever willing to detail the documents and intelligence that Pollard stole, then officials here might be willing to drop their strong opposition to letting him go.

"David Ensor, CNN, Washington."

I could hear Soledad O'Brien, but just barely, as I turned up the volume of my earpiece. "Elliot Goldenberg wrote the book *The Hunting Horse: The Truth Behind the Jonathan Pollard Spy Case*," she began. "He joins us this evening from Miami."

I could see myself on a split screen with O'Brien, and with a superimposed Miami skyline behind me.

"Good evening," O'Brien said, "nice to see you."

I was still having trouble hearing her.

"Hi, hello, how are you," I replied.

O'Brien: "I'm well, thank you. And thank you for joining us… Even Pollard's lawyers admit he spied for Israel. So what do you think are the grounds for cutting his sentence short?"

Goldenberg: "I'm sorry?

O'Brien: "Are you having trouble with audio?"

Goldenberg: "Yes."

O'Brien: Let me repeat my question for you. Even Pollard's attorneys would say, yes, he spied for Israel. So give me a sense of why you think his sentence should be cut short?"

Goldenberg: "Well, you know, first of all he spied for an American ally. He was the only person in the history of the United States who ever got a life sentence for spying for an ally. It's never happened before. No sentence has ever been close to that. So there is more to this case than meets the eye. That's for sure."

O'Brien: "Pollard supporters—and we have to include you among that group—believe he is an idealist, a patriot. You don't see him in any way as a traitor to this country?"

Goldenberg: "Well, you know, he certainly was never even accused of treason. He was accused of passing one—he was accused of passing classified information to an American ally, in the so-called Weinberger memo, which was given to Judge Aubrey Robinson after the damage assessment report.

"It—words like treasonous conduct were used which implied that Pollard committed treason. There's really a lot to this. As far as spying, you know, his information winding up in the hands of the Soviets, there's never been any proof of that. The person who did the damage assessment report on Pollard that was read by Caspar Weinberger, or allegedly did the damage assessment report, was none other than Aldrich Hazen Ames, who was the head of Soviet and Eastern bloc counterintelligence for the CIA.

"So it was a perfect frame. I mean, here's Ames trying to protect himself. And he does the damage assessment on Pollard that's read by Weinberger. And there were other Soviet—there were certain spies working behind the Iron Curtain that we did lose. They were rolled up, meaning they were executed.

"The thing is, who gave up these people? Whose information caused these people to be killed? Well, Ames admitted that it was his information after his arrest. And after the arrest of spy Robert Hanssen, the FBI spy, that was verified. So it seems that Pollard ..."

O'Brien: "Ames is ..."

Goldenberg: "I'm sorry?"

O'Brien: "Forgive me for interrupting you. I just wanted to make a point that Aldrich Ames was convicted, as you say, and is serving a life sentence in prison."

Goldenberg: "Right."

O'Brien: "Elliot Goldenberg, we're out of time, but I do want to thank you for joining us this evening."

Goldenberg: "Thank you."

Relieved I got through my interview relatively unscathed, I then watched on the monitor as Soledad O'Brien turned to the ubiquitous Wolf Blitzer who was in studio in New York.

"Our own Wolf Blitzer not only covered the Pollard story for CNN," O'Brien began, "but he also interviewed Pollard and wrote a book about him, *Territory of Lies: The Rise, Fall and Betrayal of Jonathan J. Pollard.* Wolf's taking a little break from prepping for the 8 o'clock show tonight to give us a little perspective.

"You've heard what Elliot had to say. He basically says that he doesn't think Pollard merits life in prison because he was spying, yes, but for an ally. Do the critics of Pollard see the difference and shades there?"

"Look," Blitzer replied, "the damage that Pollard did is not as bad as his worst enemies would suggest, but it's not as lenient as some of his supporters would suggest.

"Pollard pleaded guilty to spying for Israel. There's no doubt about that. There was no trial. He pleaded guilty as part of a plea bargain agreement with then-U.S. Attorney for the District of Columbia Joe deGenova.

"He was promised a substantial, a significant sentence, but his lawyers were assured, as part of the agreement, he would not get the maximum sentence, which was life in prison.

"So the attorneys themselves, and the U.S. Attorney, Joe de-Genova, agreed he wouldn't get the maximum sentence. At the same time, when Judge Aubrey Robinson, the federal judge, heard the evidence and saw the Weinberger document, as Elliot Goldenberg points out, it was a significant piece of evidence. It's still classified all these years later. The judge, on his own, decided to throw out the plea agreement and give him life because he was so outraged by the damage he believed Pollard caused the United States."

"Israeli leaders Netanyahu, Barak, Sharon, have all said that they would like to see a release or a cut in the sentence," O'Brien said. "Does the U.S. government take these pleas with any weight, any merit, do you think?

"They take them very seriously," Blitzer said. "And when I covered the White House, Bill Clinton was pressed repeatedly by Netanyahu and other Israeli leaders to do something to let Pollard get a reduced sentence.

"I have to say that when all these reviews were done, there was some mixed analysis between the civilians and the military. People in the U.S. intelligence community, though, by and large still hate Jonathan Pollard. And, as George Tenet made clear to Bill Clinton, if Bill Clinton would have reduced the sentence, he would have resigned as director of the CIA. And there are still a lot of hard feelings—eighteen years later."

That evening I drove home in a tropical storm, yet I was on such a high I was almost oblivious to it. I had with me a copy of a videotape of the Pollard segment. I didn't know if this would somehow help support a movie deal. But since image is very big in the land of make-believe, and I totally didn't blow my "fifteen minutes of fame"—or at least I didn't look like "Barney Fife" on national television—I knew it probably couldn't hurt.

That being said, on October 18, 2003, it was reported that Brad Pitt and Jennifer Aniston had bought the rights to the

Daniel Pearl story (*Mighty Heart*), written by Pearl's wife, Mariane. Pearl was the ill-fated *Wall Street Journal* reporter who was murdered in Afghanistan. To me, while it was obviously poignant, Suzanne and I wondered whether it was the kind of a story that people would pay to watch on the silver screen. Perhaps it would have been a far better story if Pearl had been saved, like Jessica Lynch during the second war with Iraq. But, unlike with our story, the Pearl story was politically correct, there would be no controversy or fallout, and there was a meaty part for Aniston if she wanted it.

"Does this knock us out of the box with Brad Pitt?" I asked Suzanne. She seemed to think it did.

To paraphrase Doc Holliday in *Tombstone*, I felt like someone had just walked over my grave.

CHAPTER THIRTEEN

CATCH-22

ON FEBRUARY 1, 2004, it was being widely reported that Israeli cabinet member Natan Sharansky—the onetime "face" of Soviet repression against Jews—would be visiting Jonathan Pollard at North Carolina's Butner prison. It didn't surprise me that Sharansky was doing this. What did surprise me was that the media was reporting it.

In 2002, when "Bibi" Netanyahu, a former Israeli prime minister, had visited Pollard at the same prison, the visit wasn't reported at all—at least in the mainstream media. In fact, I never knew about Bibi's visit until I saw the story on Esther-Zeitz Pollard's website. Then, two years later, a visit from an Israeli cabinet minister was being made into a national story by the Associated Press. Why?

True, there was a "hook" to the Sharansky story. As the AP reported, Sharansky had himself spent nine years in a Soviet prison, for "anti-state activities" and "spying," in connection with his efforts on behalf of Soviet Jews. Labeled a "refusnik," the brave Sharansky, who became a hero in America for standing up to what Ronald Reagan called the "evil empire," was freed in a prison exchange, in 1986, and flown to Israel—which, of course, is exactly what many of his supporters hoped would happen with Pollard.

According to the AP, Sharansky's visit with Pollard was confirmed by Sharansky's spokesperson, Iris Goldman, and would take place that week. While the trip was proposed at an Israeli cabinet meeting, Goldman declined to elaborate on the purpose of the visit.

Certainly, the media coverage of Pollard's appearance before a judge in Washington, on September 2, 2003, may have had something to do with the coverage of Sharansky's visit with Pollard five months later. One day prior to Pollard's September 2 court appearance, both Wolf Blitzer and I had appeared with Soledad O'Brien on CNN and were able to give some good sound bites about the case. I would like to think that made a difference in any follow-up coverage, but there was no way to know for sure.

As 2003 came to a close, Suzanne was working on developing our movie project and traveling back and forth between Fort Lauderdale and LA. One problem still facing us, however, was that actors and directors don't like to make commitments without scripts; working "A-list" screenwriters don't write scripts without funding; you can't get the funding without a studio deal; and you can't get a studio deal without a quality name actor or director. It's the perfect "Catch-22."

On the other hand, when a huge name like Brad Pitt, for instance, is associated with your project, your movie is probably going to get made. No surprise there. That's exactly why the Brad Pitts of the world are able to command such astronomical fees.

When she was back in California, Suzanne spent some time with television personality Diane Glazer—Suzanne called her the "Barbara Walters of Jewish television"—and Diane's husband, Gil, the nephew of Harry Busch. Harry, who was married to Suzanne's mother, Jean, had passed away the year before at the ripe old age of 103, and was the stepfather of two billionaires: the late Lawrence Tisch, onetime owner of CBS, and Larry's brother, the late Preston Robert (Bob) Tisch, co-owner of the New York Giants football team. Bob was also the father of Steve Tisch, one of the producers of the Academy Award-winning motion picture *Forrest Gump*.

Diane had a popular talk show on the Jewish Telegraphic Network, based in LA, and, in an ironic twist of fate, one of her soon-to-be guests was to be former Secretary of Defense Caspar Weinberger, who, while doing Diane's show, would stay at her spacious Bel Air estate.

It was Weinberger, of course, who had written the infamous memo to the judge in the Pollard case, basically ensuring that Pollard remained locked up behind bars for the rest of his life. One of the great unanswered questions surrounding that memo was what, exactly, was in it. With the exception of Pollard's first attorney, Richard Hibey (who apparently only had time to glance at it), I was told that none of Pollard's subsequent attorneys— including Ted Olson, who rose to become Solicitor General of the United States—ever got to fully examine what that memo to Judge Aubrey Robinson contained.

As for Diane, she needed at least a few "hardball" questions to toss Weinberger's way. Diane told this to Suzanne, and Suzanne said she'd come up with a few pages of questions for the former secretary of defense, a savvy and seasoned political veteran.

After being briefed on what to ask Weinberger, the first question Suzanne proposed—a rhetorical one—dealt with the very pro-Arab Bechtel Corporation. During the Carter administration Weinberger was the general counsel for Bechtel, and

George Schultz—who later replaced Gen. Alexander Haig as Ronald Reagan's secretary of state—was the company's CEO. The question was whether the Justice Department ever brought suit against Bechtel for honoring the Arab boycott against Israel.

The next question dealt with the U.S. Marine barracks in Lebanon that were destroyed in October of 1983, courtesy of Hezbollah. Noting that Weinberger allegedly ordered the casualties flown to the American Army Hospital in Germany, some seven hours away, and refused to let them be treated at Rambam Hospital in Haifa, Israel, only fifteen minutes away, the question was why Weinberger did that—especially in light of the fact that several of the seriously wounded Marines died en route to Germany.

Another loaded question touched on Weinberger's supposed labeling of his two indictments for perjury, over his testimony on the Iran-contra affair, as "political." The question was: "Since the Iran-contra special prosecutor, Lawrence Walsh, of Oklahoma, was a life-long Republican, appointed to the bench by a Republican president, what did you mean by political?"

The next question touched on the "Level Battlefield Doctrine," the premise of which was that if the Arab states were brought up to a military parity with Israel, peace would follow.

Such a premise was, quite frankly, ludicrous. But many had long thought this "doctrine" existed and that Weinberger was its chief architect. The thinking of its detractors was that, rather than prevent war, the Level Battlefield Doctrine caused the Six Day War, the Yom Kippur War, and, even, the first Gulf War. "What possessed the Reagan White House to attempt this approach when its end result was always predictable?" Suzanne wanted to know.

If the other questions failed to raise Weinberger's blood pressure, this one certainly would. "In keeping with the Level Battlefield Doctrine, and in an effort to shore up the flagging fortunes of Saddam Hussein during the Iran-Iraq War (1980-88), you secretly provided military materiel, intelligence and military advisors (from the Intelligence Support Activity) to the Iraqi army," Suzanne stated. "The Iraqi army deployed chemical and biological agents against Iranian forces on Majnoon Island. Did it not occur to you that these same weapons of mass destruction presented a clear and present danger to Israel, our non-NATO ally, and, for that matter, to Iraq's Arab neighbors?"

The next question addressed Weinberger's role, if any, in the re-establishing of diplomatic relations with Saddam Hussein, prior to the first Gulf War, and the scheme to utilize a Department of Agriculture loan guarantee program which secretly funded America's military support of Iraq. Suzanne also suggested that Diane ask Weinberger to explain why Col. Oliver North once said about him: "Weinberger's anti-Israel tilt was an underlying current in almost every Middle East issue."

Finally, the last question dealt with Pollard. "During the Reagan administration, through the first Bush administration, and into the Clinton administration," Suzanne wrote, "the American intelligence community lost many of our agents in place: our spies within the Soviet Union. You and our intelligence community initially blamed this on Jonathan Pollard. It turned out, however, that it was Aldrich Ames at the CIA, and Robert Hanssen at the FBI, who burned our agents. Still, you and the American intelligence community remain steadfastly against Jonathan Pollard's release. Why?"

***

In the coming months Suzanne continued pursuing our motion picture deal and taking meetings in Hollywood, while I stayed at my job as the senior writer for the Jewish Federation of Broward County, Florida. The job was at times stressful, but it also afforded me the opportunity to meet and interview some truly amazing people. One of those people was attorney Alan Dershowitz, who wrote the Forewords to both my books on the Pollard case: *The Hunting Horse* and *The Spy Who Knew Too Much*.

As busy as he was, Alan not only found the time to write the Forewords to those books; he did so pro bono. When we briefly chitchatted at the Federation event I was publicizing—and in which Alan spoke—he signed a copy of his own latest book for me.

"To Elliot, who does so much for so many," he wrote in the cover page of *The Case for Israel*. It was an extraordinary compliment from an extraordinary human being.

CHAPTER FOURTEEN

SYNCHRONICITY

ON MARCH 22, 2004, Sheik Ahmed Yassin, the terrorist leader of Hamas, had the top of his head blown off by a missile fired from an Israeli helicopter. It was a good day for the Israeli Defense Forces.

Not surprisingly, there was an immediate uproar in the Arab world. In the Gaza Strip, where the wheelchair-bound Yassin was a hero of epic proportions, more than two-hundred thousand Palestinians poured into the city's streets. Many were sobbing and shouting for revenge, while Yassin's coffin, along with the coffins of the eight other victims, including Yassin's bodyguards, were held aloft.

In a statement, Hamas said the "Zionists" would not have dared to carry out their operation without "getting the consent of the terrorist American Administration." Palestinian prime minister, and Arafat puppet, Ahmed Qureia, called it "one of the biggest crimes Israel has committed." As was reported by the Associated Press, an unnamed aide to Yasser Arafat stated: "[Arafat] is like a man who was hit on the head, because they killed

Yassin, and now they could kill him. He feels his turn is next, and he is sad and worried."

A week later, in what seemed to be an unrelated incident, four American workers employed by a security company were ambushed and killed in the pro-Saddam Hussein stronghold of Fallujah, Iraq. The *New York Times* reported that the workers' bodies were subsequently dragged through the streets of downtown Fallujah as a jubilant mob of Iraqis cheered. The mutilated and burned corpses were later seen hanging from a bridge over the Euphrates River. Among those killed in the attack was Scott Helvenston, a former U.S. Navy SEAL who had once been a consultant in the motion picture *G.I. Jane* starring Demi Moore.

According to an Associated Press article, the names of Saddam Hussein, or his Baath Party, were "not mentioned when frenzied mobs dragged the burned and mutilated bodies through the streets." However, the AP reporter, Sameer N. Yacoub, went on to say that "some of the mob carried pictures of Sheik Ahmed Yassin."

Upon reading the story of the Fallujah attack—which shocked most Americans, whether they agreed with the Bush policy in Iraq or not—I couldn't help but think of the Lanarca incident which took place during Jonathan Pollard's watch as a U.S. Naval Intelligence analyst. That story unfolded in Lanarca Harbor, Cyprus, back in September 1985, when a group of PLO terrorists—part of Arafat's "Force 17"—hijacked a yacht with one Israeli woman and two Israeli men aboard.

In a poignant letter he wrote to me, Pollard recalled how horrified he was when, after the terrorists murdered the Israelis and the story was reported worldwide with photos, a gory picture of the female victim, Esther Paltzur—her dead body hanging over the ship's bow—was pinned up over the coffeemaker near his office at the Navy's Anti-Terrorist Alert Center (ATAC). Next to the photo, Pollard said, were the handwritten words: "Force 17: 3—Mossad: 0."

According to an Israeli source of mine, who knew a great deal about the Lanarca terrorist attack and had seemingly firsthand knowledge about the subsequent Israeli response, Paltzur was killed first, but the other two Israelis—Paltzur's husband, Reuven Paltzur, and Avraham Avneri—were hog-tied, but left alive. After being alerted by Cypriot authorities, Israel dispatched a team of AMAN (Israeli Military Intelligence) officers, from Unit 504, to the scene. The Israeli planners also sent gunboats racing to Cyprus in case the terrorists attempted to escape by sea.

However, the Cypriot government refused an Israeli request to allow an anti-terrorist team to storm the boat. "So the negotiations continued for almost 24 hours," my source said. "In the end, seeing no way out, the three terrorists gave themselves up to the Cypriot authorities, but not before they executed their two Israeli captives by cutting their throats."

The terrorists, Elias Nassif, Mahmoud Khaled Abdullah and Ian Michael Davison, who was British, were immediately arrested. According to my source, one of the AMAN officers "was allowed to interrogate Ian Davison under scopolamine, which left the British terrorist in a catatonic state."

The Israeli Air Force, meanwhile, planned a far more aggressive response to the terrorist attack; one that would ensure that the PLO got the message. Chief among the planners was Col. Avi Sella, who had also helped plan the 1981 raid against the Iraqi nuclear facility at Osirak, an act that, at the time, drew a loud condemnation from some members of the Reagan administration, including Defense Secretary Caspar Weinberger and Deputy Director of the CIA Adm. Bobby Inman, but apparent approval from President Reagan and CIA head William Casey.

It was Sella, of course, who also "ran" Pollard (some say it was the other way around) in the early stages of the Pollard spy operation.

Recalled my Israeli source: "On the afternoon of October 1, 1985, Israeli fighter bombers suddenly appeared over PLO headquarters at Hamman Lif, outside Tunis, Tunisia, more than 1,500 miles from Israel. They destroyed the entire complex, Arafat's personal quarters, and the Tunisian air defense positions protecting them. They killed sixty-one Palestinian terrorists, including Mohammed Natour, the commander of Force 17, and twelve Tunisians working in the complex. After the longest strike in Israeli Air Force history, all planes returned safely to base.

"The Arabs were stunned. The nightly news broadcast pictures of Yasser Arafat standing dumfounded in acres of ruin that was formerly his plush headquarters."

As is noted in *The Hunting Horse*, at least some of the intelligence the Israelis used to ensure the success of this operation was provided by Jonathan Pollard.

"American intelligence was impressed," my source said. "It was obviously superior information which allowed the Israeli strike package to negotiate the entire North African coast, bobbing and weaving through hostile radar coverage and state-of-the-art Soviet made air defense systems. They had even managed to avoid detection by naval units of the American Sixth Fleet."

Back in 1985, when the Israeli attack on Arafat's headquarters in Tunis took place, the Palestinian leader was a pariah and a hunted man. Eight years later, that same Arafat would receive a Nobel Peace Prize after extending his arm in front of Bill Clinton and shaking hands with Israeli Prime Minister Yitzhak Rabin on the White House lawn. By 2004, Arafat had apparently gone full circle: he was back to being a terrorist—as if he had ever stopped being one—who Israel may again have had in its crosshairs.

Still, when I read Arafat's alleged comments after Yassin's assassination—implying that the Palestinian leader feared for his life—I was puzzled by why he was so worried about being killed by the Israelis. Wasn't this the same man, who, after emerging from house arrest by the Israelis nearly two years earlier, shouted in front of the TV cameras the words, "martyr, martyr," meaning he was proud to die as a martyr, and was even resigned to dying as a martyr? After all, Arafat had given orders, or at least turned a blind eye and a deaf ear, to Palestinian suicide bombers who believed their deaths would be glorious and that they would meet up with seventy-two virgins in heaven. How could Arafat ask these young men (and women) to turn themselves into human bombs, all in the name of the Palestinian cause, while their great leader feared for his life? Didn't Arafat know that he, too, would be welcome in heaven and into the arms of those seventy-two virgins?

Well, maybe not.

While Sheik Ahmed Yassin was meeting his maker, the U.S. government was reportedly again trying to end the life of Terry Nichols—the co-conspirator and close friend of Timothy McVeigh who, nearly three years earlier, was executed by the state of Oklahoma for allegedly masterminding the Oklahoma City bombing. Sources of mine still felt there was also a Middle Eastern connection to the bombing of the Alfred P. Murrah Federal Building that resulted in the deaths of one hundred and sixty eight men, women and children. If a connection did in fact exist, I wondered if any of that connection would be revealed during Nichols' new trial.

Meanwhile a far bigger story was also breaking on March 22, 2004: one that was front-page news and would force the Bush administration to circle their wagons and dodge the bullets. According to *Against All Enemies: Inside America's War on Terror*, a bombshell memoir to be released that day by Richard A. Clarke—George W. Bush's onetime counter-terrorism coordinator—on the evening of September 11, 2001, a stunned Bush had met with a small group of aides in the Situation Room of the White House.

As reported by Barton Gellman in the *Washington Post*, according to Clarke's book, Bush hoped to find a link between the horrific attacks earlier that morning and Saddam Hussein. "Go back over everything, everything," Bush reportedly said. "See if Saddam did this."

"But Mr. President, al Qaeda did this," Clarke recalled replying.

"I know, I know, but ... see if Saddam was involved," the president reiterated. "Just look. I want to know any shred."

While Saddam Hussein, as evil as he was, could not be directly linked to the September 11 attacks, the acquiescence of our purported ally, Saudi Arabia, may have been a far different matter. Indeed, a controversial new book by Craig Unger, while not getting nearly as much hype as Clarke's book, was about to hit the bookstands as well. Its title was *House of Bush House of Saud: The Secret Relationship Between the World's Two Most Powerful Dynasties*.

Book reviewer John Freeman noted that on September 11, 2001, the United States imposed a nationwide no fly zone, and yet one hundred and forty individuals were permitted to leave the country. According to Unger, nearly all of them were Saudi, and roughly two-dozen were kin to Osama bin Laden. "What kind of intelligence failure," Freeman asked, "allowed this to happen?"

Also, given that fifteen out of the nineteen hijackers were Saudi, Freeman posed the question: "What was the rush in squandering a potential intelligence mother lode?"

But, considering the political climate in the country prior to 9-11, George W. Bush may have been doing as much as was humanly possible in the war against terror. At the same time, the relationship between the Bush family and the Saudi kingdom was not only complex, but troubling. As Freeman noted in his review of Unger's book: "What emerges from Unger's narrative is a portrait of how Bush senior helped develop a way of doing business with the world's worst thugs that was duplicated and transplanted to other regions with staggering naiveté. Our allegiance with the Saudis had proved so convenient that it was again used to prop up the Mujahedin in Afghanistan." Not surprisingly, perhaps the greatest beneficiary of that support was none other than bin Laden himself.

After reading Freeman's review what really stood out in my mind was not what was in Unger's book, however, but that a mainstream house, such as Scribner, would actually publish it. Back in the "old days" few publishers would take on something so controversial. One of the few houses that did, SPI, and its publisher Ian Shapolsky, were familiar to all of us who wrote in this genre: people like Unger, Joel Bainerman (*The Mafia, CIA and George Bush*), Yossi Bodansky (*Target America*) and even myself. Unfortunately, Ian Shaplosky's publishing house went belly up. Fortunately, times changed and all of us were able to find other outlets.

Some of us even became "respectable." Bodansky, who, prior to 9-11, wrote a book on bin Laden, was a media star and much-interviewed "talking head" after the attack. Steve Emerson, an

"A-List" talking head, proved, as much as anyone, that being a terrorism expert was suddenly in vogue.

Author and journalist Brigitte Gabriel—an extraordinarily brave woman who, as a young girl, survived the devastation of the war in Lebanon brought on by Syria and Hezbollah, and went on to found the watchdog groups "ACT For America" and "American Congress for Truth"—also appeared often on cable news shows and was lauded by Emerson in Gabriel's book, *Because They Hate*. Noted Emerson: "Brigitte Gabriel reminds America what is truly at stake in this struggle against terrorism: our families, our way of life, and our hopes."

Years earlier I had spoken with Craig Unger by telephone when I called to discuss certain implications of his article titled "October Surprise" that appeared in the October 1991 issue of *Esquire* magazine.

It had long been alleged by some in the Justice Department that there was a so-called "Mr. X" in the Jonathan Pollard spy case—an important Jewish leader or Reagan administration official, who, like Pollard, was feeding information to the Israelis behind then-Defense Secretary Caspar Weinberger's back. Unger wrote: "In a sworn affidavit, signed by (former U.S. Attorney) Elliot Richardson on behalf of one of his clients, (former Israeli intelligence operative) Ari Ben-Menashe states that (National Security Advisor) Robert McFarlane had a 'special relationship' with Israeli intelligence, McFarlane having been recruited by Rafi Eitan ..."

This was the same Rafi Eitan who oversaw Avi Sella, and who Pollard took his orders from, as a "walk-in," when Eitan was the head of LAKAM, the special scientific intelligence gathering unit of the Israeli Defense Ministry.

Unger came up with an interesting scenario. He quoted Ben-Menashe as stating that "Robert McFarlane was the infamous 'Mr. X' in the Pollard case." When I spoke to Unger, he said he was told this personally by Ben-Menashe, who happened to be one of Pulitzer Prize-winning journalist Seymour Hersh's inside sources for his book *The Samson Option*.

In a 1988 interview with *Playboy* Magazine, Yasser Arafat also linked McFarlane to the Israelis. Pollard had already admitted passing U.S. satellite data to Israel showing the exact location of Arafat's headquarters in Tunis, which the Israelis subsequently bombed. Could someone else have done the same thing without Pollard knowing about it? During the *Playboy* interview Arafat bluntly stated, "We know that the United States supplied Israel with sensitive information, satellite photographs of our headquarters in Tunis, before they bombed it in 1985. Robert McFarlane did this."

"The same McFarlane who was, at the time, using the Israelis as intermediaries in the Iran-Contra deal?" interviewer Morgan Strong asked.

"Yes," Arafat replied. "We know it is true."

CHAPTER FIFTEEN

SILVER BULLET

SPEAKING BEFORE A congressional committee looking into the 9-11 terrorist attacks, National Security Advisor Condoleezza Rice was on top of her game, causing one of the New York tabloids to rave on its front cover, "The Lady is a Champ," while many Democrats, not surprisingly, painted her as evasive.

"There was no silver bullet that could have prevented the 9-11 attacks," Rice said, testifying for three hours, under oath, on April 8, 2004. Some of the exchanges with committee members were heated, especially between Rice and Nebraska Senator Bob Kerrey, a former Navy Seal and recipient of the Congressional Medal of Honor.

Rice argued that the threat of terrorism had been building for years, and the main problem was "institutional, cultural and legal barriers among the FBI, CIA and other intelligence agencies."

Whether anyone wanted to hear that or not, the national security advisor was right. Surely, there was a complexity of reasons why the intelligence community was asleep at the switch. No doubt, part of it was incompetence. Another reason it was so difficult to act against Islamic terrorist cells prior to 9-11, however, was the climate of "political correctness" in America.

In truth, prior to 9-11, if the FBI had put "bugs" in every mosque in the United States, for instance, we no doubt would have been far safer, and our intelligence would have been far greater. But would it have all been legal? And what would the outcry have been when this ploy was discovered? Wouldn't the same people who continued to decry the Patriot Act—hotly debated between liberals and conservatives—have called the bugging of mosques not only unconstitutional, but a blatant attack against Islam in general?

Perhaps they would have been right. At the same time, before the 9-11 attacks the FBI and CIA often found their hands tied when attempting to deal with this insidious new enemy that, burrowing under our national radar screen, had begun building a terrorist network right here in the United States.

Of course, not everyone was asleep at the switch.

According to a report by terrorist expert Steven Emerson's watchdog organization, The Investigative Project, former White House counter-terrorism czar Richard Clarke—whose explosive new book had precipitated the congressional hearings—had been "so frustrated" by the FBI's inability to identify Islamic radicals within the United States that he turned for help to Emerson, "a freelance terrorism expert whose work was deeply resented by top bureau officials."

Dan Abrams, host of "The Abrams Report" on MSNBC, said: "The bottom line is that there were few people like Clark and terrorism expert Steve Emerson who were screaming for years that al Qaeda's coming."

Oliver "Buck" Revell, former FBI assistant director in charge of counter-terrorism, and a person who may have been one of the few "top bureau officials" who was not threatened by Emerson, apparently welcomed Emerson's input. "It may be that Mr. Emerson is actually better informed in some areas than the responsible agencies of government," Revell candidly wrote in the back of Emerson's book, *American Jihad: The Terrorists living Among Us.*

An Investigative Project report noted, also, that, according to Clarke, both Emerson, and Emerson's former associate, Rita Katz, regularly provided the White House with a "stream of information" about possible al Qaeda activity inside the United States that appears to have been "largely unknown by the FBI prior to the September 11 terrorist attacks."

Both in confidential memos and briefings, Emerson and Katz furnished Clarke and his staff with the names of radical Islamic websites, the identities of possible terrorist front groups, and the phone numbers and addresses of possible terror suspects—data they were unable to get from elsewhere in the government.

According to Clarke, "this private pipeline of information—which began under President Clinton and continued under Bush even after September 11—irritated top officials at FBI headquarters, especially when much of the private research bore fruit and was later used to help develop a U.S. government list of banned organizations whose assets were frozen by the Treasury Department."

In an interview Emerson later quipped: "Al Qaeda would have been more welcome at FBI headquarters than me."

While not particularly popular with the FBI, Emerson—as is noted earlier in this book—was thoroughly despised by Muslim extremists, and summarily dismissed by pro-Palestinian spokespeople. One such spokesperson, James Zogby, president of the Arab-American Institute, once said of Emerson: "This is a guy who started out riding an anti-Arab hobby horse, and then transformed it into an antiterrorism hobby horse. His material should be taken with a grain of salt."

Fortunately, Richard Clarke was smart enough not to take Zogby's advice. Reportedly, within days of his first request, in 1999, Clarke received from Emerson a list of radical Islamic websites that Clarke then passed on to the Justice Department and the FBI. According to The Investigative Project, the Justice Department nevertheless couldn't act on the information because of "how difficult it was to prosecute 'free speech' cases."

The memos from Emerson covered more than websites. One 1999 memo revealed that Osama bin Laden's international terrorist infrastructure was at the time operating across the United States—something our intelligence community may also not have been aware of.

It's easy to understand why, since guidelines imposed back in the 1970s barred agents from attending meetings of "religious groups"—not to mention bugging their phones—unless there was specific reason to believe a federal crime had been committed. Those guidelines were only changed during John Ashcroft's tenure as U.S. attorney general.

As for the beleaguered Ashcroft, it was not surprising that he would consistently come under heavy fire. Considering how unprepared the FBI was in fighting—and sometimes even identifying—terrorists, it's probably not too shocking that on April 20, 2004, the *New York Sun* reported that Marwan Kreidie, an Arab-American activist who publicly denounced Ashcroft as a "lunatic," was actually given a community service award by the FBI's Philadelphia field office. According to reporter Ira Stoll, the year before the FBI had also decided to give a similar award to an Arab-American leader in Michigan, "but then changed its mind after protests."

Kreidie used the announcement of his award as an opportunity to take a shot at Ashcroft. "Every time he comes to Philadelphia, we hand him a copy of the Constitution," Kreidie said.

According to the *Sun*, Special Agent Linda Vizi, a spokeswoman for the FBI in Philadelphia, rationalized that Kreidie, a so-called "leader" of the Arab-American community, had been "very helpful to the FBI."

Author and Jewish activist Daniel Pipes, who lives in Philadelphia—and, like Steve Emerson, has been as vilified by anti-Israeli spokespeople—saw Kreidie in a far different light. Pipes called Kreidie's receiving of the prestigious FBI award a "travesty."

Emerson agreed. "This is someone who has compared the U.S. to authoritarian regimes in the Middle East, attacked the seizure of Hamas terrorist funds, and portrayed nearly all post 9-11 U.S. anti-terrorist initiatives in inflammatory language as racist," Emerson said, as reported in the *Sun*. "This sends a terrible message to genuine moderates in the Arab and Muslim communities who have courageously stood up for the United States."

When he appeared with Chris Matthews on *Hardball*, a week earlier, Emerson expounded on why the hands of the FBI had once been bound so tightly behind their collective backs. "The fear of God was instilled in every FBI agent that they could not shut down the charitable conduits, the religious covers, that provide money to al Qaeda or Hamas," Emerson said.

Stressing that a number of "charities" that allegedly funneled money to terrorist organizations had their assets frozen after 9-11, Emerson explained that the intelligence about the organizations was nevertheless gleaned years earlier. "That means [prior to 9-11] they just didn't have the political will or mandate to do anything. They were afraid of being tarred with the brush of being anti …"

Emerson was about to say "Muslim," but Matthews interrupted. Matthews wanted to know if the FBI agents were also afraid of losing their jobs.

Emerson replied that, more than being fired, the agents were worried about being sued. "Therefore, nobody would really step out on a limb at this point," he said.

And unless there was a command from the top of the FBI food chain, saying they needed to bust the front groups in the U.S. that were allegedly raising money for terrorist organizations in the Middle East, the agents certainly weren't going to act on their own.

Emerson argued that when people with suspected ties to al Qaeda were interrogated by the FBI in the years prior to 9-11, they often called the ACLU.

Recalled Emerson, the so-called "advocacy groups," which in reality were fronts for terrorist organizations, "screamed bloody murder" at the FBI, and the FBI backed off. According to Emerson, the FBI was worried about a backlash, not only by Muslims in the United States, but throughout the Muslim world.

"So the same congressmen complaining and bitching today about how the CIA and FBI didn't do their job," Matthews said, "would have been the first ones on the phone for some religious group."

"Absolutely," Emerson said. "And, after 9-11, there are still issues where the FBI is constrained from investigating some of the radical Islamic groups—because they use the cover of religion."

Whether this would have any influence on our possible movie deal, I wasn't quite sure. But the film industry, for better or for worse, is a place that tilts to the "left" more than it tilts to the "right." Case in point: Michael Moore, as controversial as he is, not only gets a documentary made in Hollywood, but wins the Palm d' Or at the Cannes Film Festival in France.

As for Jonathan Pollard's plight, it had never been adopted by either the "left" or the "right." Then his wife, Esther, came into the picture, arguably made enemies out of onetime allies, and, in the opinion of some, unwittingly sabotaged whatever grassroots efforts there had been to win her husband's freedom.

Another obstacle was that, for many in Hollywood, Pollard just wasn't a particularly sympathetic character.

That being said, we were nevertheless living in an era when conspiracy theories once again seemed to be in vogue. With all the nonsensical babble about how "Bush may have known ahead of time about 9-11," or how the war in Iraq was strictly a way to line the pockets of Haliburton executives and their allies in the Bush White House, our motion picture project could have been seen by some as "anti-establishment."

And, in Hollywood, that might not have been such a *bad* thing.

William Northrop (L) author of The Ghost of the Sealed Rooms; journalist Forrest Sawyer; Suzanne Migdall

The late Dr. Florence Ross, a Pollard advocate, with William Northrop

A young Jonathan Pollard and his sister, Carol

President George H. W. Bush, the former head of the CIA who also served as vice president under Ronald Reagan (The George Bush Library, College Station , Texas)

Elliot Goldenberg at a 1993 speaking engagement with Paula Morse of the National Council of Jewish Women, Plantation, Florida Section

Elliot Goldenberg

Pollard's parents, Dr. Morris Pollard and Mollie Pollard

Former Israeli Prime Minister Yitzhak Shamir. (Israeli Press Office)

Former Israeli Prime Minister Yitzhak Rabin and President Bill Clinton
(Official White House photograph)

Meir Rosenne, Israel's ambassador to the U.S. at the time of Pollard's arrest (Israeli Press Office)

Israeli Prime Minister Benjamin "Bibi" Netanyahu. (Israeli Press Office)

Former Israeli Prime Minister Shimon Peres. (Israeli Press Office)

Former Israeli Prime Minister Ariel Sharon. (Israeli Press Office)

Elliot Goldenberg and William Northrop

Motion picture producer Suzanne Migdall with actor Stanley Tucci at the
Sundance Film Festival

Suzanne Migdall testifies at a congressional hearing on Gulf War illnesses

Carol Pollard (L), Suzanne Migdall

Alan Dershowitz

Jonathan Pollard

August 5, 1996

Mr. William Northrop
4920 North Meridian
Oklahoma City, OK 73112

Dear Mr. Northrop:

Enclosed please find airline tickets for you and Ms. Migdall. You
will be met in the baggage claim area by a driver from Cloverdale
Car Company. He will have a sign with your name on it. You will
be picked up at the hotel on Friday morning at 7:15 for the trip back
to LaGuardia.

Please call us at 456-7320 after you are settled at the Empire. Forrest
would very much like to have a meeting with you at the office before dinner.

If I can be of further assistance, please do not hesitate to call me.

Sincerely yours,

Mary Thomas Joseph
Assistant to Mr. Sawyer

William Northrop and Suzanne Migdall were scheduled to be flown to New York to
be interviewed by ABC's Forrest Sawyer on Gulf War illnesses

CHAPTER SIXTEEN

GOLDA'S TOYS

POLLARD'S VISION, A thoroughbred stallion, was a twenty-to-one shot to win the 2004 Kentucky Derby. The horse—named after "Red" Pollard, the real-life half-blind jockey played by Tobey Maguire in the Academy Award-nominated movie *Seabiscuit*—went blind in his right eye at the age of fifteen months. The colt's owner, David Master, was blind in his left eye. So Pollard's Vision winning at Churchill Downs would have made for a great story—and perhaps would have been prophetic for motion picture producer Suzanne Migdall and myself—but it was not to be. In actuality, this horse was closer to "Mr. Ed" than he was to the great "Biscuit." Totally outclassed by the eventual Derby winner Smarty Jones, Pollard's Vision finished second to last on horse-racing's greatest stage.

On April 13, 2004, Israeli Prime Minister Ariel Sharon got a green light from President Bush for Israel to unilaterally withdraw from the Gaza Strip while holding on to some of the disputed land in the West Bank, thereby softening a decades-old U.S. policy. Just days later, Israeli helicopter gunships incinerated the car the Gaza-based terrorist Abdel Aziz Rantisi was riding in.

A high profile Palestinian leader, and the most public voice of Palestinian extremists in Gaza, Rantisi, a pediatrician, had served as Hamas' new leader, succeeding Sheik Ahmed Yassin, who died in a similar helicopter missile strike less than a month before. Long a spokesperson for Hamas, Rantisi seemed resigned to his fate. "It's death, whether by killing or cancer," he reportedly said. "It's the same thing. Nothing will change if it's an Apache [helicopter] or cardiac arrest. But I prefer to be killed by an Apache."

Mordecai Vananu, who worked as a technician at Israel's Dimona nuclear power plant—and, in 1986, received an eighteen-year prison term for revealing Israel's nuclear weapons program—fared a little better. Within days of Rantisi's assassination, Vananu, a Moroccan-born Jew who converted to Christianity, was at last freed.

Over the years, Vananu's fate had been linked by some to that of Jonathan Pollard's. Both were Jewish spies whose espionage involved Israel. Both had access to top-secret intelligence during approximately the same time period: In 1984 and 1985, while Pollard was passing U.S. military information to Israel, Vananu was still working at Dimona. Both Vananu and Pollard received long prison sentences for revealing state secrets. And both men had their share of supporters as well as their share of detractors. In Vananu's case, for every Israeli who labeled him a traitor, another considered him a whistle-blower.

Unlike Pollard, however, Vananu showed little, if any, remorse. "To all those who are calling me a traitor," Vananu boasted upon his release, "I am saying I am proud and happy to do what I did."

In an interview published April 5, 2004 in the Israeli newspaper *Yediot Ahranot*—the same newspaper that broke the story about the possible Islamic terrorist connection to the Oklahoma City bombing—Pollard was asked to compare himself to the Israeli nuclear spy.

"You feel that the grossly disproportionate sentence you received may have been exacerbated in vengeance by certain elements within the American security establishment," said interviewer Shimon Shiffer, who got permission to interview Pollard, outside his cell at Butner prison, as long as they were both within earshot of a representative of U.S. Naval Intelligence. "Do you see any room to compare yourself to Mordecai Vananu?"

"My case is no way like that of Vananu," Pollard replied. "It is unthinkable to even attempt a comparison. Unlike Vananu, I was never accused, indicted, or convicted of treason. I was never even accused of intent to harm the United States. And if there had been any evidence to support such heinous charges against me, believe me, the Justice Department would have presented them, and rightly so, in my opinion. But there was no such evidence."

"In Vananu's case, he was tried in an untainted legal forum," Pollard continued. "In my case the judicial process was subverted from the onset—and continues to be to this day."

Of course, with or without Vananu, Israel's membership in the nuclear fraternity had never been much of a secret. But, as Michael Matza reported in the *Miami Herald*, Israel had never officially acknowledged its nuclear arsenal, either, and that made for an important distinction.

Israel, after all, had not been a signatory of the 1970 Nuclear Nonproliferation Treaty, which prohibits the transfer of nuclear weapons, devices and technology. As an important rule of thumb, the United States would not give foreign aid to governments that had not signed the treaty. Notwithstanding, under a U.S-Israel understanding negotiated in 1969 by President Nixon and Israeli Prime Minister Golda Meir, the U.S. gave a de facto green light to the Dimona Plant, as long as Israel did not go public with the news that the tiny nation had in fact gone nuclear.

As Seymour Hersh noted in his book *The Samson Option*, "[Nixon] turned a blind-eye toward Israel's growing nuclear capacity" while paying lip-service to the goal of nuclear non-proliferation.

"Richard Nixon and [Secretary of State] Henry Kissinger approached inauguration day on January 20, 1969 convinced that Israel's nuclear ambitions were understandable," Hersh wrote. "Once in office they went a step further: they endorsed Israel's nuclear ambitions."

According to Hersh, Nixon's and Kissinger's support for Israel's nuclear weapons program was "widely known" to the Israeli leadership. "The Nixon administration made a judgment that would become American policy for the next two decades," Hersh stated. "Israel had gone nuclear, and there was nothing that the United States could, or wanted to, do about it."

In their book, *Friends In Deed: Inside the U.S.-Israeli Alliance*, authors Dan Raviv and Yossi Melman came to a similar conclusion. The authors recalled Golda Meir's first visit to the White House, in September 1969. According to Raviv and Mellman, Nixon surprised the prime minister by asking, "Tell me, do you have any toys?"

Noted Raviv and Mellman: "[Meir] did not understand, but [Nixon] persisted. 'Military toys', Nixon said. 'I'm talking nuclear.' Finally understanding that he was gently probing about Israel's secret arsenal, Meir replied, 'No, Mr. President.'"

The cagey Meir was not being totally truthful. Nevertheless, while Israel was "secretly" turning into a nuclear power, the White House apparently didn't seem to mind. Nixon and Kissinger were so unconcerned, Raviv and Melman explained, they "stopped the inspections of the atomic plant at Dimona."

As is noted in *The Hunting Horse*, a January 7, 1992, interview with Ted Koppel on ABC's *Nightline* also touched on what Nixon knew during his presidency about Israel's nuclear capabilities. Officially at least, those capabilities remain secret even to this day. While there are many who (rightly or wrongly) believe Nixon and Kissinger actually betrayed Israel with false intelligence during the 1973 Yom Kippur War—in the hope that Israel would take enough casualties to force it to make concessions to the Arabs, specifically over the Palestinian question—most would agree that Nixon had little problem with Israel becoming a full-fledged nuclear power.

During his interview with Nixon, Koppel began to question the ex-president about Israel's ability to reduce its Arab enemies to dust.

"You state, categorically, that the Israelis have atomic weapons," Koppel said. "You know that the Israelis have never admitted this publicly. But since you state this as a former president of the United States, you must know what you're talking about."

"I'm not going to divulge any of my so-called secret information and so forth," Nixon replied. "But I will say this: If I were an Israeli I wouldn't indicate that I had them and I wouldn't indicate that I didn't have them. Let me just say, most experts in the area assume that the Israelis have nuclear weapons."

"But you don't qualify it here this evening," Koppel said, "and you didn't qualify it in your book …"

Nixon, as if he knew something Israel's enemies couldn't be sure of, stopped Koppel in his tracks. "Because," the thirty-seventh president warned, "the Israelis will use them."

Today, while the world knows that Israel's nuclear weapons obviously exist, Israel's understandably evasive policy concerning its nukes makes it possible for the U.S. Congress to continue with aid programs to Israel to the tune of $3 billon a year.

According to Yoel Cohen, author of *The Whistle Blower of Dimona: Israel, Vananu and the Bomb*, one problem with a free Vananu is that, if and when he testifies before Congress, he could conceivably jeopardize Israel's aid—although, considering how much support Israel has in Congress, that would seem highly unlikely. Still, citing security reasons, among the conditions of Vananu's parole are that he will not be allowed to contact foreigners or tell his story to the media. Any violation could conceivably send him back to prison.

With Vananu's prison term finally over, I wondered what was going on in Jonathan Pollard's head. Was he buoyed that this would in some way help his own cause? Or was he envious of Vananu's newfound freedom?

In his interview with Pollard that appeared in *Yediot Ahranot*, Shimon Shiffer eloquently described the beauty of North Carolina in the spring—a place of "white blossoms, rich perfume of magnolia, bright greenery and verdant fields that stretch to the edge of the horizon, dotted with peaceful country homes." It seemed like a pleasant enough place for a man to spend the rest of his life.

That is as long as he wasn't looking at it all from behind bars.

CHAPTER SEVENTEEN

COCKTAIL FOR DISASTER

SPC SABRINA HARMON, of the 372ⁿᵈ Military Police Company, was one of a growing number of American soldiers involved in the Abu Ghraib Prison scandal that rocked the Bush administration, again landed Secretary of Defense Donald Rumsfeld in hot water, and gave Arabs an additional excuse to hate us, as if they ever needed one.

Newsweek reported that Harmon, who allegedly took photos of naked Iraqi prisoners as they were being "abused and humiliated," was also charged with attaching electrodes to the finger, toes and penis of a hooded prisoner who was told he would be electrocuted if he fell asleep. Harmon told the *Washington Post* that her job was to "make it hell so they would talk."

If these people being "abused and humiliated" were terrorists, or were linked to terrorists, perhaps what was done to them wasn't a bad idea. On the other hand, maybe it was a bad idea since, instead of being left in the hands of trained interrogators, whatever took place at Abu Ghraib was apparently the work of non-professionals. The taking of the photographs only made matters worse.

But should the blame have fallen into the lap of the secretary of defense? As *Newsweek* reported, when grilled by the Senate Armed Services Committee, Rumsfeld was willing to fall on his sword. "If there's a failure, it's me," he admitted. "These events occurred on my watch. As secretary of defense I am accountable for them—and I take full responsibility."

In an interview with Chris Wallace on Fox News, Sen. Lindsey Graham (R-SC)—the only U.S. Senator at the time in the U.S. Army Reserves—admitted that, at the very least, there was a breakdown of discipline in the prison. "These people were poorly trained and the prison was poorly staffed," Graham said. "It was a cocktail for disaster."

During the next few weeks stories on the abuses at the prison continued to spread like wildfire. Investigative reporter Seymour Hersh got perhaps the most media mileage when he attempted to link the scandal directly to Rumsfeld. As David Johnston reported in the *New York Times*, according to Hersh, both Rumsfeld and Stephen Cambone, the under secretary of state for Intelligence, authorized the expansion of a secret program that permitted the same types of harsh interrogations of al Qaeda to be used against prisoners at Abu Ghraib. The goal was to extract better information from Iraqi prisoners to counter the growing insurgency threat in Iraq.

In his article which appeared in the May 24, 2004 issue of *The New Yorker*, Hersh —who had once written a scathing piece in *The New Yorker* about the alleged damage Jonathan Pollard did to America's intelligence apparatus—stated that, "according to interviews with several past and present American intelligence officials, the Pentagon's operation, known inside the intelligence community by several code words, including 'Copper Green,' encouraged physical coercion and sexual humiliation of Iraqi prisoners in an effort to generate more intelligence about the growing insurgency in Iraq."

Newsweek was glowing in its praise of Hersh. "Thirty-two years after breaking My Lai, he's still out there scooping everyone," the weekly magazine said. "If there's a journalistic equivalent to Viagra, [Seymour Hersh] is on it."

Hersh, as he often does (and as I admittedly do as well), used anonymous sources for some of his information. Hersh's sources allegedly gave him the inside scoop as to whose responsibility it was—and how far up the chain of command that responsibility went—for ordering the mistreatment of the prisoners. One of Hersh's main claims was that, when either suspected terrorists or terrorist sympathizers were rounded up, totally innocent people were sometimes caught in the net. Among those being "abused and tortured," Hersh stressed, were Iraqis who were absolutely "no threat" to the United States.

"But how do you wind up in prison if you're just innocent and didn't do anything?" host Bill O'Reilly asked Hersh on *The O'Reilly Factor*, soon after Hersh's story broke. "Our commanders and our embedded reporters tell me that they were too busy to be rounding up guys in the marketplace and throwing them into prison. So I'm going to dispute your contention that we had a lot of people in there with just no rap sheets at all, who were just picked up for no reason at all. The people who were in the prison were suspected of being either al Qaeda, or terrorists who were killing Americans and knew about [the killing of Americans]."

"The problem is that it isn't *my* contention," Hersh calmly replied. "It's the contention of Major General [Antonio] Taguba, who was appointed by [Lieutenant] General [Ricardo] Sanchez to do the investigation. It's his contention, in his report, that more than sixty percent of the people in that prison—detainees and civilians—had nothing to do with the war effort."

To O'Reilly, that still seemed like an exaggeration. Nevertheless, O'Reilly appeared generally complementary of Hersh's reporting. At the same time, O'Reilly appeared to chide Hersh, just a bit, for totally trusting his unnamed sources. "I don't believe you made any of this stuff up," O'Reilly said, "but [the unnamed sources] may have been using you."

Perhaps, I thought to myself, it wasn't the first time.

As is noted earlier in this book, Hersh, using another anonymous source, claimed that, in the mid 1980s, Israeli Prime Minister Yitzhak Shamir handed the Soviet Union sanitized U.S. Intelligence information that was initially provided to Israel by Jonathan Pollard. One of his sources, Hersh acknowledged, was former Israeli intelligence operative Ari Ben-Menashe. A second Israeli source, Hersh said at the time, "cannot be named."

It is no longer a secret that the U.S. intelligence apparatus operating behind the Iron Curtain was decimated during those years, and that many of the Soviet moles working for the United States were subsequently discovered and executed. (I spoke about this on Labor Day, 2003, when I appeared as a guest on CNN.) Although U.S. officials have never admitted this, a rationale for Pollard's harsh punishment was that at least some of what Pollard passed on to spymaster Rafi Eitan, the director of LAKAM (the Israel Defense Ministry's Office of Scientific Liaison), wound up in the clutches of the KGB, thereby exposing those moles.

But, as we now know, the double agents were instead exposed by two other people—CIA spy Aldrich Ames and FBI spy Robert Hanssen—and not Pollard. Regardless, Pollard apparently paid for these crimes with his life sentence.

In an article that appeared in the January 18, 1999, issue of *The New Yorker*, Hersh, a Jew, had taken dead aim at America's most famous Jewish spy. Hersh alleged there were yet other reasons, in addition to the exposing of the agents, why Pollard's espionage activities were so damaging. It was because of this, Hersh explained, that U.S. intelligence officials were "up in arms" when, toward the end of his presidency, Bill Clinton was seriously considering executive clemency for Pollard.

Noted Hersh: "The president's willingness to consider clemency for Pollard so upset the intelligence community that its leaders took an unusual step: they began to go public. In early December (1998), four retired admirals who had served as directors of Naval Intelligence circulated an article, eventually published in the *Washington Post*, in which they argued that Pollard's release would be 'irresponsible' and a victory for what they depicted as a 'clever public relations campaign.' Since then, sensitive details about the secrets Pollard gave away have been made public by CBS and NBC."

It was intriguing to me that this so-called "information" had not been made public before. As for Hersh, I have to admit: his article on the Pollard case was both comprehensive and well written. It's not by accident that Hersh is considered one of the most respected investigative journalists in the world.

Among the many claims he made, Hersh stated that the documents Pollard turned over to Israel were not only focused exclusively on the *product* of American intelligence: analytical reports and estimates. The documents also revealed *how* America was able to learn what it did: "a most sensitive area of intelligence defined as 'sources and methods'."

According to Hersh, Pollard gave the Israelis "vast amounts of data" dealing with specific American intelligence systems and how they worked. For example, Hersh wrote, "he betrayed details of an exotic capability that American satellites have of taking off-axis photographs from high in space. While orbiting the earth in one direction, the satellites could photograph areas that were seemingly out of range. Israeli nuclear missile sites, and the like, which would normally be shielded from American satellites, would thus be left exposed and could be photographed."

In other words, one of Pollard's greatest crimes was that he helped keep the U.S. from spying against Israel. "We monitor the Israelis," Hersh recalled one unnamed intelligence expert telling him, "and there's no doubt the Israelis want to prevent us from being able to surveil their country."

Well, that's probably true. Of course, it's debatable whether Pollard could have even had access to any of this information. As Hersh's fellow investigative journalist, John Loftus, argued, Pollard, as a GS-12 civilian Naval Intelligence analyst, never had "Blue-Stripe" clearance. And, as is noted earlier in this book, intelligence insider Angelo Codevilla also doubted Pollard, as a GS-12 analyst, could have gotten his hands on any of this intelligence flow, as Hersh alleged.

But say, for argument's sake, that Hersh is right. Would the passing along of these secrets have caused any great damage to the United States? Perhaps the real question was whether it was Pollard's "information" that not only wound up in the Knesset, but also in the Kremlin? According to Hersh, the possibility of this happening may have been the smoking gun in the top-secret declaration—the Weinberger memo—that was presented to the court before Pollard's sentencing.

"There was little doubt, I learned from an official who was directly involved, that Soviet intelligence had access to the most secret information in Israel," Hersh wrote. "The question, the official said, was 'whether we could prove it was Pollard's material that went over the aqueduct. We couldn't get there, so we suggested in the Weinberger affidavit that the possibility existed.'"

In other words, there was no proof, just conjecture. Pollard plea-bargained and nevertheless was sentenced to life in prison by the well-respected District Court Judge Aubrey Robinson. If he had instead opted for a trial, it's doubtful that any jury in the land would have convicted Pollard on the most serious charges.

***

When motion picture producer Suzanne Migdall returned to Fort Lauderdale from a trip to Los Angeles, in late May of 2004, she brought with her a tape of the Caspar Weinberger interview on the *Diane Glazer Show*. Before that interview, Diane had asked Suzanne for some good questions to ask the former defense secretary. Unfortunately, Diane was unable to get the questions approved by Weinberger prior to the broadcast.

At the same time, Weinberger also told Diane, confidentially, that, regarding the issue of Pollard, he would no longer stand in the way of any efforts to free him. At least publicly, though, Weinberger said he didn't want to speak on the matter. "I have already answered questions about Pollard many, many times," he said. "I don't want to go there again."

He would be open to speak about Israel, he reiterated, but not about Pollard. So, during the interview, Diane instead focused primarily on a hot topic: the war in Iraq.

Weinberger, in his mid-eighties but his mind as sharp as ever, skated through Diane's questions with ease. He appeared extremely warm, likeable and scholarly during the interview, in which he smartly defended President George W. Bush's policy in Iraq. In his calm and relaxed California manner, Weinberger, for some reason, reminded me of the great UCLA Bruins basketball coach John Wooden, the professorial "Wizard of Westwood," who won all those NCAA championships in the 1960's and '70s, and always handled himself with such dignity and class.

In his half-hour interview, Weinberger stressed that, while mistakes were made by the present Bush administration, the world was generally a better—and safer—place with the destruction of Saddam Hussein's regime.

On camera at least, Weinberger was a far cry from the ogre that some in the Pollard camp—myself included—had often portrayed him as ever since he wrote that secret memo to Judge Aubrey Robinson that sealed Jonathan Pollard's fate.

And, per Weinberger's request, the subject of Pollard was never once brought up.

CHAPTER EIGHTEEN

SMOKE AND MIRRORS

ON JUNE 3, 2004, George Tenet, who had once threatened to resign as CIA director if President Bill Clinton commuted Jonathan Pollard's life sentence, finally did step down in the wake of the ongoing Iraqi crisis. Tenet's resignation came amidst charges, from various quarters, that there was a critical intelligence failure in connection with what many felt was a growing "quagmire" in Iraq; that he didn't do enough to prevent the terrorist attacks on 9-11; and that, as the Director of Central Intelligence, he relied far too much on erroneous information concerning Iraq's alleged weapons of mass destruction.

Three days later, on the sixtieth anniversary of D-Day, the world learned of the death of Ronald Wilson Reagan, the fortieth president of the United States and the person many credited for winning the Cold War.

Pollard had links to Reagan as well.

It was during the Reagan presidency that Pollard worked as a civilian Naval Intelligence analyst; and he, and his first wife, Anne, even attended Reagan's second inauguration. Indeed, Pollard was—according to his father at least—every bit the Reagan Republican. Swept up in the Reagan revolution, Pollard, an admirer of the "Great Communicator," came to Washington to be a small part of a re-igniting of the American spirit. Even when he spied for Israel during Reagan's tenure in the White House, Pollard remained a Reagan supporter. His problems, he always said, were with some of the president's underlings and their apparent "pro-Arab" policy, not with the president himself.

While Reagan, to many, was a breath of fresh air, the national mood seemed to reach its low ebb during the years when Reagan's predecessor, Jimmy Carter, sat in the Oval Office: a period that included a landmark peace agreement between Israel and Egypt, yet a period that was more defined by the takeover of the American Embassy in Tehran, and the holding of eighty U.S. hostages, for over four-hundred days, by the radical young followers of the Ayatollah Khomeini.

Carter was a moral and a decent man, who, both at home and abroad, was perceived as far too weak to be the "most powerful man in the world." Reagan, on the other hand, was the "cowboy." He saw things in black and white, didn't waver in his beliefs, and meant what he said. At least that was the perception.

But perception or fact, there was something very American about Ronald Wilson Reagan. It may have been the reason there was there was such a genuine outpouring of love and affection when we all learned of his death.

While my business partner Suzanne Migdall remained optimistic, she and I still wondered whether the political climate was ever going to allow our motion picture to get made. Watching Sly Stallone being interviewed by Bill O'Reilly—and telling

O'Reilly that he, too, was having problems securing a motion picture deal—was, in its own way, telling.

It was from a Los Angeles studio that Stallone appeared on the May 24, 2004 edition of *The O'Reilly Factor*. Stallone explained why he filed a lawsuit against MGM, which he believed was preventing him from putting together another *Rocky* movie. MGM had called Stallone's lawsuit "sad, desperate and pathetic."

According to Stallone, in 2002, Kirk Kerkorian, who owned MGM, asked Stallone if he would want to make another *Rocky* film. True, the last *Rocky*—where the aging fighter loses everything and has to go back to his roots—didn't do particularly well at the box office. But the other movies did, making a great deal of money for their investors and obviously a household name out of their star.

Stallone told O'Reilly that, after speaking to Kerkorian, he then called the studio head, who, according to Stallone, was irate that the actor had avoided him by speaking to Kerkorian about *Rocky*.

O'Reilly interjected that Kerkorian could have solved the whole issue by saying, "we want to do the movie," but he never did that.

"He didn't want to step up at all," Stallone said.

According to Stallone, Irwin Winkler, who produced the previous *Rocky* films, also came down hard against Stallone, saying he had "veto rights" on any new Rocky deal.

Stallone said he asked Winkler, "Why would you want to veto it?"

Recalled Stallone, Winkler then told him the movie would be made "only if his son directed it."

While watching all this, it reminded me of the challenges that Suzanne had been facing while negotiating her way through the Hollywood landmines.

"What this reinforces," O'Reilly said, "is what we all think about Hollywood, Mr. Stallone—that it's full of egotistical weasels and that you have to kiss their butts to get anything done. And if you cross them, or even if they think you crossed them, they go out for revenge. So your lawsuit—whether it has merit or not, I don't know—reinforces what a jungle Hollywood is."

Stallone agreed, but only in part. Echoing what Suzanne had told me after her meetings with several Hollywood studios—and what I had seen for myself—Stallone explained there is also a "kinder and gentler" side of Hollywood.

"Hollywood is a tough place," Stallone acknowledged. "But there are really a lot of very good, ethical, wonderful filmmakers out there. And they do play it straight."

Stallone eventually did get his film made. Titled *Rocky Balboa*, I felt it was a great story with terrific acting and a wonderful script.

While over the years Suzanne had spent time with Stallone and his family, the closest I came to rubbing shoulders with him was when I went to a UFO lecture by an unusual fellow named Eddie Page, who, to me, physically resembled the late actor Warren Oates.

Eddie spoke for over two hours at this lecture without notes, claimed he was a by-product of an alien abduction, that his "father" was from the Pleiades, and that he once flew in a flying saucer. As bizarre as his whole story was, the strangest part was that Eddie, a trucker with no more than a high school education, was able to give an in-depth explanation of how these UFOs got here, and seemed to have an understanding of quantum physics while relating it to space travel and sounding more like the British physicist Stephen Hawking than some Florida "cracker."

So how, exactly, did Sly Stallone fit into all of this?

Well, Eddie said he knew, through telepathy, when the saucers were near, and told us of the exact spot where a saucer once picked him up: near a lonely stretch of highway in central Florida. I told Suzanne about Eddie's lecture and Suzanne went with me to meet with Eddie at his home in a sleepy Florida town called Lakeland. We brought with us Suzanne's friend, Gary Sax, a musician and cameraman who had worked on a number of projects with Suzanne.

Here was the deal: We would go with Eddie to the exact spot where his "close encounter" allegedly took place. If another saucer came within a hundred yards of us or so—as, according to Eddie, they often did in that area—Gary would shoot the footage.

That's where Stallone came in. Gary joked that we would tape Stallone separately, and, as the saucer approached, get him to say "Yo, Alien!"

It all sounds funny. But some Hollywood producer at Universal Studios offered Suzanne *one million dollars* if we could get a close-up of that UFO on tape, which would then be made into a blockbuster TV program sure to garner enormous ratings.

Sufficed to say, we never did see Eddie's space ship.

On June 11, 2004, the day the nation watched as Ronald Reagan was finally laid to rest, Pollard's name was once again in the news. The Associated Press reported that, in a ruling a few days before, the Circuit Court of Appeals in Washington, D.C. had allowed Pollard to continue the fight to appeal his 1987 conviction. Specifically, a U.S. Court of Appeals panel ruled that Pollard's attorneys would have the opportunity to argue the merits of his case before the appellate court.

As the AP reported, a three-judge panel would hear arguments, probably later in the year. However, the panel would not decide on whether Pollard's sentence was too harsh; only whether he could take the next step in his legal fight. Notwithstanding, it was a rare victory for Pollard and his attorneys, Eliot Lauer and Jacques Semmelman.

"The court could also grant a request from Pollard's current lawyers to see partly classified documents used at Pollard's sentencing," AP reporter Anne Gearan wrote. "The lawyers say they need to see the material to rebut government arguments against any new appeal or against presidential clemency."

The AP story stated that Pollard had already exhausted his regular appeals and would need special permission from a judge to take the case further. "U.S. District Court Judge Thomas Hogan turned him down last fall, and the case could have ended there," Gearan explained. "Lawyers for Pollard asked the appeals court to reconsider Judge Hogan's ruling, a request that is routinely denied. The appeals court instead agreed to take up the matter."

Semmelman called the ruling "a significant development."

"This is a major advance in Jonathan Pollard's quest for justice," added Lauer. "After eighteen years in prison, the U.S. Court of Appeals is now committed to taking a serious look at the circumstances that led to Pollard's life sentence. It is apparent that the Court of Appeals believes we have raised serious issues that warrant further judicial scrutiny."

A press release sent out by the two attorneys' law firm—Curtis, Mallet-Prevost, Colt & Mosle LLP—stated some of the facts: that, prior to his conviction, Pollard pleaded guilty to a single count of conspiracy to commit espionage; and that, despite agreeing to a plea bargain, and cooperating with the U.S. government, on March 4, 1987, he nevertheless received the maximum sentence: life imprisonment.

The U.S. government's "aggressive pursuit" of the maximum sentence was therefore "in direct violation of its plea agreement with Pollard," Pollard's attorneys insisted. "But the material breach went unchallenged by Pollard's original attorney, who failed to object, or even file a one page notice of appeal from the constitutionally defective sentence, thereby precluding appellate review."

At the same time, Lauer and Semmelman stressed, the U.S. government was continuing to block the two of them, who were security-cleared, from viewing Pollard's sentencing file docket, while at the same time making "repeated false statements" to the court regarding their security clearance and "need to know."

"No one representing Pollard," they said in a statement, "has seen the file since the day he was sentenced."

Many in the Pollard camp wondered: Would the Pollard file actually be opened? What, exactly, was inside it? Were there any deep, dark secrets that none of us knew about? Would the file serve to condemn this man, who had already been condemned?

Or like when Geraldo Rivera opened up Al Capone's vault, would the contents amount to nothing—little more than smoke and mirrors?

CHAPTER NINETEEN

BIBI AND BUBBA

ON MONDAY, JUNE 28, 2004—in a move that took Islamic extremists and the rest of the world by surprise—interim Iraqi Prime Minister Iyad Allawi, who in the 1990s worked with the CIA to try and undermine Saddam Hussein's regime, officially took over the reigns of the new Iraqi government. With President Bush's blessings, the long planned transfer of power came two days before scheduled.

"The story behind a handoff that critics once said could never be done by June 30, let alone earlier, offers a peak into the administration's secretive decision-making and its desire to bolster a crucial ally and keep a ruthless insurgency off balance," wrote Eric Schmidt in *The New York Times*. "Bush said he was persuaded to alter the timing because Allawi and the other Iraqi officials had demonstrated a firm hand in running the ministries they had taken over."

The most important consideration, of course, were the fears that insurgents, led by the radical Shiite cleric Moqtada al-Sadr and the Jordanian terrorist Abu Musab al-Zarqawi, would try to

disrupt the scheduled transfer of power with nationwide terrorist attacks. The radicals, like the American media, were caught
completely off guard by the Bush administration's shrewd move.

When, in March 2003, Michael Moore took the stage after
winning an Academy Award for his documentary *Bowling for
Columbine*, he lashed out at his favorite target, President George
W. Bush. "We live in a time when we have fictitious election
results that elect a fictitious president," the average-Joe-looking
filmmaker said to a worldwide audience estimated to be more
than a billion people. "We live in a time where we have a man
sending us to war for fictitious reasons. Shame on you, Mr. Bush
… Shame on you."

Hollywood, for the most part, is a liberal enclave, yet many
in the "industry" felt that the Academy Awards was neither the
time nor the place to get into a political rant. While a majority of
his peers may have agreed with Moore, he was therefore greeted
that evening with a rising chorus of boos.

Over a year later, on the day that the new Iraqi prime minister and the rest of his cabinet were sworn in, a "national town
meeting" to turn up the heat on Bush—and at the same time
to promote Michael Moore's new movie, *Fahrenheit 9/11*—was
being held in homes throughout the U.S. Most of the reviews of
Fahrenheit 9/11, a quasi "documentary," went from good to bad
generally depending on which side of the political fence the reviewer sat on. Since much of the media, like much of Hollywood,
has a liberal bent, more often than not the reviews of the new
film were positive.

As David Gates noted in *Newsweek*, the core narrative of
Moore's labor of love went something like this: The Bush administration seized power by a "fraudulent vote" in Florida, and ex-
ploited the September 11 terrorist attacks to "pump up fear, tamp

down dissent, enrich its cronies, and, ultimately, to launch an ill-advised war against Iraq on the dubious grounds that Saddam Hussein was somehow in league with al Qaeda."

Philip Shenon wrote in *The New York Times* that, according to Moore's film, Bush and his administration also "jeopardized national security" in an effort to placate Bush family cronies in Saudi Arabia, and that the White House helped members of Osama bin Laden's family flee the U.S. after September 11.

The fact that Moore didn't always get his facts straight admittedly didn't seem to bother him. He saw himself as a filmmaker, after all, not a journalist. As was noted earlier in this book, it was the legendary screenwriter and wit Ben Hecht who allegedly once said: "Never let the facts get in the way of a good story." However, Hecht would have said that tongue-in-cheek while the opinionated Moore was at least somewhat serious about what he was doing.

According to Shenon in *The New York Times*, Moore, readying for a conservative "counterattack" after his controversial film hit the theatres, hired outside fact checkers. Shenon reported that Moore's backtracking fact checkers said they "do not view the film as straight reporting." Shenon quoted Dev Chatillon, the former general counsel for *The New Yorker*, as saying: "This is an op-ed piece; it's not a news report. This is not *The New York Times*."

Moore himself said in an interview aired on ABC: "[The movie] is an op-ed piece. It's my opinion about the last four years of the Bush administration. And that's what I call it." Obviously taking a shot at the Fox network and its biggest news star, Bill O'Reilly, Moore added: "I'm not trying to pretend that this is some sort of, you know, fair and balanced work of journalism."

O'Reilly, in his syndicated column, reacted to Moore's statement. "As responsible columnists know, all op-ed pieces are supposed to be grounded in truth," O'Reilly said, "and facts should be cited in backing up one's op-ed opinion."

In the June 28, 2004 edition of *Newsweek*, Michael Isikoff then asked the question that many others were asking: "Can Michael Moore be believed?"

Isikoff reported that one of Moore's many allegations was that in the days after 9/11, when airspace was shut down, the White House approved special charter flights so that prominent Saudis—including members of bin Laden's family—could leave the country. My old source Craig Unger—with whom I had discussed the Pollard case in the past, and who had recently authored the new book *House of Bush House of Saud*—appeared on camera in *Fahrenheit 9/11* and claimed that bin Laden family members were never interviewed by the FBI before they flew back to Saudi Arabia.

According to a report from the 9-11 Commission, however, that was simply untrue. Wrote Isikoff: "The report confirms that six chartered airplanes flew one hundred and forty two mostly Saudi nationals out of the country, including one carrying members of the bin Laden family. But the flights didn't begin until September 14—after airspace reopened. Moreover, the report states the Saudis were screened by the FBI, and twenty-two of the twenty-six people on the bin Laden flight were interviewed. None had any links to terrorism."

In actuality, Michael Moore—who literally became his own cottage industry—did Suzanne and me a favor by making politically charged material more popular. In the past, our Pollard project had been called politically "too hot to handle" and "too thorny" by some of the Hollywood decision makers Suzanne came in contact with. But, in part because of Moore and his commercial appeal, conspiracy theories were once again in vogue. Hopefully, Michael Moore had opened up some doors.

***

In his well-received autobiography, *My Life*, which hit the newsstands in June of 2004, former president Bill Clinton recalled the night he met with Ariel Sharon at the Wye River Conference Center in Maryland, in October 1998, as the Israeli, Palestinian and American delegations were working around the clock to try to get the "peace process" back on track. Benjamin "Bibi" Netanyau, not Sharon, was the Israeli prime minister at the time, and Clinton's meeting with Sharon—with just the two of them present—lasted well into the evening.

Clinton couldn't help but notice that, earlier that same day, Sharon had been the only member of the Israeli delegation who would not shake hands with the leader of the Palestinian delegation, Yasser Arafat. "I enjoyed hearing Sharon talk about his life and his views," Clinton said, "and, when we were finished, at nearly three in the morning, I had a better understanding of how he thought."

Clinton said one of the things that surprised him most about Sharon was "how hard he pushed me to pardon Jonathan Pollard, A U.S. Navy Intelligence analyst who had been convicted in 1986 of spying for Israel." Actually, Pollard was sentenced in 1987, not 1986. But the point was that, according to Clinton at least, Sharon took a presidential pardon for Pollard very seriously, contrary to the oft-stated beliefs of Pollard's wife, Esther.

Clinton noted that Netanyahu, and the late former Prime Minister Yitzhak Rabin, had previously asked for Pollard's release as well. "It was obvious that this was an issue in Israel's domestic politics, and that the Israeli public didn't think the United

States should have punished Pollard so severely since it was to an ally that he had sold sensitive information," Clinton said. "The case would come up again before we finished."

Whether Pollard "sold" information to Israel for cold cash, as Clinton opined, or whether he passed that information on for remuneration so that he could continue with his little spy shop, is a matter for debate. Regardless, Clinton was apparently convinced of the former, not the latter, and this may have affected his decision concerning a pardon for the Jewish spy.

In his book, Clinton also recounted when King Hussein of Jordan, dying of cancer and weakened by chemotherapy, appeared at the conference center to help move the talks along. "He said he would come to Wye if I thought it would help," Clinton wrote. "I told Hussein we could use all the help we could get."

As Clinton noted, one major sticking point in the negotiations had been Arafat's demand for the release of one thousand Palestinian prisoners being held by Israel. Clinton recalled Netanyahu telling him that he couldn't release Hamas members, or others "with blood on their hands," and that no more than five hundred of the Palestinians could be let go.

During what Clinton believed to be a breaking point in the negotiations, he asked Hussein to come to a large cabin where all the parties were dining. There, the courageous king personally spoke to both the Israeli and Palestinian delegations, asking them each to make concessions. After a drained Hussein finally left, the meeting continued on with everyone collected around different tables in the dining room. "My strategy for success now boiled down to endurance," Clinton said. "I was determined to be the last man standing."

As Clinton foresaw, it turned out to be a very long night. By Clinton's recollection, everyone kept "plowing ahead" until a deal was finally worked out at about 7 a.m.

But there was one more obstacle.

"Netanyahu was threatening to scuttle the whole deal unless I released Pollard," Clinton recalled. "[Netanyahu] said I had promised him I would do so at an earlier meeting the night before, and that's why he had agreed on the other issues. In fact, I had told the prime minister that, if that's what it took to make peace, I was inclined to do it, but I would have to check with our people."

According to Clinton, for all the sympathy Pollard generated in Israel, his was a "hard case to push in America."

"He had sold our country's secrets for money, not conviction," Clinton said, again reinforcing a point that may well have been erroneous. "For years he had not shown any remorse."

It was obvious that whatever Clinton knew about the Pollard case was based mostly on intelligence reports written by people who had a vested interest in not seeing Pollard set free. Clinton said that when he talked to National Security Advisor Sandy Berger, and CIA Director George Tenet, "they were adamantly opposed to letting Pollard go, as was [Secretary of State] Madeleine Albright. George said that after the severe damage the Aldrich Ames case had done to the CIA, he (Tenet) would have to resign if I commuted Pollard's sentence. Tenet's comments closed the door."

Clinton explained that one reason he didn't want to alienate Tenet was that security, and commitments by the Israelis and the Palestinians to work together against terror, were "at the heart of the agreement we had reached." The president apparently believed Tenet's leadership at the CIA was critical if the whole process was to be successful.

"Tenet had helped the sides to work out the details and had agreed that the CIA would support their implementation," Clinton said. "If [Tenet] left, there was a real chance Arafat would not go forward. I also needed George in the fight against al Qaeda and terrorism."

Clinton told Netanyahu that he would nevertheless review the Pollard case "seriously," and try to "work through it" with Tenet and the national security team. But Clinton added the caveat that Netanyahu was better off with a security agreement he could count on than he would have been with the release of Pollard.

"Finally, after we talked again at length, Bibi agreed to stay with the agreement," Clinton said, "but on the condition that we would change the mix of prisoners, which Arafat considered problematic."

An agreement was finally reached, Clinton said, with Israel getting "unprecedented cooperation (from the Palestinians) in the fight against violence and terror." It was an agreement, of course, that Arafat never intended to live up to.

As for Pollard, a pawn in an international chess game, he would remain exactly where most of the intelligence community wanted him to remain—in a securely locked cell, in a medium security prison, out of sight and out of mind.

CHAPTER TWENTY

FAILURE OF IMAGINATION

HE LARGER THAN life Marlon Brando, looking nothing like the young, strapping, Stanley Kowalski in *Streetcar Named Desire*, the fighter who "could have been a contender" in *On the Waterfront*, or the motorcycle-riding tough in *The Wild One*, died in a Los Angeles hospital on July 2, 2004. That same day the world got its first glimpse of a much thinner, but still defiant, Saddam Hussein, months following the dictator's capture by the U.S. military.

Defiant in his own right, Brando had once said about Hollywood that it is "ruled by fear and the love of money," which may be accurate. "But it can't rule me," the legendary actor claimed, "because I'm not afraid of anything—and I don't love money."

Like most of us mere mortals, filmmaker Michael Moore hardly felt guilty about making money, however, and may not have been above stretching the truth just a tad in the name of artistic license. Swimming against the current, Suzanne Migdall was, at the same time, shopping a project in Hollywood that was not yet being heartily embraced by either the political left—or the political right.

Moore, meanwhile, had not only found his niche; he had found a philosophical home. He was the darling of the George W. Bush-hating rabid left, especially with a presidential election coming up. And whether the basic premise of his *Fahrenheit 9-11* was fictitious, or not, hardly seemed to matter to his millions of adoring fans.

Of course, not everyone loved him.

In a scathing article, the sardonically brilliant Christopher Hitchens, writing for *Vanity Fair*, called Moore a "silly and a shady man."

"To him, easy applause, in front of credulous audiences, is everything," Hitchens, noted. As for Moore's entertaining and admittedly funny film, Hitchens said that to describe it as "dishonest and demagogic would almost be to promote those terms to the level of respectability. To describe it as an exercise in facile crowd-pleasing would be too obvious. *Fahrenheit 9-11* is a sinister exercise in moral frivolity, crudely disguised as an exercise in seriousness. It is also a spectacle of abject political cowardice masking itself as a demonstration of 'dissenting bravery.'"

Hardly a "right-wing fanatic," Hitchens had once written a book in which he accused Henry Kissinger of war crimes. His shots at Moore therefore had to carry far greater weight than if they had been delivered by card-carrying Conservatives such as Ann Coulter or Sean Hannitty. After I read his article the first thing that came to my mind was: Christopher Hitchens could care less about being politically correct; he just wanted to get it right. He was definitely a man after my own heart.

When the *9-11 Commission Report* hit the bookstores in mid July 2004 it became an immediate bestseller. Contrary to the protestations of many Bush detractors, the bipartisan 9-11 Commission did not condemn the president—nor did it condemn his predecessor, Bill Clinton—for the tragic events that took the lives of more than three thousand innocent people.

On the *Abrams Report*, telecast July 22, 2004, 9-11 Commission Chair Thomas Kean, a Republican and the former governor of New Jersey, explained that on September 11, 2001, we were, quite simply, unprepared. "We did not grasp the magnitude of a threat that had been gathering over a considerable period of time," Kean said during a taped segment.

Kean was careful to say "we," not President Bush. After all, al Qaeda had strengthened during Clinton's watch as well as Bush's. To Kean, there was clearly enough blame to go around. "This was a failure of policy, management, capability, and, above all, a failure of imagination," Kean said.

Also in a taped segment, the 9-11 Commission vice chair, U.S. Rep. Lee Hamilton, an Indiana Democrat, rhetorically asked: "Who is in charge? Who ensures that agencies pool resources, avoid duplication, and plan jointly? Who oversees the massive integration and unity of effort necessary to keep America safe? Too often, the answer is no one."

It was Rep. Hamilton who, in 1987, did a favor for Dr. Morris Pollard by getting Dr. Pollard's son, Jonathan, transferred out of the Springfield Medical Center for Federal Prisoners—which basically housed the criminally insane. Pollard wound up in Marion Penitentiary in Marion, Illinois—one of America's harshest prisons—but that was not Hamilton's intent.

When he appeared as a guest, the following day, on CNBC's *Scarborough Country*, terrorism analyst Steve Emerson explained to his listeners and host Joe Scarborough that the 9-11 Commission Report was basically divided into three sections: the outline of the plot and the history leading up to the attacks; recommendations; and footnotes. Emerson described the footnotes as "absolutely mesmerizing in their detail."

"They're an amazing, shocking list of revelations, that are going to be bombshells as they get disclosed and refined over in the media as well as in Congress," Emerson said. "I've been absolutely in shock, and I'm not using any exaggeration as to the degree to which the United States of America was thoroughly compromised by Islamic extremist groups going back to the early 1990s."

Acknowledging that Emerson was one of the most respected terrorism experts in the country, Scarborough said: "You have been sounding warning bells for years about Islamic extremism and al Qaeda, and about Osama bin Laden. Are you telling us here, tonight, that, after reading the 9-11 report, it's much worse than you ever imagined?

"Absolutely," Emerson replied.

Emerson has long been despised by many of the apologists in the Muslim world—people who claim that the hatred of radical Muslims for America is rooted in America's support for the State of Israel. This isn't true, it's merely a rationale. The real reason these people hate America and the west is because they hate everything America and the west stand for. Ideals like democracy and freedom have no place in the fanatical world of militant Islam—which was why the Bush gambit of trying to bring a western-style democracy to Iraq was so risky. The perception that Muslim civilization had somehow been "left behind" in the annals of history has only intensified radical Muslim anger. As a result, America and the west have been involved in its most deadly struggle since Europe was enveloped by the dark clouds of the Third Reich.

***

When Sandy Berger appeared on *Meet the Press* during September of 2000, moderator Tim Russert asked Bill Clinton's national security advisor about Jonathan Pollard, since the question of clemency for the former spy, first brought to Clinton's attention in 1996, was again on the table.

"As you know the spy Jonathan Pollard, who was convicted of espionage for transferring secrets to Israel, requested clemency in the past, and he's requesting it again," Russert said.

Russert emphasized that Clinton, who had rejected Pollard's original clemency request four years before, seemed to agree with then-Attorney General Janet Reno that the original sentence imposed by the court was warranted.

"Has anything changed?" Russert asked.

"We've made no judgment that is contrary to that," Berger replied. "I know this is a very controversial matter. People have different views. But I believe that the judgment the president made in 1996 was the correct one."

"In the year 2000?" asked Russert.

"That's my judgment, yes," Berger replied.

When he was spying for Israel, Pollard always gave the Israelis the "finished product" to which they felt they were entitled, not the "cooked" information they were officially being given by the United States. Ninety percent of Pollard's material would be a report and would have attachments of some of the raw data. The analysis would be on various subjects. The Israelis would tell Pollard what subjects they wanted and Pollard would go to the library at Naval Intelligence and take the relevant information out. He would bring the material somewhere else, photocopy it, and then return the original information back to the library.

Pollard had little choice but to leave the library at Naval Intelligence in order to have the intelligence data copied. After all, if he had the copies made at Naval Intelligence he might have drawn some unwarranted attention. As one of my sources told me: "If you as much as check out a piece of paper [from Naval Intelligence] there is a safeguard on that paper. There is a computer listing on that paper. And if you don't check it back in—I mean these people in counterintelligence are not stupid—people will begin to notice."

Whereas Pollard was removing documents, copying them, but always returning them, former National Security Advisor Sandy Berger—who had gone on record as being against executive clemency for Pollard—apparently had a different plan. When the story broke on July 20, 2004, that Berger was himself removing classified documents—in this case from the National Archives—it seemed unlikely that Berger meant to place all those documents back from where they came. As was reported by the Associated Press, Berger was actually the focus of a criminal investigation for removing those highly classified terrorism documents and hand-written notes from a secure reading room during his preparation for the September 11 Commission hearings.

"Berger's home and office were searched earlier this year by FBI agents armed with warrants after he voluntarily returned documents to the National Archives," the AP report stated. "However, some drafts of a sensitive after-action report on the Clinton administration's handling of al Qaeda terrorist threats, during the December 1999 millennium celebration, are still missing."

According to the AP, the FBI searches occurred after National Archives employees told agents they believed they witnessed Berger place documents in his clothing while reviewing sensitive Clinton administration papers.

Berger's lawyer admitted that his client knowingly removed some handwritten notes, sticking them in his jacket and pants, and "inadvertently took copies of actual classified documents in a leather portfolio."

"In the course of reviewing thousands of pages of documents on behalf of the Clinton administration, in connection with requests by the September 11 commission, I inadvertently took a few documents from the archives," Berger explained. "I deeply regret the sloppiness involved, but I had no intention of withholding documents from the commission."

Berger insisted that, once he was informed that the documents were missing, he returned "everything I had except for a few documents that I apparently had accidentally discarded."

FBI officials said those missing documents not only included critical assessments of the Clinton administration's handing of the millennium threat, but also focused on the administration's lack of preparedness concerning America's terrorism vulnerabilities at airports and seaports.

In his syndicated column, conservative columnist Cal Thomas opined that Berger's need to "slip some of the classified documents in his jacket and stuff others in his pants may say something about his true motive."

"If Berger was behaving lawfully, why would he not follow lawful procedures, including asking permission to remove notes he took from the classified documents?" Thomas wrote. "Imagine the reaction if National Security Advisor Condoleezza Rice had done such a thing and made a similar excuse. Democrats and the *New York Times* would be calling not only for her head, but demanding she be sent to prison for breaking the law. And 'accidentally' and 'inadvertently' would not absolve her in their minds."

Paul Brachfeld, inspector general for the National Archives, also wasn't about to cut Berger any slack. "Why did he get away with it?" Brachfeld rhetorically asked during a report on Fox News aired years later. "He got away with it because he *was* Sandy Berger."

"It all adds up to a huge cover-up," Republican congressman Tom Davis added during that same report. "We just don't know what was being covered up."

CHAPTER TWENTY ONE

A STACKED DECK

WHEN I APPEARED as a guest on CNN during Labor Day of 2003—the day before Jonathan Pollard appeared in front of U.S. District Court Judge Thomas Hogan—I was one of two people interviewed in the CNN Pollard segment who were openly in favor of the Jewish spy's release from prison. The other Pollard supporter was Congressman Anthony Weiner, a Democrat from New York. (Journalist Wolf Blitzer, who also appeared in the Pollard segment, didn't voice his opinion.)

Eleven months later, on August 7, 2004, Weiner—who years later, following a sex scandal, would resign from Congress in disgrace—sent a letter to President Bush, urging the president to finally commute Pollard's sentence.

"Today is Mr. Pollard's fiftieth birthday," Weiner wrote. "This is the nineteenth year he has celebrated his birthday in prison. No other person convicted of espionage on behalf of a United States ally has ever been imprisoned for so long."

Weiner noted that Pollard "cooperated fully" with the investigation into his activities, and waived his right to a jury trial.

According to Weiner, the life sentence Pollard was serving was "not a reflection of the severity of the crimes he committed, but rather the result of ineffectual counsel."

In his letter, Weiner used the words of United States District Judge George N. Leighton who wrote: "The evidence shows that the government engaged in serious misconduct that went unchecked by an ineffective defense counsel, and these constitutional violations severely prejudiced Mr. Pollard and resulted in his sentence of life in prison." To Judge Leighton, the deck had obviously been stacked against Pollard getting a fair shake.

Weiner stressed, also, that Pollard still hadn't submitted a formal petition to the pardon attorney of the Justice Department. The reason, Weiner stated, was because of the Justice Department's continuing refusal to permit Pollard's attorneys to access portions of five sentencing documents in the court's docket, totaling approximately thirty-five to forty pages of material.

"The attorneys have the appropriate security clearances to see those court documents, and they plainly have a 'need to know' what is in their client's court file," Weiner wrote. "Until they have been afforded access to these materials, they believe it is premature to submit any application for executive clemency or similar relief."

On August 11, 2004, David Sanger reported in the *New York Times* that President Bush had nominated Rep. Porter Goss, the longtime chair of the House Intelligence Committee, to head the CIA "at a moment of heated debate about both the agency's shortcomings and how to execute the broadest overhaul of U.S. Intelligence operations in more than half a century." Bush praised Goss as "a leader with strong experience in intelligence and in the fight against terrorism."

"He knows the CIA inside and out," Bush said. "He's the right man to lead this important agency at this critical moment in our nation's history."

A week after Congressman Weiner sent his letter to the president—urging Bush to commute Jonathan Pollard's sentence—I wrote an op-ed on Goss, the president's choice to replace George Tenet.

It was noted on Esther Zeitz-Pollard's website, Justice 4JP, that Goss, a Republican from Florida, was among the authors of a 1999 proposed House resolution stating that Jonathan Pollard should serve the full term of his life sentence, "and should not receive pardon, reprieve, or any other form of executive clemency from the president of the United States." According to the Zeitz-Pollard website, Goss was quoted as saying, "He (Pollard) is one of the worst traitors in our nation's history. There is absolutely no reason to let this guy out of jail—none."

I didn't personally know Porter Goss, but I had met with, and genuinely liked, both of Florida's U.S. senators at the time of Goss's appointment by Bush: Bob Graham and Bill Nelson. Democrats Graham and Nelson—who supported fellow Floridian Goss—were affable and smart, and, each year, Graham's office would send me a calendar published by the United States Capitol Historical Society, which Graham always signed. His office would also send me a "Seasons Greetings" card, which of course was sent to other reporters as well. It wasn't by accident that Graham, who courted the media, never had a problem getting re-elected.

As much as I respected Graham's and Nelson's opinions, however, I had a bone to pick with Goss. The title of my op-ed was: "An Intelligent Choice to Lead the New CIA?" I sent it to all the "usual suspects," including the local mullet wrappers such as the *South Florida Sun-Sentinel* and the *Miami Herald*, as well as the *New York Times*, *Washington Post*, and the *Los Angeles Times*.

I immediately got a call back from Oren Rawls, the Opinion Editor of the *Forward*, a newspaper published in New York since 1897, with a large circulation, that dealt with Israel, the Middle East, and just about anything of interest to Jews. Rawls decided to go with my piece, with just a few cosmetic changes.

My op-ed, as originally written, began:

I have never met Republican Congressman Porter Goss, nor have I ever spoken with him. Still, as the author of *The Hunting Horse: The Truth Behind the Jonathan Pollard Spy Case*, the fact that Goss could be the new director of Central Intelligence gives great me cause for concern.

First of all, let me say that I am not a George W. Bush basher. Second, I am not particularly bothered by the fact that, in 1999, Goss wrote a scathing article, picked up by the *Washington Times*, in which the Florida congressman was adamant that Pollard, an American who spied for Israel, should never be released from prison—even though I totally disagreed with Goss on this matter.

The problem I have with Goss is that, when it came to the Pollard spy case, he simply didn't have his facts straight. And he should have. A former CIA operative and chairman of the House Select Committee on Intelligence, Goss appeared, instead, to be parroting what he heard from others in the CIA who had an agenda. Goss simply took the faulty information, and ran with it. Today, with al Qaeda breathing down our necks, ready, willing, and perhaps even able, to destroy our way of life, I do not want a director of Central Intelligence who is little more than an empty suit and a spin doctor.

I want a bold DCI who can make sound decisions based on quality information. Most importantly, I want a DCI who will tell his commander-in-chief the truth—and not necessarily what the president wants to hear.

Goss noted in his article about Pollard—a former GS-12 civilian Naval Intelligence analyst—that "Pollard's ideology was not what motivated him; it was primarily his greed." Well, that's Goss's opinion. I disagree, but that's subjective and I won't argue it. However, Goss goes on to say that Pollard "approached three, and perhaps four, countries with the secrets he had pledged to protect." Goss continues: "Two were predominantly Christian countries, one predominantly Buddhist, and one was a sectarian Muslim state. In 1984, he approached Israeli military intelligence and found a buyer."

Aside from Israel, exactly what countries did Pollard approach? Yes, I've heard the rumors. But if Goss knows, he should let us know. He can't, of course, because his friends in the CIA, who passed this "information" on to him, were mostly blowing smoke. If those countries were in fact named, then good journalists could have investigated and asked to see the proof.

Goss goes on to say that Pollard's "betrayal compromised this nation's most sensitive sources and methods, causing excessive damage to our national security, while adding risk to the lives of brave Americans who protect our country."

But Goss is not specific. He can't be specific, because, again, this is a gross exaggeration of the damage Pollard actually caused. Truth be told, as a GS-12 analyst Pollard never had access to much of the material he was alleged to have passed on to the Israelis from 1984-85 (and that some claim was then passed on to the Soviets). Simply put, he didn't have the necessary clearance.

Goss also notes that "upon his release, the thousands of dollars that are most likely still being deposited into a foreign account by Israel would surely make (Pollard) a millionaire. If he is released, Pollard's treacherous crimes will pay, and handsomely."

Well, many of us have "thousands of dollars" in our bank accounts, but we are not millionaires. In actuality, the Israelis were supposed to place $300,000 in a Swiss bank account for Pollard, if he worked for them for ten years—that's $30,000 a year, which barely covered Pollard's expenses—but the account was never activated.

Goss then states that releasing Pollard "would now risk further damage to our national security; he still has secrets to sell."

Did Porter Goss realize that Pollard was arrested in 1985? What intelligence secrets could he possibly have had to sell in 1999?

Finally, Goss notes that Pollard's life sentence is a "fair punishment for the hardship and excessive damage he has caused. It is not unreasonable to assume that in war times Pollard could have been sentenced to death for his betrayal."

Pollard was officially accused of one count of passing classified information to an American ally—Israel. For that he could have been given the death penalty? Is Porter Goss delusional?

The bottom line is that the world we live in today is a very dangerous place. The DCI needs to be a tough-minded individual who is willing to do whatever it takes to change the Agency for the better. As the president picks the right man—or woman—for the job, this is hardly the time to make a mistake.

On August 20, 2004, my article—with the few changes made by Oren Rawls at the *Forward*—appeared on the Justice4JP website. I was pleased to see it there. At the end of the article, however, a caveat was included that stated: "The only source of information J4JP recommends is the Justice for Jonathan Pollard Web Site. J4JP does not endorse any book(s) on the Pollard case."

Well, at least they didn't say not to buy my book.

CHAPTER TWENTY-TWO

DÉJÀ VU ALL OVER AGAIN

I T WAS, IN the immortal words of Yogi Berra, "Déjà vu all over again."

On August 28, 2004, on the eve of the Republican National Convention, a story broke that an analyst for Douglas J. Feith, an undersecretary of defense and the number three ranking official in the Pentagon, may have acted as a spy for Israel. The still unnamed analyst had reportedly taken classified information, having to do with secret White House deliberations on Iran, to his contacts at the American Israel Public Affairs Committee (AIPAC), which allegedly then passed this information on to the Israelis.

Not surprisingly, Jonathan Pollard's name was again being brought up by the media because of the obvious parallels to the Pollard case.

As Curt Anderson noted in an Associated Press article, "Despite the close U.S.-Israeli relationship, this is not the first allegation of spying for Israel. Jonathan Pollard, a former Naval Intelligence officer who gave top-secret documents to Israel, has been a point of contention in U.S.-Israeli relations. The Israeli government has repeatedly pressed for his release, but intelligence officials have called the information he passed on to the Israelis highly damaging."

The timing of the new "spy" story was interesting to say the least. Was the story "leaked" just before the convention to hurt President Bush, who had such a close relationship with Israeli Prime Minister Ariel Sharon? Was it in retaliation for the Sandy Berger incident? Or was a legitimate piece of news?

The person at the center of the new storm of controversy—identified the following day as Lawrence A. Franklin—was a career analyst at the Defense Intelligence Agency who specialized in Iran. Franklin, who was not Jewish, had served in the Air Force reserve, rising to the rank of colonel. According to a story in the *Washington Post*, early in the Bush administration Franklin had moved from the DIA to the Pentagon's policy branch headed by Feith, where he continued his work on Iranian affairs. It was reported on ABC News that Franklin could soon be arrested on charges ranging from mishandling classified information to espionage.

AIPAC—Israel's main lobbying group in the United States—meanwhile denied any involvement and released a statement saying it was "fully cooperating" with U.S. authorities. The statement added that AIPIC "would not tolerate any violations of U.S. law or interests."

The Associated Press reported that David Siegel, a spokesperson for the Israeli embassy in Washington, also categorically denied the allegations, calling them "completely false and outrageous."

Alon Pincus, the former Israeli consulate general in Washington, shared those sentiments. "This whole thing seems to me to be totally ludicrous," Pincus said on Fox News, doubting that the people at AIPAC, notoriously cautious, would ever take such a risk. He added: "The level of international cooperation (between Israel and the United States) is at such a high level that we would never need a lower level operative for something like this."

On August 28, Prime Minister Sharon's office issued an official statement saying that Israel "does not engage in intelligence activities in the U.S. We deny all these reports."

Obviously, Iran's nuclear aspirations were no secret to the Israelis. A month earlier, in July of 2004, Lieutenant General Moshe Yaalon, Israel's military chief of staff, had publicly accused Iran, which bankrolled and embraced Islamic terrorists around the world, of continuing to develop nuclear weapons. "We have to pay serious attention to Iran's intentions to arm itself with nuclear capabilities," Yaalon said. "This should not only concern Israel, but all the countries of the free world."

Yaalon's statements were just part of an escalating war of words taking place between Israel and Iran. Alluding to Israel's preemptive strike against the Osirak nuclear reactor in Iraq in 1981, which destroyed that facility, Iranian leaders cautioned Israel not to try the same thing against them. If the Israelis launched such an attack, the Iranians warned, there would be "dire consequences" for Israel. Specifically, Iran threatened, as retaliation, to destroy Israel's Dimona nuclear reactor.

Back on December 14, 2001, former Iranian president Ali Akbar Hasehemi Rafsanjani, who some considered a "moderate," had even suggested that Iran should one day annihilate Israel with nuclear weapons. "If the day comes when the world of Islam is duly equipped with the arms Israel has in its possession," Rafsanjani reportedly said at Tehran University, "the strategy of colonialism would face a stalemate because application of an atomic bomb would not leave anything in Israel—but the same thing would just produce damages in the Muslim world."

Rafsanjani continued: "Jews shall expect to be once again scattered and wandering around the globe the day when this appendix is extracted from the region." Rafsanjani went on to describe the establishment of Israel as "the worst event in history."

Perhaps Rafsanjani was just blowing smoke. As an Iranian president he had to know that Israel not only had nuclear weapons; it was a major nuclear power that could reduce Iran to ashes. At the same time, before getting to the point where they would have little choice but to make all of Tehran "glow in the dark," it's logical to assume the Israelis had a desire to know all about U.S. policy concerning Iran, especially what was going on behind the scenes. While Israel, at the very least, would not think twice about launching a pre-emptive strike against an Iranian reactor—regardless of Iran's threats—the Sharon government surely had a keen interest in knowing, ahead of time, exactly what the United States, burdened by Iraq, was itself planning to do about a possible nuclear Iran.

Interestingly, according to James Risen in the *New York Times*, Lawrence Franklin was one of two Defense Department officials who traveled to Paris for a secret meeting with Manucher Ghorbanifar, an Iranian arms dealer who, nearly two decades earlier, had been a central figure in the Iran-contra affair—during which the Reagan administration allegedly back-channeled arms to Iran during that country's war with Iraq. Israel, as an intermediary, had been involved as well. According to *The New York Times*, Secretary of Defense Donald Rumsfeld confirmed that this latest secret meeting with the Iranians did, in fact, take place, but defended the meeting as "an appropriate diplomatic effort," adding that the talks "went nowhere."

In his book *Veil*, author Bob Woodward notes that Ghorbani-far had long been known to the CIA, but was not particularly trusted. In 1984, Woodward writes, the CIA "issued a formal 'burn notice,' warning that Ghorbanifar was a 'talented fabrica-tor.' ... [Director of Central Intelligence William] Casey was alert to the danger of Ghorbanifar, but the man was the sort of person who often became an intelligence agent: sleaze was no barrier to usefulness." Ghorbanifar would wind up being the Iranian point man in the trading of American hostages, held by Islamic radicals, in exchange for TOW anti-tank missiles. Israel would be the "middleman."

However, Woodward notes in his book: "Execution of the arms sale was complicated by distrust between Iran and Israel. Iran did not want to pay until it received the weapons, and Israel would not provide the TOW missiles until they were paid for. To break the impasse, Ghorbanifar came up with a 'bridge loan' from Saudi American businessman Adnan Khashoggi, who put up $5 million for what became the purchase of 508 TOWs. On September 15, 1984, the Reverend Benjamin Weir, an American hostage, was released."

I assumed that one of my Israeli sources may have also person-ally dealt with Ghorbanifar, at least somewhere down the line, but I never specifically asked him. In his book *The Secret War Against The Jews*, author John Loftus alleged that Casey asked one of his old friends in the oil business to contact Khashoggi, whom Loftus described as a business partner of Cyrus Hashe-mi. Noted Loftus, Khashoggi had his own investors who could privately finance the arms deal as well as "extensive contacts in BCCI (Bank of Credit and Commerce International) Monaco to ensure discretion. About the same time, in the spring of 1985,

Manucher Ghorbanifar was told to see if he could lure Khashoggi and the Israelis into taking over the arms for hostages game."

Back in April 1986 a group of Israelis were indicted by a federal grand jury in New York, along with retired Israeli general Avraham Bar-Am and Sam Evans, an attorney for Saudi arms dealer Khashoggi, for conspiracy to sell American-made weapons to Iran. After getting caught in the net, Hashemi, who had been involved with the group, was set to testify against his former colleagues in an attempt to wriggle out and save his own skin.

The $2 billion arms deal was purportedly the biggest arms deal in U.S. history. The charges against the group, known as the "Bermuda Five" (following their arrest in Bermuda), were dropped, in July of 1986, after the shady Hashemi, an Iranian merchant banker, died in London under mysterious circumstances.

The question has long been asked: Why, in the mid-1980s, were the Israelis willing to help arm Iran? I believe there are three reasons. First, Iran was engaged at the time in a war with Iraq, and the Israelis considered Saddam Hussein and his regime to be a far greater threat to Israel than the mullahs in Tehran. Secondly, the Israelis did it for the money. Third, when it came to dealing with Iran, the Israelis were smart enough to hedge their bets.

During Iran's war with Iraq, Israel was in fact moving so much material to the Iranians, an Israeli source once told me, that there was always the off chance that, somewhere down the line, the Iranians would turn Israel's own material against them. At the same time, Iran's "order of battle" was the same as Israel's in that it was American (and not Soviet) based: hence Iran needed the spare parts for their air force that either Israel or the U.S. could provide.

"Now there are parts—an example is a radar system made by Westinghouse, the APQ-120 radar—that are installed in a wonderful airplane called the Phantom," my source explained to me. "The Phantom, without modification, has two engines that pull in tandem. So you can't pull one Phantom engine out and make it work on one airplane. Meanwhile the computers hooked into the APQ-120 radar do everything for the pilot except make him coffee. As for the lock-on systems for the mid-range Sparrow missiles, fire, direction, everything, goes through this system. In that radar system they have a particular little box—lets call it a continuous wave multiplier—that burns out. What this does is it jacks an electric impulse up and holds the radar beam on the enemy target while the Sparrow missile rides the beam to the target."

When the Phantom was first designed in the late 1950s, my source continued, engineers could not "culture" 45-megahirt crystals, but they could culture 15-megahirt crystals. They therefore had to make a box big enough to hold three 15-megahertz crystals.

These days, my source went on, one 45-megehertz crystal was adequate to do the entire job. "So you had empty space in this box. And the box never reduced in size because the whole APQ-120 radar system was built around having a box this size.

"So what we would do is inside the box we would put a little pyrotechnic device that had a small UHF receiver. And if the Iranian Phantoms were ever to come toward Israel, one of the first things that would happen was the leader of an interceptor wing would switch to a particular megahertz, give it a pulse, the pulse would go out to these little receivers, the receiver would react by igniting the pyrotechnic charge, and the APQ-120 would shut down. Now, after your APQ-120 shuts down, if you're a Phantom driver you can do one of two things. If it's a clear day you can land. Or, you can crash. You can't do anything else. You can't shoot your guns; you can't shoot your missiles; you can't call home. This was known as a 'Shanghai Surprise.' This device was put in a great number of the spare parts—especially the aircraft spare parts, since the Iranian Air Force was deemed the primary threat against Israel.

"And in the unlikely event that the Iranian Air Force ever attacks Israel, there are many, many thousands of these Shanghai Surprises sitting right there waiting for them."

On August 29, 2004, *The New York Times* reported that investigators in the Lawrence Franklin case still didn't know whether Israeli intelligence officers had "tasked" intermediaries at AIPAC to seek specific information for Franklin to obtain, which, as reporters David Johnston and Eric Schmidt noted, would "make the case more serious."

Regardless, according to Johnston and Schmidt, Franklin appeared to be an "unlikely candidate" for intelligence work. "[Franklin] was at the bottom of the food chain, at the grunt level," the reporters recalled being told by a senior defense official.

In the September 6, 2004 edition of *Newsweek*, reporters Michael Isikoff and Mark Hosenball also questioned whether Franklin could have been a "mole." According to Isikoff and Hosenball, while some U.S. officials warned against exaggerated accusations of spying, at least one administration source, however, described the case as the "most significant Israeli espionage investigation in Washington since Jonathan Pollard."

Ephraim Sneh, a member of Israel's Knesset and a retired general who had been monitoring the development of nuclear weapons in Iran for years, nevertheless insisted that Israel would be "crazy to spy on its best friend."

"Since Pollard, we avoid any intelligence activity on U.S. soil," Sneh explained in an interview reported by *Newsweek*. "I know the policy; I've been in this business for years."

The retired general then made sure he was crystal clear. "We avoid anything that even *smells* like intelligence-gathering in the U.S," he said.

SPOCK'S BRAIN

PAT BUCHANAN, PERHAPS the only Conservative "talking head" in America who rails against Israel, was up to his old tricks. In an op-ed that appeared in early September 2004, Buchanan gave his personal spin to the story involving suspected mole Lawrence Franklin, who may or may not have handed a draft copy of a National Security Presidential Directive on Iran to his friends at the American Israel Public Affairs Committee (AIPAC), which allegedly then passed that directive on to the Israelis.

The potential scandal had temporarily ceased getting media play, but that didn't stop Buchanan from trying to fan whatever flames were still there.

Referring to Jonathan Pollard, who Buchanan called an "American traitor," Buchanan noted that, "Washington is today rife with reports that the FBI has been investigating whether or not a nest of Pollardites inside the Pentagon has been funneling secrets, through the Israeli lobby AIPAC ... to Prime Minister Ariel Sharon."

Buchanan continued: "With the mullahs (in Iran) apparently pursuing atomic bombs, Israel wants the United States to attack, denuclearize and bring down its number one enemy, the regime in Tehran."

Buchanan—who, whether you agree with him or not, is a snappy writer and a crack journalist—proceeded to make a strong circumstantial case that Franklin did exactly what some in Washington had suspected him of doing. Buchanan tried to link Franklin's alleged actions to Franklin's boss, Douglas Feith, who according to Buchanan, had close ties to Israel's Likud Party. Buchanan also attempted to show that "neo-conservatives" Richard Perle and Paul Wolfowitz—two very pro-Israeli advisors to George W. Bush—may have had their own fingerprints all over the Iran directive that supposedly wound up on Ariel Sharon's desk.

"In my new book, *Where the Right Went Wrong*, there is a line that now appears prophetic," Buchanan wrote: "America needs a Middle East policy made in the U.S.A., not in Tel Aviv, or at AIPAC ..."

Unfortunately for Buchanan, his feelings about Israel were notably quite different from those of Democratic presidential nominee John Kerry, a longtime unequivocal supporter of the Jewish State. They were also out of whack with the views of his own political party, not to mention his commander-in-chief. "An attack on Israel is like an attack on the United States," George W. Bush had once said while addressing AIPAC. "This is what Israelis must know, and this is what the world must understand."

Yoko Ono was far, far to the left of Pat Buchanan, but it appeared that she, like Buchanan, had a bone to pick with the Israeli government. On September 17, 2004, it was announced that Ono, who gained fame and fortune by marrying the late John Lennon, awarded $50,000 "peace grants" to two individuals: journalist Seymour Hersh and Israeli nuclear whistle-blower Mordechai Vananu. Ono was quoted as saying that the honorees were "people who have spoken out for the benefit of the human race by overcoming extreme personal difficulties, and, in doing so, have allowed the truth to prevail."

In the May 24, 2004 edition of *The New Yorker*, Hersh had written a scathing story about the abuse of Iraqi prisoners by American guards at Abu Ghraib prison. The prolific Hersh was also completing a new book: *Chain of Command: The Road From 9-11 to Abu Ghraib.*

Vananu, a former technician at Israel's Dimona nuclear power plant, served eighteen years in prison for revealing information about Israel's nuclear weapons program.

Perhaps what Ono should have said was that her so-called peace grants are given to Jews who apparently have some serious issues with the Jewish State, since Hersh also wrote an "expose" about Israel's nuclear capabilities when he penned *The Samson Option*. Hersh, as I've documented in this book, was a major critic, as well, of spy Jonathan Pollard.

I have never met Yoko Ono, but I did meet John Lennon. Once, in the early 1970s—I can't remember the exact year—the former Beatle struck up a conversation with me in a Manhattan bar called "The Home," which was located just a few blocks away from the exclusive Dakota Building where the rock star and Ono were then living. Lennon had just broken up with Ono— although they would soon be back together—and, on the day I met him, Lennon was like a rudderless ship.

A few years later, I read an account in a Lennon biography in which the writer—I'm paraphrasing what he wrote—recalled a forlorn Lennon telling him how, in years gone by, he was so famous he could have "slept with any woman in the world (he used far more colorful language than that), but now people don't even know I exist."

In a televised interview after Lennon's death, Ono's longtime publicist, Elliot Mintz (who my partner Suzanne Migdall once had lunch with) implied that Lennon wasn't wired that way, and that the writer had to have fabricated the conversation. I knew otherwise. Because when I met Lennon, who appeared to be totally ripped on whatever was his drug of choice at the time, he said virtually the exact same thing to me—*word for word.*

Of course, by no stretch did that make Lennon a bad guy. But, like all of us mere mortals, he, too, was flawed, and had his own set of demons. Contrary to what many of his admirers felt about him—that he was some kind of highly-evolved pop-culture "guru"—the man who wrote "Imagine" didn't have all the answers, at least in his own personal life. And the fact that Yoko Ono could still get such positive press for her causes, simply by trading off on her late husband's good name, shows that we live in a society in which image is too often more valued than substance. Considering how dangerous our world has become, I find that to be an alarming trend, to say the least.

On September 14, 2004, it was reported that Jonathan Pollard's pro-bono attorneys, Eliot Lauer and Jacques Semmelman, filed a brief on Pollard's behalf in the United States Court of Appeals for the District of Columbia Circuit. The brief was in regard to their motion, originally filed in 2000, to vacate Pollard's life sentence based upon ineffective assistance of counsel during Pollard's original sentencing hearing, and to finally gain access to the classified portions of Pollard's court docket.

Oral arguments were scheduled for January 13, 2005, before a three-judge panel of the United States Court of Appeals in Washington, D.C.

On September 22, 2004, U.S. Rep. Porter Goss, who represented Florida's Sanibel Island area, was confirmed as the new director of the CIA. Seventy-seven senators voted in favor of Goss, a Republican, while seventeen people—all Democrats—voted against him.

Although a Democrat, Bob Graham was quoted in the South Florida *Sun-Sentinel* as saying that his personal experience as chairman of the Senate Intelligence Committee led him to believe that Goss—who served in the same capacity as chairman of the House Intelligence Committee—was "uniquely qualified" for the post. Once he had gotten Bob Graham's approval, many felt Porter Goss was a virtual lock.

The first week of October 2004 saw the first debate between President George W. Bush and his Democratic challenger John Kerry. The derisive attacks leveled against Bush by the Liberal elite, the MoveOn.Com people, and the Al Frankens and Michael Moores of the world, had the effect of possibly turning people off to Kerry. Nevertheless, Kerry said some things during that debate that many of us in the pro-Israel camp wanted to hear: both about Israel and our national defense. If elected president would Kerry stand by his words? Kerry certainly *seemed* strong enough, and tough enough, to lead our country.

On October 10, 2004, a review of Seymour Hersh's explosive new book *Chain of Command: The Road from 9-11 to Abu Ghraib*, that originally appeared in the *Baltimore Sun*, was picked up by the *South Florida Sun-Sentinel*. The book had its genesis in a series of "extensively researched" *New Yorker* articles about prisoner abuse at Abu Ghraib in Iraq, David W. Marston wrote in his review. Those articles were then turned into a book, with the addition, Marston noted, "of some meandering chapters on Pakistan, Israel, Turkey and the Kurds ..."

Marston referred to Hersh's winning his Pulitzer Prize for exposing the My Lai massacre in Viet Nam, and how "eight books, countless articles and a few swirling controversies later, Hersh is still making headlines." Marston noted that Hersh had received a Grant for Peace from Yoko Ono, because, as Ono believed, Hersh "epitomized John Lennon's song *Gimme Some Truth.*"

But was the grant deserved? Marston had his doubts.

Hersh's charge—that Defense Secretary Donald Rumsfeld and Vice President Dick Cheney were directly responsible for the prisoner abuse at Abu Ghraib—was reduced to an "unsubstantiated claim that Rumsfeld and [President] Bush created the conditions that allowed abuse to occur," Marston wrote. "*Chain of Command* is further undermined by Hersh' aversion to annotations and affection for blind sources ... By book's end, Hersh abandons any pretense of objectivity, concluding with a frothing attack on Rumsfeld, Cheney and Bush."

Somewhere along the way "Sy Hersh morphed into Michael Moore," Marston concluded, "and his investigative reporting dissolved into a relentless 'Bush Bash.'"

***

Back in November of 2002, Leonard Nimoy, who had put together a book of his photographs, but was far better known for his portrayal of the pointy-eared Vulcan "Mr. Spock," was the keynote speaker at the Annual Jewish Book Month held at the sprawling Posnack Jewish Community Center in Davie, Florida.

One of the perks of my job at the Jewish Federation was occasionally covering events such as these and doing the PR for them. After writing many of the press releases and media alerts prior to Nimoy's appearance, I met him for the first time, just minutes before he spoke, as we were both going to the men's room.

I recalled that incident when one of the funniest articles I had read in a long time, by Dan Neil of *The Los Angeles Times*, appeared on October 16, 2004, in the *South Florida Sun-Sentinel*. In it, Neil paid homage to the recent Emmy Award-winner, William Shatner, a.k.a. Captain James T. Kirk.

"Shatner's Emmy is four decades overdue," Neil wrote, tongue-in-cheek. "Go back and watch the original [*Star Trek*] series. How many actors can sell a line like 'What have you done with Spock's brain?' Sir Laurence Olivier? Anthony Hopkins? Please."

What struck me was that I had interviewed literally hundreds of people in the past, and dozens of local, national and even world leaders. During the same year that I introduced myself to Leonard Nimoy, I also interviewed Gen. Wesley Clark, who was appearing as a guest of the Federation—the Jewish Federation, not the Federation of Planets—in a large closet at the new Westin Diplomat Hotel in Hollywood, Florida, so we could both get away from all the noise.

But for whatever reason, nothing was as memorable to me, or as strange for that matter, as bumping into Mr. Spock in the men's room.

On November 2, 2004, George W. Bush was re-elected president of the United States. Many pundits gave their reasons why they thought Bush won, such as John Kerry not "defining" himself enough. But one possible reason was hardly being addressed, if it was being addressed at all. That's that the left had helped to sabotage Kerry's campaign by implying that "W" was not a particularly bright bulb. This didn't sit particularly well in the American heartland where the people felt that "W" was one of them. If they think *he's* stupid, these people must have thought—then what do they think about me?

Just days after the election, an email, allegedly written by Michael Moore, was circulated to tens of thousands of Americans. It was a humorous attempt to find a bright side to another four years of George W. Bush, and listed seventeen reasons for optimism.

It was pretty funny. Point number ten, however, showed why Michael Moore still sometimes made me cringe. Moore wrote: "Five more African-Americans were elected as members of Congress, including the return of Cynthia McKinney of Georgia. It's always good to have more blacks in there, fighting for us and doing the job our candidates can't."

Cynthia McKinney? Yes, the affable and hard-working congresswoman being lauded by Michael Moore was the same Cynthia McKinney who allegedly stated that President Bush had advance knowledge of the 9-11 attacks; the same Cynthia McKinney who stated that the U.S. should not support Israel; and the same Cynthia McKinney who called the Supreme Court racist. In *Slate* magazine Chris Suellentrop wrote about McKinney: "All of us have voices in our heads, whispering insanities. Rep. Cynthia McKinney's problem is that she lets hers speak."

On November 11, 2004, Yasser Arafat, whose name and face were synonymous with terrorism, finally died in a Paris hospital after a weeklong deathwatch. Tim Collie, a terrific reporter for the *South Florida Sun-Sentinel*, wrote a comprehensive piece about the Palestinian leader.

A year and a half earlier, Collie had been in the room with a number of reporters, including myself, when former Israeli Prime Minister Ehud Barak spoke at Temple Beth Israel in Sunrise, Florida. Barak had just finished making a condolence phone call to the father of Israeli astronaut Col. Ilan Ramon—who had perished aboard the space shuttle Columbia—and was about to address the local media assembled there.

Barak began to reminisce about the daring 1981 Osirak raid in which Israeli jets destroyed the Iraqi nuclear facility near Baghdad. As was noted earlier in this book, it was an act that, at the time, drew condemnation from a number of President Ronald Reagan's closest advisors, including Defense Secretary Caspar Weinberger and Deputy Director of the CIA Adm. Bobby Inman, but apparent approval from the president and his CIA director, William Casey. Ramon, then a very young pilot, was one of the ten Israeli fliers who took part in that mission.

As has also been noted in this book, the first information spy Jonathan Pollard ever gave the Israelis dealt with satellite overheads of the Osirak raid. The person Pollard handed those overheads to was Israeli Col. Avi Sella, who helped plan the Osirak operation and would later become Pollard's de-facto "handler."

Collie, in his article which came out just hours after Arafat's expected death, described the Palestinian leader as "among the last of the charismatic revolutionaries who dominated developing world politics in the late 20th century—a group that included Ernesto 'Che' Guevera, Fidel Castro and Nelson Mandela."

It was an interesting observation, although calling Arafat a "charismatic revolutionary" made me think more of someone like Pancho Villa or fellow bandito Emiliano Zapata than a ruthless, cold-blooded killer of women and children.

"To his enemies," Collie wrote, Arafat was a murderer. "But to his people, Arafat was the embodiment of Palestinian nationalism."

While Collie in fact revealed many of the sides of the complex Arafat, some "reporters" wrote about the terrorist's passing as if he had been Mother Teresa.

Jeff Jacoby, of the British publication *The Globe*, was one who got it right when he noted: "Yasser Arafat died at age 75, lying in bed surrounded by familiar faces. He left this world peacefully, unlike the thousands of victims he sent to early graves."

However, Jacoby's countryman, Derek Brown, wrote in another British mullet-wrapper, *The Guardian*, that Arafat's "undisputed courage as a guerilla leader" was exceeded only by his "extraordinary courage as a peace negotiator."

Reporter Barbara Platt, of the BBC, was equally glowing in her praise of Arafat. "When the helicopter carrying the frail old man rose above the ruined compound I started to cry," Platt reported from Ramallah when Arafat was being airlifted to Paris. "I remembered when the Israelis re-conquered the West Bank more than two years ago, how they drove their tanks and bulldozers into Mr. Arafat's headquarters, trapping him in a few rooms, and throwing a military curtain around Ramallah. I remember how Palestinians admired his refusal to flee under fire. They told me, 'Our leader is sharing our pain; we are all under the same siege'—and so was I."

After reading this I couldn't help but think that when Hitler reared his ugly head the Brits were damned lucky that, instead of Barbara Platt, they had Winston Churchill.

In fact, when it comes to the relationship between Israel and the Palestinians, the wit and wisdom of comedian Dennis Miller stands in sharp contrast to the ignorance and abject stupidity of those on the radical left—on either side of the Atlantic. As Miller noted in an "analysis" that was widely distributed on the Internet: "The Palestinians want their own country. There's just one thing about that: There are no Palestinians. It's a made-up word. Israel was called Palestine for two thousand years. 'Palestinian' sounds ancient but it is really a modern invention. Before the Israelis won the land in the 1967 war, Gaza was owned by Egypt, the West Bank was owned by Jordan and there were no 'Palestinians.'

"As soon as Jews took over and started growing oranges as big as basketballs, what do you know, say hello to the 'Palestinians' weeping for their deep bond with their lost 'land' and 'nation.'"

Miller opined that the Palestinians still could have had their own country, but they turned down the chance at Camp David when Arafat, once again, balked at what he was being offered by a magnanimous Ehud Barak. "If you have your own country, you have to have traffic lights and garbage trucks and chambers of commerce," Miller explained, "and worse, you have to figure out some way to make a living."

It was Israeli statesman Abba Eban who once said about the Palestinians: "They never miss an opportunity to miss an opportunity." Now that Arafat was gone, there *would* be opportunities. There might also be chaos. It was quite possible that Jonathan Pollard would be named the new director of the CIA before a Palestinian leader emerged who could forge a workable peace agreement with Israel.

Of course, we all hoped that, during his second administration, George W. Bush would find a way to do what no other American president had been able to do—and that there would finally be peace between the two peoples who shared an ancient land.

That, most of us felt, would be nothing short of miraculous.

CHAPTER TWENTY-FOUR

THE BARGAINING CHIP

ON JANUARY 19, 2005, Tony Blankley, editorial page editor of the *Washington Times*, wrote an op-ed highly critical of investigative reporter Seymour Hersh, after Hersh wrote yet another controversial piece that appeared in the *New Yorker*. In his article, that received wide media attention, Hersh alleged that the Bush administration had been conducting secret reconnaissance missions inside Iran.

"Much of the focus is on accumulation of intelligence and targeting information on Iranian nuclear, chemical and missile sites," Hersh wrote. "[The] American commando task force has been set up in South Asia and is now working closely with a group of Pakistani scientists and technicians. The American task force has been penetrating eastern Iran from Afghanistan in a hunt for underground installations ..."

Blankley stressed that 18 United States Code section 794, subsection (b) prohibits anyone "in time of war, with intent that the same shall be communicated to the enemy [from publishing] any information with respect to the movement, numbers, or disposition of any of the Armed forces of the United States, or supposed plans or conduct of any military operations, or any other information relating to the public defense which might be useful to the enemy ...[this crime is punishable] by death or by imprisonment for any term of years or for life."

Simply put, some might argue that what Hersh did actually bordered on treason.

Blankley expressed how "shocked" he was, therefore, when he read Hersh's piece in the *New Yorker*. "Mr. Hersh is revealing to all the world, including the Iranian government, that our commandos are currently behind enemy lines in Iran on a dangerous and vital military assignment," Blankley explained. "Moreover, he helps the enemy by writing that our commandos have been penetrating eastern Iran from Afghanistan." Argued Blankley, that information "considerably reduces the areas the Iranian military and counterintelligence forces have to search and monitor to try to catch our brave commandos."

Hersh also alleged that American commandos were working with "a group of Pakistani scientists" who had previously worked with Iranian scientists. "Such information might further assist Iranian security forces with their investigation," Blankley wrote.

In addition, Hersh alleged that American commandos had been working with local Iranian agents to "plant detection devices around known or suspected nuclear plants."

"This gives the enemy insights into our commandos' specific method of operation and alerts Iranian intelligence to be looking for local Iranians as well as Americans," Blankley stated.

"This is not just any military operation," Blankley continued. "The purpose of this operation is to protect the world from a possible nuclear attack once the fanatical Iranian Islamist regime gets its hands on a nuclear bomb."

Of course, in all fairness to Hersh, he's an investigative reporter and not a member of the National Security Council. So whatever information he had, and then used in the *New Yorker*, may have been purposely sent his way by one or more high-ranking U.S. government officials. So was Iran *supposed* to find out about all this? Was this "leak" to such a prominent reporter as Hersh made to simply confuse the Iranians? And would that leak make it difficult for Tehran to distinguish between any disinformation, and accurate information, that their intelligence people might uncover?

Still, it's ironic that Hersh had once labeled Jonathan Pollard a traitor in that 1999 article he wrote in the *New Yorker*. For would-be "patriot" Seymour Hersh, it may have truly been a case of the pot calling the kettle black.

For a long time there were rumors swirling that Jonathan Pollard's life sentence in prison was based on some "smoking gun" in his case, and that what Pollard allegedly did, by spying for Israel, was a lot worse than what we actually knew. This was alluded to by Seymour Hersh in his article "The Traitor" that appeared in The *New Yorker* magazine (Jan. 1999).

One of the allegations, as has been mentioned throughout this book, was that some of the classified information Pollard gave Israel also wound up in the hands of the KGB, exposing many of our assets behind the Iron Curtain and causing their capture and executions. The net result was that our intelligence apparatus in the Soviet Union and its satellite states had literally gone blind, resulting in enormous harm to the security of the United States.

These allegations may be part of what was implied or stated in the secret Weinberger memorandum, given by then-Secretary of Defense Caspar Weinberger to District Court Judge Aubrey Robinson, in 1987, before the judge handed Pollard a life term in prison, irregardless of that fact that Pollard had plea bargained, in good faith, for a lesser sentence.

It was later learned, however, that the exposure of our agents was not caused by Pollard at all; it was caused by the treasonous acts of the head of Soviet and Eastern Bloc Counterintelligence for the CIA: Aldrich Hazen Ames. And while other agents were also exposed, they, too, were not exposed by Pollard, as some originally thought, but by FBI spy Robert Hanssen.

The well-respected diplomat Dennis Ross was the former American Special Envoy to the Middle East under President Bill Clinton and the author of the book *The Missing Peace*. In his book there is a whole section on Pollard. With a new hearing on the Pollard case coming up, I was curious about what one of America's top negotiators and Middle East experts had to say.

There would be no surprises; no smoking gun. In fact, Ross neither stated nor implied in his book that what Pollard did, by passing U.S. intelligence to Israel, was particularly damaging or harmful to the United States. To Ross, the imprisoned Pollard's greatest "crime" may instead have been the value he had as a bargaining chip when it came to the negotiations surrounding the Middle East peace process.

During the Wye River accords, in October 1998, when Benjamin "Bibi" Netanyahu was Israeli prime minister, Ross was asked by Clinton about Pollard.

"He (Clinton) wanted to talk about releasing Jonathan Pollard," Ross recalled. According to Ross, Clinton wanted to know if the Pollard case was a big political issue in Israel, and, secondly, if releasing Pollard would help Netanyahu politically.

"'Yes,' I replied," Ross said, "because [Pollard] is considered a soldier for Israel and there is an ethos in Israel that you never leave a soldier behind in the field. 'But if you want my advice,' I continued, 'I would not release him now. It would be a huge payoff for Bibi; you don't have many like this in your pocket. I would save it for permanent status. You will need it later, don't use it now.'"

In a footnote in his book, Ross said he was personally in favor of Pollard's release, believing that he had "received a harsher sentence than others who had committed comparable crimes."

"I preferred not tying his release to any agreement," Ross wrote, "but if that was what I was going to do, then I favored saving it for permanent status."

It's important to note that when Pollard's name first came up in conversation, Clinton did not say, "Dennis, what you don't understand is that what Pollard did was so terrible that we cannot ever release him." Nor did he tell Ross that there were circumstances surrounding the Pollard case that Ross didn't know about.

Contrarily, if Pollard committed crimes that justified a life sentence, I have to assume that Clinton would have let Ross know about it, or would have at least hinted at it. And I doubt there was anything Pollard did that Clinton may not have been aware of. As President of the United States, it's safe to say that Clinton was in the loop. Or at least he should have been.

As Ross alluded to, it was apparently all about keeping Pollard in play as a bargaining chip.

Bargaining chip or not, when CIA Director George Tenet learned that Clinton was considering releasing Pollard, Tenet, as has been well-documented, went ballistic. Still, Tenet didn't say to Clinton that what Pollard did was so heinous that the president couldn't release him—at least he didn't say anything like that within earshot of Ross.

As Ross recalled, National Security Advisor Sandy Berger had arranged for himself, Ross and George Tenet to sit with the president to discuss the Pollard matter. "Sandy began explaining that the president was considering releasing Jonathan Pollard," Ross noted. "In the president's presence, [Berger] explained that this is what it might take to do the deal, and that he wanted to be able to take this step if necessary."

According to Ross, it was at that point that the Director of Central Intelligence "blew up."

"Mr. President, you can't do this!" Ross recalled Tenet saying. Tenet explained that Pollard's release would "signal that spying could take place with impunity and, further, that it would damage the morale of the intelligence community which he (Tenet) had worked so hard to restore."

"If you are considering a release," Tenet added, "have a procedure in which all the agencies can express their view—otherwise you will be savagely criticized."

Noted Ross, the president remained "largely impassive."

"With George still sputtering, he and I went out to the boardwalk," Ross recalled. "He told me that if the president released Pollard he would have no choice but to resign from the CIA."

Clinton, to Netanyahu's displeasure, eventually did follow Tenet's advice.

The bottom line was that, to the Clinton administration Pollard remained a valuable bargaining chip; to Netanyahu he became a sought-after prize; and, to the CIA, which had been duped by Aldrich Ames, he was, perhaps more than anything else, a stain and an embarrassment.

On March 15—the anniversary of the Ides of March, the day Julius Caesar was stabbed in the back by those he trusted—Pollard once again had his day in court. As with the ill-fated Caesar, Pollard's future had apparently also been plotted by his enemies in advance.

A day before, Pollard's wife, Esther, was nevertheless optimistic. "I have a strong sense we've already won," Esther recalled telling her husband while sitting in his prison cell just hours before his hearing in a U.S. Appeal's Court.

There were reasons for optimism. The arguments Pollard's pro-bono attorneys, Eliot Lauer and Jacques Semmelman, were going to present to the three judge panel were legally sound. Still, they weren't enough. Associated Press reporter Pete Yost noted that two of the federal appeals court justices—Judge David Sentelle and Judge Judith Rogers (the other was Judge Karen Henderson who didn't speak)—suggested that Pollard was on "weak legal ground."

"Reviving Pollard's case would mean that you've 'opened the floodgates' for hundreds of other prisoners sentenced long ago," Yost quoted Sentelle as telling Pollard's attorneys during their forty-five minute argument in front of the judges. According to Yost, Judge Rogers also questioned whether Pollard was entitled to further court challenges to his sentence.

Lauer and Semmelman, as they had in the past, argued that the U.S. government had lied to Pollard about his plea agreement, and that his original attorney, Richard Hibey, "failed to defend him properly." Judge Sentelle disagreed, calling Hibey "one of the most highly regarded criminal defense lawyers in the country."

Matthew Berger, writing for the Jewish Telegraphic Agency, quoted Sentelle as stating that the attorneys' claims about Hibey's ineffectiveness were subjective, calling Hibey an "eloquent" and "excellent" attorney.

The judges also did not see a problem with attorney Hibey neglecting to file a notice of appeal in time. "Sentelle pointed out that Pollard had pleaded guilty," Yost noted, "and, in those days, lawyers just did not file a notice of appeal after guilty pleas."

Pollard's new lawyers also wanted the court to grant them access to certain classified documents: Specifically, they wanted to see everything that was in the infamous Weinberger memorandum read by Judge Robinson before he imposed his life sentence on Pollard. Lauer said he needed the classified documents to assist the executive branch in determining Pollard's clemency claim.

"The classified material will help Pollard's legal team demonstrate that the harm to national security that the government said was attributable to Pollard's spying," Lauer argued, "was in fact attributable to others."

The judges were not swayed. Noted Berger, Sentelle said there was "no precedent for granting access to documents for the purpose of clemency."

Sentelle suggested that Pollard would still be able to "exercise relief" through the parole process. Pollard's attorneys stressed that it would be hard to argue for parole, however, without the classified information that they were being denied.

Upon listening to the comments of the judges, a disappointed Esther Zeitz-Pollard called the hearing "a mockery of justice." She added that while "excruciating care was taken by the bench to dismiss any attempt by the attorneys to actually address the merits of the case," she was proud of the work done by Lauer and Semmelman. "In spite of what can only be viewed as open contempt from the bench," Zeitz-Pollard said, "Lauer and Semmelman never missed a beat, never lost focus, and rose to the challenge with true professionalism and grace."

Julius and Ethel Rosenberg were relatively low-level spies—there is some debate whether Ethel was a spy at all—who, early in the cold war, were executed for allegedly passing American nuclear secrets to the Soviets. As attorney Alan Dershowitz notes in his best-selling book *Chutzpah*: "Julius and Ethel Rosenberg were prosecuted by Jewish lawyers and sentenced to death by a Jewish judge." The Rosenbergs, both Jews, were in fact the only spies ever executed in the United States during peacetime.

Many felt the severity of the punishment handed out to the Rosenbergs was a warning to a suspected Jewish "fifth column" then operating in the U.S. The question has often been asked: If the Rosenbergs were not Jews would they have met the same harsh fate? And was it mere coincidence that, to make it all look "kosher," the prosecutors in the Rosenberg case, one of whom was the infamous Roy Cohn, were Jews, while the judge, Irving R. Kaufman, also happened to be a Jew?

A few days following the Pollard hearing, Suzanne Migdall received an email from her sister Maxine, a Dade County, Florida judge.

"I think [Pollard] really has an uphill battle," Maxine said. "The law is against him; the politics are against him. And, although some people might disagree, the fact that he is Jewish is reminiscent of the Rosenberg case of the 'fifties.'"

CHAPTER TWENTY-FIVE

SIX DEGREES OF SEPARATION

ON APRIL 1, 2005, as Pope John Paul II, the best friend the Jews ever had in the Vatican, was living out his last day on earth, National Security Advisor Sandy Berger—who had gone on record as being against executive clemency for Jonathan Pollard when his boss, Bill Clinton, was in the Oval Office—pleaded guilty to taking classified documents from the National Archives. As was reported in the Associated Press, Berger's plea agreement, if accepted by a judge, would end a "bizarre episode in which the man who once had access to the government's most sensitive intelligence was accused of sneaking documents out of the Archives in his clothing."

***

In yet another strange coincidence reminiscent of Kevin Bacon's "Six Degrees of Separation," years earlier Suzanne Migdall had piqued the interest of movie producer Marvin Worth in our Pollard project (prior to the publication of *The Hunting Horse*). Marvin, at the time, was also trying to develop a project about the life of actor James Dean and was talking to Leonardo Di-Caprio about the starring role. At the same time, he was committed to a picture called *City Hall* starring Al Pacino. The writer of the movie's script was Nick Pileggi.

Among Pileggi's many other credits were *Goodfellas* and *Casino*. Joe Pesci, who played a deadly "wiseguy" in *Goodfellas*, played a similar role of an out of control hood in *Casino*, which also starred Robert DiNiro and Sharon Stone. While the names of the characters in *Casino* were fictionalized, their real identities were never much of a secret, especially to the insiders in Las Vegas. Pesci's "Nicky Santoro" was really the hot-tempered Anthony "The Ant" Spilotro, who hated and once tried, unsuccessfully, to "whack" my old friend, the late Bill Roemer, perhaps the most honored agent in the history of the FBI, and a person who, while attending law school at Notre Dame University, just happened to become friendly with a research scientist there, Dr. Morris Pollard, whose son, born a few years later, would be named Jonathan.

***

On May 4, 2005, the *Los Angeles Times* reported that Pentagon analyst Lawrence Franklin, who had been under investigation for passing U.S. secrets to Israel, was arrested and officially charged with disclosing classified information to two members of the pro-Israeli Washington lobby group, AIPAC—the American Israel Public Affairs Committee. Noted Richard Schmidt in the *Los Angeles Times*: "A focus of the inquiry has been whether a group of pro-Israeli conservatives in the Pentagon crossed a line in sharing the nation's secrets, and whether that same ally may have broken the rules about access to government data in an attempt to gain sensitive intelligence to protect itself from such foes as Iran and Iraq."

Notwithstanding, the complaint did not allege Franklin engaged in espionage or that he directly shared secrets with Israel.

As Warren P. Stroebel, another reporter covering the story, wrote: "Franklin's is the first major case involving leaks of classified information to a staunch U.S. ally since 1985 when U.S. Navy analyst Jonathan Pollard was arrested and convicted of espionage."

In an interview he gave that appeared in the April 22, 2005 edition of the Israeli periodical *Makor Rishon*, Pollard charged that, soon after his November 1985 arrest, it was the Mossad, Israel's version of the CIA, that not only betrayed him, but provided the American authorities with the erroneous information that helped seal his fate. He insisted that AIPAC, whether inadvertently or not, also had a hand in it.

"After I was arrested, the FBI investigators who were debriefing me purposely allowed me to see the statements that the Israelis had made about me," Pollard said. "The Mossad cast all the blame on Rafi Eitan (Pollard's handler), and on LAKAM (the Office for Informational Cooperation which Eitan headed). They wanted to bury me. It was the Mossad that was the source of all the disinformation about me and my character. The lies that I used cocaine and was a mercenary—selling secrets to countries other than Israel—it all came from them. It was clear that the Mossad had three goals: to bury me, to destroy LAKAM, and to protect AIPAC at all costs. To this day, this remains the policy of the Mossad."

At around the same time the story of Lawrence Franklin's arrest made headlines, a story also broke that James Woolsey, former head of the CIA—and once one of Jonathan Pollard's harshest public critics—apparently was having some second thoughts concerning Pollard. In an interview with reporter

Carolyn Glick that appeared in *The Jerusalem Post*, Woolsey, who served as Director of Central Intelligence from 1993 to 1995, even implied that the president should consider commuting Pollard's life sentence.

"[In the past] Pollard may not have been a prime candidate for commutation," Woolsey reportedly said, "but twenty years is a very long time. At a certain point it is time to ask if enough is enough—that is in regard to his release, not to diminishing the seriousness of his actions. There is an obligation to have a different approach to spies for friendly countries."

Stressing that he had "studied the Pollard case closely," Woolsey said the claims that information Pollard gave Israel was subsequently leaked to intelligence services in countries like China or the former Soviet Union were simply untrue. Notwithstanding, Woolsey acknowledged that, at the time of Pollard's arrest, there were legitimate U.S. fears that Israel's intelligence services could have been penetrated.

"Part of [this information], if it had found its way into the hands of a hostile country, would have presented a danger to the United States' ability to collect intelligence," Woolsey reasoned. "No intelligence apparatus is immune to penetration, not even Israel's."

Apparently, former Defense Secretary Caspar Weinberger—as he admitted privately to Suzanne Migdall's friend Diane Glazer—would also no longer stand in the way of Pollard being set free. When, in 1987, Weinberger passed his secret memo to Judge Aubrey Robinson, alleging that Pollard had done "great and irreversible damage to the national security of the United States," the secretary of defense may well have based his damage assessment on a report given him by the head of Soviet and Eastern Bloc Counterintelligence for the CIA at the time: Aldrich

Hazen Ames—although, as was stated earlier in this book, the CIA denied that Ames ever wrote that report.

As was also stated in this book, during an interview with Weinberger in 2002, author and investigative journalist Edwin Black asked the former defense secretary why the Pollard spy case was never mentioned in Weinberger's latest book, *In the Arena*.

Weinberger's response was illuminating. "Because it was, in a sense, a relatively minor matter," Weinberger said. "It was made bigger than its actual importance."

Pollard received more press in late May of 2005 when First Lady Laura Bush toured the Middle East with Israeli officials. During Bush's visit the *Washington Post* reported that armed Israeli security forces held back protesters during a "religiously and politically-charged visit" to two of the world's holiest shrines.

"In one of the most intense situations she has experienced as first lady," reporter Jim Vandehei wrote, Bush encountered a number of vocal Israelis protesting Jonathan Pollard's continued incarceration. Vandehei described a scene in which protesters, many of whom were women wearing pictures of Pollard, chanted "Free Pollard Now, Free Pollard Now!"

The first lady was also confronted by Muslim protesters denouncing her visit to the Dome of the Rock. According to Vandehei, Israeli police were forced to "lock arms and form a human fence" to keep protesters at Bay while Bush was ushered to her motorcade in Jerusalem's Old City.

Just days before Laura Bush's plane landed in Israel, the *New York Post* reported that Danny Ayalon, Israel's ambassador to the United States, had gone to North Carolina to visit Pollard in prison and to see, firsthand, the status of Pollard's health.

Israeli officials were expressing "new optimism" about persuading the U.S. to finally release Pollard, *New York Post* reporter Uri Dan wrote. According to Dan, Prime Minister Ariel Sharon also raised the subject of a possible pardon for Pollard, when, a month earlier, he met with Secretary of State Condoleezza Rice in Texas.

"It went without saying," Dan wrote, quoting from an anonymous source in the Israeli government, "that Pollard's release would greatly help Sharon shore up his domestic support when he carries out the withdrawal of Jewish setters from the Gaza Strip this summer."

As for Pollard's wife, Esther, she felt she had been down this bumpy road before and paid short shrift to Ayalon's visit. "It's just another of Sharon's 'cheap tricks'," she said.

***

During the first week of June 2005, the true identity of "Deep Throat"—the secret source to reporters Bob Woodward and Carl Bernstein who helped bring the Nixon presidency to its knees during Watergate—was finally revealed. There were mixed opinions about ninety-one year-old W. Mark Felt, once the number two man in the FBI whose name was known by few outside the bureau. As Katherine Q. Seeyle noted in *The New York Times*: "W. Mark Felt's disclosure that he was Deep Throat has sparked a debate about whether he should be praised as a hero or condemned as a traitor for going outside the legal system."

Years earlier I had interviewed Bernstein who, not surprisingly, declined to tell me who Deep Throat was. When I began doing research on my first Pollard book, *The Spy Who Knew Too Much*, I wondered whether Pollard, in order to reveal the secret U.S. policy during the Reagan years to arm Iraq with the technologies to make biological and chemical weapons, thereby endangering Israel, could have done what Deep Throat did and found his own Woodward or Bernstein, instead of risking everything to become a spy.

***

On June 7, the Miami Heat, with an injured Dwyane Wade and Shaquille O'Neal, were eliminated in the NBA's Eastern Division Finals by the World Champion Detroit Pistons. That same day, the long-awaited trial of former University of South Florida professor Sami al-Arian finally began in Tampa.

Al-Arian's name had been mentioned often in terrorism expert Steve Emerson's book, *American Jidad*. Al-Arian had also been named in a lawsuit filed by author and TV and radio personality John Loftus who claimed that al-Arian was part of a massive Saudi network to finance Islamic terrorists.

Appearing on *At Large with Geraldo Rivera*, during the eve of the al-Arian trial, Steve Emerson told Rivera that al-Arian was one of the leaders of the Palestinian Islamic Jihad, and, in essence, was critical to the operations of the terrorist group.

Al-Arian's attorney William Moffitt, Rivera's other guest, immediately got into a heated argument with Emerson.

"The fact of the matter is that your supporters, and the supporters of Mr. al-Arian, have consistently stated that he is the subject of some type of racial profiling and stereotyping and that he is innocent," Emerson said. "Come on now, are you going to disavow that?"

"I don't have any supporters; I'm an attorney," Moffitt said.

"Somebody pays you. Who pays you?" Emerson asked.

"None of your damn business," Moffitt snapped.

CHAPTER TWENTY-SIX

THE HORSE'S MOUTH

ON JULY 7, 2005, a day after London was named as the site of the 2012 Olympics, three explosions, the work of terrorists calling themselves "The Secret Organization of al Qaeda in Europe," rocked England's capital city, killing more than fifty people while injuring over seven-hundred on a London subway. "Whatever we do," British Prime Minister Tony Blair said about the bombers, "it is our determination that they never succeed in destroying what we hold dear in this country and in the civilized nations throughout the world."

A day earlier, freedom of the press in America arguably also took a hit when Judith Miller, a reporter for the *New York Times*, author of *God Has Ninety-Nine Names*, and one of the country's most knowledgeable people on the Middle East, was placed into custody for refusing to disclose her confidential source to a prosecutor who was investigating how the name of an undercover CIA agent wound up in print. As was reported in *The Los Angeles Times*, the Supreme Court declined to hear the appeals of the two reporters involved—Miller and Matthew Cooper of *Time* magazine—who argued that the First Amendment protected them from having to identify their sources to special prosecutor Patrick Fitzgerald.

In a statement Miller said she was "extremely disappointed."

"Journalists simply cannot do their jobs without being able to commit to sources that they won't be identified," Miller said. "Such protection is critical to the free flow of information in a democracy."

According to the *Los Angeles Times*, both the *New York Times* and *Time* magazine filed court papers seeking a hearing before Thomas Hogan, the federal district judge in Washington who, nine months earlier, had held the two reporters in contempt. It was the same Judge Hogan who, in September of 2003, refused to be swayed when he heard the arguments from Jonathan Pollard's attorneys, Eliot Lauer and Jacques Semmelman, for continuing with Pollard's appeal.

At the same time it was being debated whether freedom of the press was being attacked in the cases of Miller and Cooper, the *New Yorker* magazine once again reared its politically correct head in a story entitled "Espionage and the Israel Lobby" that appeared in its July 4, 2005 edition. In that article, which attempted to explore the ties between Lawrence Franklin, the analyst at the Defense Intelligence Agency who specialized in Iran, and the American Israel Public Affairs Committee (AIPAC), Jeffrey Goldberg, a Jew—the *New Yorker* seems to always use Jews to take shots at Israel—touched on the Pollard spy case.

Wrote Goldberg: "Twenty years ago, a civilian Naval Intelligence analyst named Jonathan Pollard was caught stealing American secrets on behalf of an Israeli intelligence cell—a rogue cell the Israelis later claimed. Pollard said that he was driven to treason because, as a Jew, he could not abide by what he saw as America's unwillingness to share crucial intelligence with Israel."

Well, of course, Pollard never said he was "driven to treason," nor implied anything of the kind, and was, in fact, never even accused of treason by either the prosecutor or judge in his case. But to make his point, Goldberg, who more often than not gets it right, decided to put his own words in Pollard's mouth. Now while the astute Goldberg may not have meant it the way it came out, I couldn't help but think that somewhere in the Bahamas his fellow *New Yorker* scribe, Seymour Hirsh, was sitting in a lounge chair, enjoying the hot summer sun, a drink in one hand, the *New Yorker* in the other, and saying to himself, "Damn good job, Jeff—I wish I wrote that one myself."

A few days later, when I first saw the book *Spy Handler, Memoir of a KGB Officer: The True Story of the Man Who Recruited Robert Hanssen and Aldrich Ames*, I was literally smacked right between the eyes. Based on the copious notes of retired KGB colonel Victor Cherkashin, and written by Gregory Feiffer, the book's front inside flap noted that, while playing a major role in global espionage for much of the cold war, Cherkashin took part in some of the KGB's highest profile cases. He was posted in the United States, Australia, India and Lebanon, and, according to the author, "tracked down U.S. and British spies around the world."

But it was in 1985, known as "The Year of the Spy," that Cherkashin scored one of the KGB's greatest coups. In April of that year, the book states, the Soviet spymaster recruited disgruntled CIA officer Aldrich Ames and became Ames' principal handler. Then, six months later, FBI Special Agent Robert

Hanssen contacted Cherkashin directly, with Hanssen "eventually becoming an even bigger asset than Ames."

In Chapter Eight of *Spy Handler* Cherkashin mentions the names of two of the Soviet bloc "moles" recruited by the CIA—Valery Martynov and Sergei Mortorin—who were found out, and subsequently executed, because of their exposure by either Hanssen or Ames. In that same chapter, Cherkashin writes of the so-called The Year of the Spy: "Among the agents exposed in 1985 was a spy whom we had nothing to do with: U.S. Naval Intelligence analyst Jonathan Pollard."

The words sent chills down my spine. For years I had insisted, along with people like Angelo Codevilla, John Loftus, and others, that it was highly unlikely that the information Pollard gave Israel ended up in Soviet hands, and, even if it did, would have had nothing to do with the deaths our agents behind the Iron Curtain. Now, Hanssen's and Ames' spymaster was implying the very same thing—not from the American or Israeli side, but, this time, from the *Soviet* side. The bottom line was that Pollard was in no way responsible for what happened to the CIA spies. And we were now getting that straight from the horse's mouth.

Unfortunately, none of that seemed to matter much to a federal appeals court in Washington. On July 22, 2005, the Associated Press reported that the U.S. Court of Appeals for the District of Columbia officially rejected Pollard's latest legal attempt to reduce his life sentence. According to the court, Pollard waited too long to try to contest his 1987 sentence, and failed to make a convincing case that he had gotten insufficient legal help. The court also ruled it had no authority to review Pollard's request to see the secret documents—part of the so-called Weinberger memo—that were submitted to Judge Aubrey Robinson before he imposed his life sentence on Pollard.

As for Pollard's faulting his original attorney, Richard Hibey, for not filing a notice of appeal in time, Judge David Sentelle, writing for the three-judge panel, called the argument that Pollard didn't realize the mistake of his lawyer "nonsensical."

"Pollard knew the facts," Sentelle said bluntly. "What he now claims not to have known is the legal significance of the facts."

A reaction was immediately posted on the Justice4JP website, stating that the decision, issued by "what was essentially a kangaroo court," came as no surprise.

"The merits of Pollard's case, which were supposed to have been heard at oral arguments in Washington in March of this year, were, in fact, never heard," the Justice4JP release stated. "At the hearing, an openly biased and hostile panel of judges, led by Judge David Sentelle, actively prevented the merits from being heard. Sentelle derided Pollard's legal efforts, invoking one of the oldest anti-Semitic devices known, and proclaiming that the problem with Pollard is that he 'thinks he is unique.' So it comes as no surprise that, in his formal decision today, Sentelle and his panel rejected both of Jonathan Pollard's motions. The court's contention that since Pollard knew the facts of his previous attorney's actions, he should have also known the judicial consequences is ludicrous. Moreover, the court's insistence on upholding the banning of Pollard's attorneys from seeing their own client's sentencing docket is reminiscent of the worst characteristics of the former Soviet system of justice. The judges' claim—that Pollard's attorneys have no 'need to know' what is in the very documents which are keeping Pollard chained to an unlimited life sentence— strains credibility to the limit."

Pollard's attorneys, Eliot Lauer and Jacques Semmelman, also issued a statement in which they noted: "We are deeply disappointed in today's ruling by the Court of Appeals in the Jonathan Pollard case, denying Mr. Pollard's appeal from the rulings of the lower court that had (a) denied, purely on procedural grounds, his motion to vacate his life sentence; and (b) refused to allow his security-cleared attorneys access to the classified portions of the court's sentencing docket. As with the lower court's ruling, this ruling is largely procedural and does not address the appropriateness of the life sentence. In 1992, Judge Stephen Williams of the very same Court of Appeals, called Mr. Pollard's life sentence 'a fundamental miscarriage of justice requiring relief.' That relief was not granted today. We are evaluating our procedural options to determine the next step in our efforts to obtain justice for Jonathan Pollard."

But how many tricks did Pollard's attorneys have left in their bag? As was reported in the New York-based *Jewish Week*, Kenneth Lasson, a law professor at the University of Baltimore and a longtime Pollard advocate, said the only legal options remaining for Pollard were an appeal for a hearing before the full Circuit Court of Appeals in Washington, or an appeal to the Supreme Court, but that "both are extreme long shots."

Certainly, Pollard's legal options had about run their course. At the same time, our Pollard motion picture project was still stuck in neutral. Perhaps, an Israeli source of mine thought, we could shake things up a bit by visiting Pollard in prison. We would hopefully be allowed to bring a tape recorder, alert the media, get some publicity, and I would write about it.

At least that was the plan. But, from what I heard, we never did get the necessary clearance.

On August 13, on Book TV, C-Span rebroadcast the January 1, 2005 appearance of Gregory Feiffer, author of *Spy Handler: Memoir of a KGB Officer*, on the *Jim Bohanan Show*. During the question and answer period following Bohanan's interview, someone from the studio audience asked Feiffer to compare Jonathan Pollard to Aldrich Ames or Robert Hanssen in terms of the damage Pollard caused. Feiffer admitted he didn't know a great deal about the Pollard case, which in itself spoke volumes. After all, if Pollard had in any way been involved with the KGB, Feiffer, while working so closely on his eye-opening book with Soviet spymaster Victor Cherkashin, would have certainly gotten wind of it.

"I didn't do any research into Pollard," Feiffer said. "I know a lot has been written about Pollard. It was a big stink. But I don't think that what Pollard did compares to what Ames and Hanssen did."

If Suzanne Migdall could have only taken Feiffer with her the next time she made a motion picture pitch. Part of the resistance she faced in Hollywood was that Pollard, allegedly, wasn't a "sympathetic enough" character. Some of the studio executives Suzanne encountered insisted on lumping Pollard with admitted traitors like Hanssen and Ames.

They were dead wrong to do that, but that's what Suzanne was up against. Then along came Cherkashin and Feiffer and Suzanne could finally say, this time with tangible proof, that Pollard wasn't anything like those guys.

Armed with that new information, Suzanne would in fact soon make a new contact: motion picture producer/director John Daly. Daly, who apparently had a real interest in the Pollard project, was exactly the kind of high-minded filmmaker Suzanne was looking for. The producer of *The Falcon and the Snowman*, *The Last Emperor*, *Platoon*, *Hoosiers* and *The Terminator*, Daly had never read *The Hunting Horse*, so Suzanne sent him a copy, along with a treatment, a tape of the *60 Minutes* Pollard interview with

Mike Wallace, and a tape of my appearance on CNN with Soledad O'Brien.

The question, still, was whether John Daly, or someone else
like him, would have the passion, guts, and wherewithal, to take
our Pollard project, as controversial as it was, and to make our
project his own.

For all of us—especially for Jonathan Pollard, reportedly now
with major health issues—the clock was definitely ticking.

CHAPTER TWENTY-SEVEN

E.T. PHONE HOME

ON **SEPTEMBER 4**, 2005, Esther Pollard arrived in Jerusalem to attend a hearing for her husband in Israel's Supreme Court of Justice. Jonathan Pollard had filed a petition four months earlier to compel the Israeli government to officially declare him a "Prisoner of Zion," which would result in specific legal obligations from the Israelis to try to secure his release from prison.

At the same time, back in the U.S. Pollard's attorneys, Eliot Lauer and Jacques Semmelman, filed a Petition for Rehearing En Banc. Essentially, this petition requested that, following the denial of Pollard's appeal by the three judge panel of the Court of Appeals in July, all the judges who sat on the District of Columbia's Court of Appeals would get to review the divided ruling.

Both of the legal maneuverings, we were told, had little chance of success.

On October 24, Hurricane Wilma struck Broward County, Florida, where both Suzanne Migdall and I live, with a ferocity that ripped roofs from homes like tin cans, uprooted massive trees, blasted out windows from office buildings, gutted trailers, took a dozen or so lives, and left more than three million Floridians, myself included, without electricity. Fortunately, both our homes survived the storm.

Soon after Wilma, a story began making the rounds that the Bureau of Prisons was projecting a 2015 release date for Jonathan Pollard. Esther Pollard gave little credence to the report. So did Pollard's lawyers. Noting that their client was arrested twenty years earlier, in November of 1985, they wrote: "Under U.S. law in effect at the time of Mr. Pollard's activities, any prisoner sentenced to life in prison is presumptively entitled to parole on the thirtieth anniversary of the date of incarceration. As a result, the Bureau of Prisons computer automatically generates the thirtieth anniversary date as the 'projected' release date. At that time, Mr. Pollard will be presumptively entitled to parole. However, the U.S. government will still be entitled to oppose parole."

As the New Year began, a new movie that had just been released was receiving a lot of press, not all of it good. While *Munich*, directed by Steven Spielberg, got mostly raves from reviewers, it received harsh words from some Jewish groups that felt the entertaining film played fast and loose with the truth.

I soon wrote an op-ed on the film that I sent out to various newspapers. The title was "Spielberg led astray on *Munich*, says former Israeli op with first-hand knowledge." I didn't use that intelligence operative's name in the piece.

That source apparently had intimate knowledge of the plan to assassinate the cold-blooded killers of eleven Israelis during the 1972 Olympics. The source, who took part in similar counter-terrorist operations as the one depicted in the movie, never heard from Spielberg, nor did he hear from anyone attached to the brilliant director. Perhaps Spielberg didn't care if he got it right, or perhaps he felt that his own version of *Munich* would make for more compelling cinema.

Regardless, the usually well-intentioned Spielberg, while being heaped with praise in some quarters (*Time* magazine called the film "a masterpiece"), may have been deserving of at least some of the criticism he was also getting.

Bret Stephens, in a wonderful piece that appeared in *The Wall Street Journal*, rhetorically asked, "Why is this movie raising such hackles among Israelis and those generally known as the 'pro-Israel' crowd? Maybe, it has something to do with his choice of screenwriter."

Indeed, Tony Kushner, the Pulitzer Prize-winning writer of *Angels in America* who some described as a card-carrying member of the far left, was hand picked by Spielberg to rework the original screenplay that was written by Eric Roth. Kushner had allegedly been quoted as once saying that the creation of the State of Israel was a "historical, moral, political calamity." Noted Stephens in *The Wall Street Journal*, Kushner also believed the policy of the government of Israel was a "systematic attempt to destroy the identity of the Palestinian people." Furthermore, Stephens wrote, Kushner had described Israeli Prime Minister Ariel Sharon—who on January 4, 2006, suffered a massive stroke—as an "un-indicted war criminal."

Stephens argued, also, that the George Jonas book, *Vengeance*, on which the film was largely based, "is widely considered to be a fabrication." Stephens added that the book was based on the recollections of a source named Yuval Aviv, who claimed to be the model for Israeli squad leader Avner Kauff-man, played in the movie by Eric Bana, but was, "according to Israeli sources, never in the Mossad."

When I contacted my own source, while he was not overly critical of Spielberg he did bring to light a few of the inaccuracies in the film.

"While the book was hyped as the 'inside story' by the leader of an Israeli hit team, known as 'Avner,' the story was, in reality, a total fabrication by an Israeli named Yuval Aviv," my source said, confirming what Bret Stephens alleged. According to my source, Aviv "never served in the Mossad—or any other branch of Israeli intelligence."

In the movie, a Frenchman who works with the Israelis praises Kauffman because he "pays better than anyone." Also in the movie, Kauffman's "team" consists of a squad of five men.

"I am aware of three 'Kidon' units (hit teams) that were active in this operation," my source said. "There was a fourth—a scratch unit pulled together on an emergency basis. Each team consisted of at least twelve individuals with specific assignments in the action.

"So there was no team of five individuals—freelancers, roaming around Europe, paying some French organization for information. That's a joke. Also, the code name for the operation was not "WOG," "Wrath of God," "Payback," or some such (as was implied in the book). The name of the operation was CAESARIA. Additionally, those participants in these actions never suffered doubts or delayed stress, and they are proud of what they did in the name of the Jewish people."

"But enough on the historical side," my source concluded. "It is entertainment—right up there with other Spielberg films like *Jaws, Close Encounters* and *ET.*"

On January 16, 2006, Israeli journalist Hillel Fendel reported that Israel's Supreme Court rejected Jonathan Pollard's request to be labeled a "Prisoner of Zion." According to the Justice4JP website, if successful, Prisoner of Zion status would have offered Pollard "a measure of protection in prison" and provide him with "specific benefits."

While it was a fantasy to assume that the Israeli judiciary would interfere with the judicial system in the United States, Pollard's wife, Esther Zeitz-Pollard, had apparently been counting on just that.

As soon as she heard the bad news, Esther insisted that Prisoner of Zion status not only would have made her husband's prison experience less harsh; it would have improved his chances of his getting released. Believing that Pollard was being treated poorly in prison, she said: "The prison authorities in the U.S. would not dare to harass someone who has been recognized this way by the Israeli government. It also would have helped smooth the way for diplomatic pressures in both Israel and the U.S."

***

On February 8, in a story written by Matthew Berger, the Jewish Telegraphic Agency (JTA) reported that Pollard's attorneys petitioned the U.S. Supreme Court to reverse a lower court ruling that denied his lawyers' access to the classified information used to sentence him for spying for Israel. "For the time being, this is the remaining action in the judiciary sphere," Pollard's attorney Eliot Lauer told the JTA. "It's conceivable that we'd do something else, but this is the only pending approach in the court system."

The odds on the Supreme Court ruling in Pollard's favor—or even hearing his lawyers' arguments for that matter—were probably slim to none. As for Pollard's twenty year long serpentine path, cutting through a maze of legal paperwork and always ending in a trail of broken dreams—it, in all likelihood, it would take him back to exactly where he started.

It would take him back to square one.

CHAPTER TWENTY-EIGHT

PIECES OF THE PUZZLE

I **READ JONATHAN POLLARD'S** interview by Charley J. Levine in the March 2006 issue of *Hadassah* magazine and was pleasantly surprised. I felt it was the first time in a decade that Pollard had done an interview in which he said all the right things, even coming across as an admirer of President Bush, the man, after all, who could give him a pardon.

When asked, for instance, who was responsible for the harshness of his sentence, Pollard referred to certain politicians—both in Israel and the United States—who understood the miscarriage of justice in his case, yet failed to do anything about it. Realizing there was no need to make enemies, he wisely didn't name names.

When asked if there was "more at stake here" than simply his imprisonment, Pollard referred to a speech once made by George Washington, of all people. By innuendo he was wrapping himself in the American flag. While answering the same question, he referred to his one-time main nemesis, former Defense Secretary Caspar Weinberger, admitting that the Pollard case was, in reality, a "very minor matter," and one that, in Pollard's words, not Weinberger's, was "blown all out of proportion to serve other ends."

If he was a political candidate in a debate, Pollard was scoring some points.

Asked if the intelligence that passed through his hands was relevant today, he said "absolutely not. The very definition of intelligence is that there is no longer one shred of relevance today."

By and large, Pollard came across as completely rational, totally sane, and confident that his actions of more than twenty years earlier neither hurt the interests of the United States, nor did they result in the loss of any American lives. He appeared a pillar of strength and righteousness.

I thought to myself: "He's finally come to his senses. He explains himself, with no commentary from his wife, makes some politically correct statements, and doesn't sabotage his case."

The same week that the *Hadassah* magazine article came out, a story also appeared in the *New York Times* in which Steve Erlanger, referring to a story in the Israeli newspaper *Yediot Aharonot*, stated that Rafi Eitan, Pollard's old handler at LAKAM, insisted that "Pollard never exposed American agents in the Soviet Union or elsewhere," an important admittance from the old spymaster who had never before consented to a do an interview on the case.

According to Erlanger, Eitan also believed that top CIA operative Aldrich Ames, who was spying for the Soviets, tried to blame Pollard for exposing the American agents in order to clear himself of suspicion.

"The information the charge was based on arrived from the CIA, and more accurately, from the counterespionage branch of the CIA," Eitan said confidently. "The person who headed the branch, and initiated the move against Pollard, was Ames."

"I have no doubt," Eitan added, "that had Pollard been tried today, in light of what is known about Ames and other agents who were exposed, he would have received a much lighter sentence."

While blaming Ames, Eitan—who, if not for the Pollard affair, may well have been named to head the Mossad—vehemently denied that Pollard ever handed to Israel information used to expose American spies in the former Soviet Union. "I'm willing to put my hand to the fire and swear in everything dear to me that those charges are a blatant lie," Eitan reportedly said. "Nothing from what Pollard delivered leaked out of the Israeli intelligence community—nothing. Besides, he never provided us with information that could have exposed American agents in the Soviet Union, or anywhere else. We weren't interested in those subjects. And he didn't provide the information."

Nevertheless, on March 20, 2006, the United States Supreme Court denied Jonathan Pollard's appeal to the highest court in the land. Noting that Pollard's attorneys had sought access to classified documents in his sentencing file, Reuters reported that, "without comment, the justices declined to review a U.S. appeals court ruling that federal courts lack jurisdiction to review claims for access to such documents for clemency purposes."

The article went on the say that Pollard's lawyers did not seek Supreme Court review of the other main part of the appeals court ruling: that Pollard had waited too long and therefore could not challenge his life sentence on the grounds that he had received ineffective legal advice.

Many Pollard supporters were convinced that the biggest roadblock preventing Jonathan Pollard's freedom had been set down two decades earlier by Caspar Weinberger. On March 27, President Ronald Reagan's former defense secretary, who was once pardoned by the senior President Bush for his alleged role in the Iran-contra affair, died, surrounded by family members, at the age of eighty-eight.

It was Weinberger's classified assessment of the damage Pollard allegedly caused to the United States that was handed to the judge who sentenced Pollard to life in 1987. With that damage assessment report remaining classified—and with Pollard's attorneys once again being thwarted in their attempt to see what it contained, this time by the U.S. Supreme Court— "Cap" Weinberger just may have taken his secrets with him to his grave.

By mid April 2006 Jonathan Pollard was again back in the news when reports once again began surfacing that Israel planned to release imprisoned terrorist and Palestinian leader Marwan Barghouti from an Israeli jail in exchange for the U.S. granting clemency for Pollard. The rationale was that the release of Barghouti would be a shot in the arm for Barghouti's Fatah faction, and could weaken Fatah's rival, Hamas—something deemed beneficial in Washington as well as in Jerusalem.

Both the U.S. and Israel denied there was anything to that story, however.

Two years earlier, when another proposed swap for Barghouti was reportedly being considered, Pollard stated that "from the outset, I have always been opposed to gaining my freedom in exchange for the release of murderers and terrorists." Pollard's Israeli attorney, Nitzana Darshan-Leitner, said Pollard would therefore not agree to any such exchange.

As reported in the *Jerusalem Post*, a senior source in Prime Minister Ehud Olmert's office also tried to douse the flames. "Barghouti has been tried in Israeli courts and convicted of murder," the source said. "This is not on the agenda."

On May 5, Porter Goss—who once said about Pollard: "There is absolutely no reason to let this guy out of jail"—resigned unexpectedly as director of the CIA.

***

After her return to South Florida from Los Angeles, in late May, I told Suzanne Migdall that Senator Chic Hecht, who had prostate cancer, had died earlier in the week. Hecht, a politically adept Nevada Republican, was the fellow who, according to John Loftus, once told Jewish leaders that Jonathan Pollard had "done something so horrible that it could never be made public."

What Hecht told those Jewish leaders, Loftus claimed in his 2003 *Moment* Magazine piece about Pollard, was that Pollard's spy operation had cost the lives of U.S. moles behind the Iron Curtain—something we now knew was the work of Aldrich Ames and Robert Hanssen.

"Chic Hecht died?" Suzanne asked. "Are you sure?"

"Yes," I said. "It was Chic Hecht, the Nevada senator."

"Elliot," Suzanne said, "don't you remember when I told you about the time I was flying to the Bahamas and sat next to a U.S. Senator? That was Chic Hecht. When I told him I wanted to do a movie on the Pollard spy case, he cringed."

Suzanne called Hecht "a very nice man who had had no ill will toward Jonathan Pollard; he was just given faulty information. He said, 'I'm still afraid to tell you everything I know about this case, but it's really bad. It's a lot worse than you think. It goes so high up, you have no idea. And I'm even afraid to talk about it now.'"

CHAPTER TWENTY-NINE

AN OLIVE BRANCH

AS JULY 2006 began, Jonathan Pollard once again found himself in the news. A press release made its way to my desk at the Jewish Federation about a new book scheduled for an August release: *Capturing Jonathan Pollard: How One of the Most Notorious Spies in American History was Brought to Justice.* According to a blurb from the book's publisher, Naval Institute Press, the author, Ron Olive, "gives details of Pollard's confession immediately following his arrest, and describes Pollard's interaction with the author before and during the time suspicion about his activities was mounting."

I had never heard of Ron Olive and Pollard never once mentioned his name in anything he sent me. Nor was his name mentioned in Wolf Blitzer's book about Pollard, *Territory of Lies*. I emailed an Israeli source of mine who had intimate knowledge of the case and asked if he knew anything about the author. According to my source, Ron Olive was one of the Naval Investigative Service (NIS) agents assigned to Pollard's case. "He was not the NIS case officer—the agent in charge—but he was assigned," my source explained. "Actually, it was an FBI case, and they, not NIS, were the lead agency on the Pollard matter. I'm not sure, but I believe that NIS does not have prosecutorial powers unless the defendant—in this case, Pollard—was a uniformed member of the Naval Service, which he was not."

Back on June 8, Abu Musab al-Zarqawi, Iraq's top al Qaeda leader who led a campaign of suicide bombings and the beheading of hostages—including the beheading of *Wall Street Journal* reporter Daniel Pearl—was killed by a U.S. air strike in an area northeast of Baghdad.

Days later, after being down two games to zero against the favored Dallas Mavericks, my beloved Miami Heat—I'm also a huge Miami Dolphins fan—rallied to win the next four games and take the NBA crown as World Champions. The great Dwayne Wade would win the Final's Most Valuable Player award; Alonzo Mourning, playing with a transplanted kidney, would finally get his World Championship ring; the "Big Diesel," Shaquille O'Neal, would live up to his promise of delivering a championship to Miami; and coach Pat Riley, who had gone eighteen years since winning his last one, finally got a huge monkey off his back.

It was a good week.

Then, on June 25, a young Israeli corporal, Gilad Shalit, was taken hostage by Palestinian guerillas during fighting in which other Israeli soldiers were killed. In response, Israeli tanks moved into Gaza.

By mid July the growing conflict in the Middle East had greatly escalated. After Hezbollah guerillas, aside from lobbing rockets into Israel, crossed into Israeli territory from southern Lebanon, killed two more soldiers, and seized three others, the

Israelis responded by imposing a naval blockade, striking two Lebanese air bases, and bombing runways at the international airport in Beirut. Israel was determined to destroy Hezbollah, would try not to destroy Lebanon in the process, and had the full backing and support of the country that mattered most, the United States. Soon, Israeli land troops were moving into southern Lebanon, going house to house to root out the enemy, and Hezbollah, like cornered rats, was fighting back with all it had.

Meanwhile, one of the most publicized victims of radical Islamic terror was about to have his story told, thanks to Brad Pitt and Angelina Jolie. As the fighting in Lebanon continued to rage, it was being widely reported that Jolie—and not Jennifer Aniston –would star as murdered *Wall Street Journal* reporter Daniel Pearl's wife, Marianne, in an adaptation of Marianne's book, *A Mighty Heart*. Pitt would produce the film.

A month later, with the war in the Middle East winding down but still not over, former president Jimmy Carter once again acted like—Jimmy Carter. In the August 15, 2006, edition of the German magazine, *Der Spiegel*, Carter was quoted as saying: "I don't think Israel has any legal or moral justification for their massive bombing of the entire nation of Lebanon. I represent the vast majority of Democrats."

Well, he certainly represented the vast majority of anti-Semites, although no one could say for certain that Carter was one himself.

On August 21, Ari Fleisher, George W. Bush's former press secretary, responded to Carter, arguably the least qualified president of the twentieth century. "I just read the transcript of your interview with the German magazine *Der Spiegel*, in which you accuse Israel of launching an 'unjustified attack on Lebanon'," Fleisher wrote. "As someone who served in the White House as a spokesman for a president, I am reluctant to criticize another president, but in this instance my conscience compels me to do so."

Fleisher called Carter's words "music to Hezbollah's ears," adding that Carter's message was a "blow to long-term peace."

"Just as you underestimated the threat of the Soviet Union in the 1970s, you underestimate the threat of radical Islam today," Fleisher continued. "Your condemnation of Israel, the victim, only encourages Hezbollah, the attacker, to bide its time and attack again... I'm sorry to see you articulate about Hezbollah and its aggression the same weak world view that encouraged Soviet aggression...Sadly, Hezbollah today is planning its next war. For the sake of peace, Israel deserves your praise, not your condemnation."

A few weeks later an interesting story appeared about the FBI evidence being displayed, regarding the Oklahoma City bombing, at the Oklahoma City Bombing Memorial and Museum. According to Associated Press writer Ron Jenkins, while hundreds of FBI agents had worked in the multi-state investigation to link Timothy McVeigh and Terry Nichols to the explosion that killed one hundred and sixty-eight people on April 19, 1995, Rep Dana Rohrabacher (R-Cal)—chair of the Oversight Investigations Subcommittee of the International Relations Committee—still planned to conduct hearings to explore "possible foreign connections to the bombing."

Strangely, Rohrabacher was also one of only twenty-one members of Congress who voted against House and Senate resolutions of support for Israel in its war with Hezbollah. Others included Illinois Democrat Jessie L. Jackson Jr., son of the reverend; Georgia Democrat Cynthia McKinney, who espoused bizarre conspiracy theories about the terrorist attacks of 9-11; and California Democrat Gary A. Condit, whose name was once linked to the murder of Chandra Levy, a young aide he was allegedly having an affair with.

On September 15, Jonathan Pollard's old spy-handler, Rafi Eitan, was once again in the news. Noted Gil Hoffman in the *Jerusalem Post*, when asked what should be done to bring about Pollard's release, Eitan said, "No one knows what could get him free." However, referring to Pollard's outspoken wife, Esther, Eitan added: "There is no doubting that his wife is in the way."

Esther immediately responded. "There has been an ongoing treacherous complicity between Rafi Eitan and successive governments of Israel, which, more than any other factor, is what is keeping Jonathan in prison," she said.

In a September 2006 issue of the Israeli newspaper *Haaretz*, following the publication of the Ron Olive book *Capturing Jonathan Pollard*, *Haaretz* correspondent Amir Oren noted allegations by Olive that "prior to Jonathan Pollard's attempt to seek refuge in the Israeli embassy in Washington, D.C., on November 21, 1985, the Federal Bureau of Investigation did not suspect that he may have been spying for Israel."

The headline of the *Haaretz* story read: "New book reveals FBI did not suspect Pollard ties to Israel."

Oren added, "In fact, even though he was a civilian analyst for U.S. Naval Intelligence, the FBI did not even know that Pollard was Jewish."

All that was true, but this information was not "revealed" for the first time in Mr. Olive's book. Truth be told, what happened to Mr. Pollard during his interrogation, and the reasons why the FBI thought that, if Pollard was a spy at all, he may have been spying for a country other than Israel, most likely Pakistan, was actually revealed in both my books on the Pollard case: *The*

Hunting Horse, which came out in 2000, and *The Spy Who Knew Too Much*, which came out in 1993.

Referring to the Olive book, Oren correctly noted that, "During his confession, Pollard gave information regarding the scale of his espionage, the methods and the payments, but led his interrogators astray when he told them that the material was given to a CBS reporter in Afghanistan who then sent it on to Pakistan or another country."

What Pollard was trying to accomplish—as he noted in letters he sent me prior to the publication of *The Spy Who Knew Too Much*—was to lead the FBI and Naval Intelligence Service (NIS) investigators on a wild goose chase while keeping the scent off the Israelis. (Chapter Eight in *The Hunting Horse*, titled The Trail of Secrets, goes into this in great depth.) Meanwhile, the Pakistani/Afghan connection proved to be quite a serpentine trail itself, involving arms dealing, heroin trafficking, the skimming of missiles, and a CBS reporter—and alleged CIA asset—named Kurt Lohbeck, who, according to Pollard, approached him and allegedly may have been working with, of all people, a then de facto U.S. ally in Afghanistan named Osama bin Laden.

An Israeli intelligence source, reacting to the *Haaretz* piece, wrote to me: "The only information that is 'new' is the identity of the agent who burned Pollard and his case officer. As you know, I have always suspected that Pollard was burned by an Israeli working for the CIA, rather than some co-worker, as Ron Olive would have us believe. Counterintelligence is just not that good. In more than ninety-nine percent of the cases, a mole is uncovered in his 'sponsor's' territory, not within the area of operations (AO)."

My source alleged it was Andrzej Kielczynski (a.k.a. Joseph Barak), a member of the Likud Central Committee, who reported the existence of the "Hunting Horse" to his CIA handler,

Thomas Votz. "You see what it does to the old saw, "friends don't spy on friends, bullshit," my source concluded.

On March 18, 2007, something strange happened as I returned to my home in Tamarac, Florida, from Fort Lauderdale-Hollywood International Airport. I had spent the day in Pinellas County, Florida, near Tampa, where I was a guest speaker at an event featuring my book *The Hunting Horse*. Unbelievably, I made every light from the airport to my home—a ride that usually takes close to forty minutes. In thirty years of living in the area; in taking dozens of trips to and from the airport, that was the first time that had ever happened.

Maybe it was some kind of an omen.

On May 21, *The Jerusalem Post* reported remarks made by the U.S. ambassador to Israel, Richard H. Jones, stating that Jonathan Pollard was fortunate he didn't receive a blindfold and a cigarette for spying for the Israelis.

"It came out in the trial, very clearly, that Jonathan Pollard took money for what he did; he sold out his country," Jones said during an address at Bar Ilan University near Tel Aviv. "The fact that he wasn't executed is the mercy that Jonathan Pollard will receive."

"This is a very emotional issue in the United States," Jones added. "I know he was helping a friend, but that's what makes it even more emotional for Americans—if a friend (Israel) would cooperate in aiding and abetting someone who is committing treason against his own country."

Esther Zeitz Pollard reacted immediately.

"Jones' declaration that Jonathan Pollard 'got off easy' because he deserved to be shot is wantonly malicious," Zeitz Pollard said, "especially since he knows that Jonathan didn't commit treason, which is the only crime which carries the death penalty."

The following day, Jones apologized for his remarks saying they were "misinformed and misleading" and that they did not reflect his own personal views, or the views of the Bush administration.

"I certainly do not personally believe that Mr. Pollard should have received capital punishment," Jones said. "I was appalled to learn that I had given that impression."

CHAPTER THIRTY

SPOOKED BY ABRAMOFF

DURING THE FIRST week of January 2008, while the Republican and Democratic primaries were going on in the U.S., President Bush was in Israel, meeting with Prime Minister Ehud Olmert and trying to once again push the peace process forward—a formidable task. In preparation for Bush's trip, Israeli Cabinet Minister Eli Yishai, of Israel's largely Orthodox and hawkish Shas Party, which was part of Israel's ruling coalition, called upon Bush to release Jonathan Pollard.

At the same time, with the Democratic and Republican primaries drawing to a close—with a woman (Hillary Clinton) and African-American (Barack Obama) vying for the nomination on the Democratic side, and a senior citizen (John McCain) on the side of the GOP—it was clear that the winds of change were upon us.

As April rolled around, former president Jimmy Carter was once again making news for himself by meeting with Islamic terrorists—this time leaders of Hamas.

Then, on April 22, a story broke that could have had major repercussions for us in regards to the climate for our motion picture getting made, although I wasn't quite sure what those repercussions would be. It was reported, in the Associated Press, that Ben-ami Kadish, an 84-year-old former U.S. Army mechanical engineer, had been arrested on charges that—more than two decades earlier—he slipped classified U.S. documents about nuclear weapons, fighter jets, and missiles, to an employee of the Israeli consulate who also had received classified information from Jonathan Pollard.

Although the AP report didn't name the employee of the Israeli consulate who conspired with Kadish, other stories leaked to the media did. Reuters concluded that Kadish's alleged handler was Yossi Yagur, who was also Pollard's "katsa," or case officer, replacing Col. Avi Sella, who was never a true intelligence operative. (The whole Pollard operation had been run by spymaster Rafi Eitan, although I didn't see Eitan's name specifically linked to the Kadish story.)

According to Reuters, the arrest of Kadish indicated that the Israeli spying revealed by the Pollard case "may have spread wider than previously acknowledged."

Not surprisingly, Joe deGenova, the former U.S. attorney who prosecuted Pollard in the mid 1980s, agreed. "It was bigger than we thought, and they hid it well," deGenova said. Reuters also reported that it was deGenova who identified Kadish's intelligence contact as Yagur.

When the frail-looking Kadish made an appearance at a Manhattan federal court following his arrest, he had no comment for reporters. Reuters, meanwhile, reported that Israeli Foreign Ministry spokesman Arye Mekel, when commenting on the four counts of conspiracy and espionage levied against

Kadish, said: "We know nothing about it. We heard it from the media."

As for Pollard, he said in an interview that he had never even heard of Kadish until he learned of Kadish's arrest.

On her website, Justice for Jonathan Pollard (J4JP), Pollard's wife, Esther, wrote: "It is not clear for how many years the U.S. has been sitting on this 'breaking news' story, waiting for the right moment to hurl new accusations against Israel, and falsely, and unfairly, target Jonathan Pollard by association."

Eitan Haber, who served as then-Defense Minister Yitzhak Rabin's assistant at the time of the Pollard affair, agreed. Haber, in an Israeli interview, said the revelation of a new "Israeli spy" was aimed at sabotaging a presidential pardon for Pollard—and thwarting any chances of seeing Pollard released before George Bush left office. "One would be a fool to believe that the timing is a coincidence," Haber said.

As for the possibility that Bush was going to pardon Pollard, Haber added: "Whoever initiated the new affair may have very well taken this into account, not wanting to see Pollard outside the prison walls. Pollard's main pursuers continue to be all of the intelligence branches of the U.S.—which are joining forces in preventing his release."

In early May, Suzanne Migdall went to Israel for the first time and, along with others in her entourage, had a private meeting with Benjamin Netanyahu. The subject of Pollard never came up.

Upon returning from Israel, Suzanne had a meeting—a chance meeting, this time—with a woman who had been stationed at the Israeli embassy in Washington, D.C. on November 21, 1985—the day Pollard was arrested. This woman had actually witnessed Pollard being turned away from the embassy and into the waiting hands of the FBI.

When Suzanne told me this I couldn't help but think about how she also sat on that flight to the Bahamas next to Senator Chic Hecht, who, perhaps more than anyone, may have been responsible for initially advising Jewish leaders to "stand down" on Pollard.

Once again the coincidences were eerie.

On May 27, it was reported that the legendary director Sydney Pollack passed away. Pollack once had a passing interest in our project, I was told, but nothing ever came of it. Notwithstanding, back in February of 2008, Christian Taylor, who was involved with Suzanne and a partner of hers on their "Huntsville Mystery Illness" project (which had to do with a Texas prison and the testing of biological germs on prisoners) —and had introduced Suzanne to Katie Haber, who was friendly with filmmakers Ridley and Tony Scott—said Mirage Enterprises, the production company run by Pollack and Anthony Minghella, apparently had an interest in the Huntsville project, while, an interest in the Pollard project had possibly been rekindled as well.

It turned out to be a false alarm. Franklin Leonard, head of Production and Development for Mirage, told Suzanne that Pollack was already too sick to consider any further projects.

Interestingly, Suzanne and her husband, Allan, had both been extras in the motion picture *Absence of Malice*, which was shot in South Florida and directed by Pollack, while Suzanne's close friend, Beverly McDermott, had been one of the films casting directors.

On June 21, Pauline Jelinek of the Associated Press reported that Israel held a large scale military exercise aimed at showing that country's ability to attack Iranian nuclear facilities. Jelinek noted that, after the Israelis sent their warplanes on a major exercise in the eastern Mediterranean, Pentagon officials said Israel's military refused to either confirm or deny that the maneuvers were practice for a strike in Iran.

The *New York Times* meanwhile also reported that more than 100 Israeli F-16s and F-15s staged the maneuver, "flying more than 900 miles, roughly the distance from Israel to Iran's Natanz nuclear enrichment facility."

According to the Associated Press, State Department spokesperson Sean McCormack would not comment on whether the United States supported, or opposed, any future Israeli strikes against Iran.

Longtime Pollard advocate Jon Voight, meanwhile, took on some of the more ardent supporters of Barack Obama. I personally liked Obama—it was hard not to—but, in an op-ed piece published in July in the *Washington Times*, Voight, an admitted Conservative, attacked the Democratic Party for "creating a God-like figure in a man who falls short in every way. If God forbid, we live to see Mr. Obama president," Voight continued, "we will live through a socialist era that America has not seen before."

Voight knew his comments could cost him work in Hollywood, which is exceedingly Liberal. He spoke his mind, just the same.

On November 2, 2008, producer-director John Daly's obituary appeared in the *Miami Herald*, two days before writer and Harvard-trained medical doctor Michael Crichton (*Jurassic Park*) also passed on, and two days before Barack Obama made history by being the elected the first black or bi-racial president of the United States. Daly had once been genuinely interested in the Pollard project and, at the time, Suzanne sent him material to look over, including a treatment.

The British-born independent producer of thirteen Oscar-winning movies, including *Platoon* and *The Last Emperor,* Daly was described by one friend as "witty, stylish and debonair—like Cary Grant."

In an article appearing in *Hollywood Today*, Daly was also hailed as "one of the first to show that you could make money and take in major awards with film market-funded projects and without big studios." According to *Hollywood Today*, Daly's company, Hemdale, was involved in over one-hundred pictures—including box office hits like *Terminator*—that grossed over $1.5 billion.

Suzanne knew that Daly, seventy-one, had terminal cancer and I called her to tell her the news of his passing. She was saddened but not surprised. Daly's death also brought to mind a story Suzanne once told me: that Daly let her know that he couldn't get involved with the Pollard project because, if he did, there would be "serious repercussions." The warning, which Daly's financial backers took seriously, allegedly came from Jack Abramoff, the former Washington lobbyist with close ties to the administration of George W. Bush.

"[Daly] was going forward with the project until, as he confided in me later, he got a call to 'stand down'," Suzanne said. "He really wanted to produce the movie, and he never did tell me, at the time, why he didn't go forth with it."

Abramoff, meanwhile, was a controversial character to say the least. On the second day of January 2006, Abramoff pled guilty in a Miami courtroom to federal conspiracy and wire fraud charges. He admitted that, along with a New York businessman named Adam Kidan, he conspired to defraud lenders in the purchase of SunCruz Casinos, a South Florida fleet of gambling ships.

On his January 3, 2006 news show, Jim Lehrer asked reporter Jay Weaver, who was covering the story for the *Miami Herald*, about Abramoff and former SunCruz owner Gus Boulis, a successful South Florida businessman and Greek immigrant who had been the founder of Miami Subs before pouring his money into the SunCruz fleet.

"For the record, the original owner of the cruise ships, the guy from Greece, he was murdered, was he not?" Lehrer asked. "There was no connection—was there ever a connection established between that murder and Abramoff?'

"Well, that's always been the $64,000 question," Weaver replied. "About five months after the sale of his SunCruz Casino empire, [Boulis] was gunned down, mob style, on the streets of Fort Lauderdale, as he was leaving his business in his BMW."

Five years later, three men were arrested in connection with the murder, but neither Abramoff nor Kidan were charged. While Abramoff has never been implicated in Boulis' murder, "Fort Lauderdale police still have their eye on Kidan," Weaver told Lehrer.

That being said, John Daly's financial backers had obviously been spooked by Abramoff, and, at the time, apparently took Abramoff's alleged threat quite seriously.

In retrospect, who could blame them?

CHAPTER THIRTY-ONE

WILL OF THE NATION

ON MAY 1, 2009, just days before the start of the American-Israel Public Affairs Committee (AIPAC) annual policy conference in Washington, it was reported that federal prosecutors asked Judge T.S. Ellis III to drop the charges against two ex-AIPAC staffers accused of passing classified information to Israel. According to Dana Boente, the acting U.S. attorney for the Eastern District of Virginia, the government would have been unable to prove that defendants Keith Weissman, AIPAC's former Iran analyst; and Steve Rosen, its former foreign policy chief, intended not only to assist Israel, but to harm the United States.

Thus apparently ended the saga that began on August 28, 2004, when a story broke that a then unnamed analyst for Douglas J. Feith, a U.S. undersecretary of defense, and the number three ranking official in the Pentagon, may have acted as a spy for Israel. The unnamed analyst—later revealed to be Lawrence Franklin—had reportedly taken classified information, having to do with secret White House deliberations on Iran, to his contacts at AIPAC, which allegedly then passed this information on to the Israelis.

Upon hearing the news that the charges were finally dropped against Weissman and Rosen, an Israeli source of mine said the case against AIPAC had always been a "smear," and opined that "those particular staffers were targeted."

Alan Dershowitz agreed. The famed attorney, whose latest book was *The Case Against Israel's Enemies*, called what some deemed a witch-hunt "the worst case of selective prosecution I have seen in forty-two years of legal practice."

On June 1, a week after a Washington meeting between President Obama and Prime Minister Netanyahu, the head of the Israel Defense Forces (IDF) Military Intelligence Research Division informed the Knesset Foreign Affairs and Defense Committee that Iran was only one year away from obtaining enough material for a nuclear weapon.

"By the end of the year, Iran may have enough fissile material for their first nuclear bomb," Brigadier Gen. Yossi Beiditz told the committee during the briefing as reported by Hana Levi Julian. According to Levi Julian, Beiditz added that Iran was developing its nuclear weaponry "at a faster pace than before and that negotiations are unable to halt the process."

***

On December 23, 2009—just a few days before Christmas—the Associated Press reported that former President Jimmy Carter, in an open letter, apologized for "any words or deeds that may have upset the Jewish community." The former president said he was offering an *Al Het*—a plea for forgiveness often said on Yom Kippur, the holiest of Jewish holidays. Carter's letter was first sent to the Jewish Telegraphic Agency, a wire service for Jewish newspapers, and then provided to the Associated Press.

"We must not permit criticisms for improvement to stigmatize Israel," Carter wrote. "As I would have noted at Rosh Hashanah and Yom Kippur—but which is appropriate at any time of the year—I offer an *Al Het* for any words or deeds of mine that may have done so."

Carter's apology was welcomed by many in the Jewish community including Abe Foxman, national director of the Anti-Defamation League, who had been a vocal critic of Carter's stated views on Israel in the past. The Council on American-Islamic Relations (CAIR), meanwhile, declined comment.

On December 29, Mordecai Vananu, who, as noted earlier in this book, worked as a technician at Israel's Dimona nuclear power plant—and, in 1986, received an eighteen-year prison term for revealing Israel's nuclear weapons program before being freed by the Israelis in 2004—was ordered under house arrest. The reason, an Israeli spokesperson said, was that the non-repentant Vananu had "met with a number of foreigners," something he was forbidden to do as one of the terms of his release.

In March of 2010, as our motion picture project still remained on hold, tensions erupted between the Obama administration and Prime Minister Netanyahu when Israel's Interior Ministry announced plans to construct sixteen hundred new housing units in an east Jerusalem neighborhood—described as "disputed territory" by the Palestinians—just as Vice President Joe Biden's plane was landing in Israel.

Conservative columnist Cal Thomas, a strong supporter of Israel, was one of many who immediately reacted to the tough comments by both Biden and Secretary of State Hillary Clinton

who condemned the project, and especially the timing of the announcement, as "destructive," an "affront," and an "insult."

"To the Palestinians and their Arab and Muslim neighbors,
most especially Iran and Syria, all of Israel is 'disputed territory',"
Thomas said. "It is difficult to understand why the U.S. State
Department thinks that not building a few houses is going to
dissuade Israel's enemies."

Another firestorm erupted in late May when Israeli commandos launched a raid at sea on a pro-Palestinian flotilla on its way
to the Gaza strip. As a result of that raid—and a violent response
by the activists aboard one of the ships, the Maru Mamri—nine
activists were killed. The aim of the flotilla—those taking part
included more than seven-hundred activists, four-hundred of
whom were Turks—had been to break the Israeli and Egyptian
blockage of the Gaza Strip while allegedly bringing in ten thousand tons of aid.

As usual, much of the world railed against Israel. However, as
the Associated Press reported, Israeli Prime Minister Netanyahu
rejected the calls to lift the blockade on Hamas-ruled Gaza, and
labeled worldwide criticism of the Israeli raid as "hypocrisy."

Andrew Rosenkranz, Florida Regional Director of the Anti-
Defamation League, agreed, noting in an op-ed that Israel im-
posed the blockade on Gaza "in response to Hamas' takeover of
Gaza four years ago, and its ongoing barrage of rockets aimed at
Israeli civilians." Rosenkranz added that, "despite the blockade,
Israel allows the flow of essential goods into Gaza every day and
ensures that humanitarian needs are met, including food, medi-
cines, fuel and electricity."

Referring to the reason for the boarding of the Maru Mamri
by Israeli commandos that led to the deaths of the nine activists,
Netanyahu said the aim of the flotilla was to break the blockade,

not to bring aid to Gaza. "If the blockade ended," Netanyahu said bluntly, "hundreds of ships would bring in thousands of missiles from Iran.

"This was not the 'Love Boat.' It was the hate boat."

On June 9, Washington lobbyist Jack Abramoff, who was sentenced in 2006 to more than five years in prison on a fraud conviction over his purchase of SunCruz casinos, and was accused by the late motion picture producer John Daly of allegedly making threats against his financiers, was set free.

The summer of 2010 turned into the fall, and, while nothing significant was happening with our motion picture deal, there were some rumblings regarding the Pollard case, thanks to an old ally. That ally, Lawrence Korb, a former assistant secretary of defense in the Reagan administration, had, in the past, been highly critical of the man he had once worked under, Defense Secretary Caspar Weinberger, whose memorandum to the judge in the Pollard case set the wheels of justice in motion that proceeded to run Pollard over.

Specifically, Pollard's name was once again popping up in the media because of an opinion piece Korb wrote that had legs once it appeared on October 28, 2010, in the *Los Angeles Times*. A senior fellow at the Center for American Progress, a Washington, D.C. think tank, Korb attempted to set the record straight about the Pollard case, with the intent of persuading President Obama to grant Pollard clemency. In his op-ed Korb acknowledged that Pollard originally deserved to go to prison but stressed that the punishment should have fit the crime. "In this case," Korb wrote, "it does not."

Korb then went on to lay out the facts in the case, arguing that Pollard had originally agreed to plea bargain to one count of passing classified information to an American ally, and the

U.S. attorney agreed that, in return, he would not seek a life sentence. Korb also mentioned the Weinberger memo; that James Woolsey, the CIA director from 1993 to 1995, believed Pollard served long enough and should be released; and that, in a 2004 interview, Weinberger himself acknowledged that "in retrospect, the Pollard matter was comparatively minor."

The fact that Korb's op-ed appeared in the *Los Angeles Times*, no doubt read by many of the movers and shakers in Hollywood, couldn't hurt our so far challenging quest to sell our project and get our film made. And the fact that the op-ed was penned by a former assistant secretary of defense, who worked under Caspar Weinberger and served in the Defense Department at the time Pollard was caught spying for the Israelis, gave even more gravitas to the arguments Pollard's supporters had been making throughout his long incarceration.

Korb's op-ed seemed to take root. In early December, Israel's Knesset speaker, Ruby Rivlin, sent a letter from the Knesset to President Obama and Attorney General Eric Holder urging them to finally release Pollard. As Israeli journalist Hillel Fendel reported, the letter was signed by the leaders of every political party in Israel, including Labor and Likud—the only exception being Israel's Arab parties—representing one hundred and nine of the one hundred and twenty members of the Knesset.

The letter stressed, first and foremost, that "the State of Israel has taken full responsibility for Pollard's actions, and has apologized for them." Besides being an apology, however, the letter was surprisingly blunt.

"We feel that we must make you aware that many citizens of Israel sense that [Pollard] is being discriminated against, in comparison with other spies caught in the U.S.," the letter stated.

"This casts a shadow over the strong friendship between our two countries ..."

The letter continued: "There is no question that twenty-five years is more than enough in meting out justice to [Pollard] and the time has come to release him immediately. Please respond to this request affirmatively."

With the perception, whether factually-based or not, that Obama hadn't been overly supportive of Israel, the Knesset letter would hopefully weigh heavily on a beleaguered president beset by falling public opinion polls. As for the attempts to finance our motion picture, Pollard's clemency, if it happened during Obama's watch, could finally bring some closure to his story, as well—and make it a far more a feasible story for Hollywood to tell.

As expected, the New Year brought new hope for Jonathan Pollard. In a speech before the Knesset, on January 4, 2011, Israeli Prime Minister Netanyahu publicly appealed to the president to release Pollard—using a far more apologetic tone than the Knesset did in its letter, and promising that Israel would never again spy on the United States.

"Jonathan has suffered greatly for his actions and his health has deteriorated considerably," Netanyahu said. "Both Mr. Pollard and the government of Israel have repeatedly expressed remorse for these actions, and Israel will continue to abide by its commitment that such wrongful actions will never be repeated."

The prime minister added: "At the time of his arrest, Pollard was acting as an agent of the Israeli government. Even though Israel was in no way directing its intelligence efforts against the United States, its actions were wrong and totally unacceptable."

Three weeks later, on January 26—as Egyptians were flooding the streets of Cairo to demand the resignation of President

Hosni Mubarak in a popular revolution inspired by events in Tunisia, with at least some of the flames being stroked by the radical Muslim Brotherhood—Gil Hoffman reported in the *Jerusalem Post* that Philip B. Heymann, a former U.S deputy attorney general, had requested that President Obama release Jonathan Pollard. According to Hoffman, Heymann—the James Barr Professor of Law at Harvard Law School, author of two books on terrorism, and the director of Harvard Law School's International Center for Criminal Justice—became the first U.S. official to state he had reviewed Pollard's complete record and found no evidence that he helped America's enemies.

Heymann also became the second senior Harvard Law School professor to write Obama, asking him to commute Pollard's life sentence to the more than twenty-five years he had already served. The first, Hoffman noted, was Charles Ogletree, who was a mentor to both the president and his wife, Michelle. .

"Having already served a severe sentence, Pollard is now supported by political and religious leaders across the political spectrum in seeking a commutation," Heymann wrote in a letter to the president. "I join them with deep conviction as to the justice of their shared cause."

While Egypt was descending into total chaos as Israel and the rest of the world watched, Jonathan Pollard was picking up another supporter—perhaps his most important ally, yet. That new ally, Republican Mike Huckabee, the former governor of Arkansas who had come up short in his 2008 bid for the presidency, but was poised to make another run in 2012, arrived in Israel with actor Jon Voight.. They both met with Prime Minister Netanyahu.

On February 1 the *Jerusalem Post* reported that Voight called Pollard's life sentence "beyond injustice," and "a clear case of anti-Semitism."

According to the *Jerusalem Post,* Huckabee stated that, as a gesture of friendship to Israel, President Obama should commute Pollard's sentence. "Right now," Huckabee said, "we don't need anything that reflects that we are anything but an absolute ally of Israel. [Freeing Pollard] would send the right message to the rest of the world: that America is not pulling back on its friendship and relationship with Israel, but it is accelerating it and making sure that we are taking every step possible to solidify those bonds."

If Mike Huckabee was a big fish, then Pollard's next major supporter was nothing short of Moby Dick. On March 3, 2011, former Secretary of State Henry Kissinger sent a letter to the president asking him to finally set Pollard free.

"I gave much thought to the question of clemency for Jonathan Pollard," Kissinger wrote. "At first I felt I did not have enough information to render a reasoned and just opinion. But having talked with [former Secretary of State] George Schultz and having read the statements of former CIA Director Woolsey, former Senate Intelligence Committee Chairman DeConcini, former Defense Secretary Weinberger, former Attorney General Mukasey and others whose judgments and first-hand knowledge I respect, I find their unanimous support for clemency compelling."

Although Kissinger didn't mention him by name, former Vice President Dan Quayle also said he was in favor of clemency.

Kissinger concluded: "I believe justice would be served by commuting the remainder of Pollard's sentence of life imprisonment."

***

According to the *Jerusalem Post*, Israeli President Shimon Peres, who had served as prime minister when Pollard was spying for Israel, also raised the issue of Pollard, on April 5, during an Oval Office luncheon with President Obama. The *Post* reported that while speaking to reporters afterwards Peres said he requested that Obama grant Pollard clemency, and also raised the issue of kidnapped Israeli soldier Gilad Schalit, who, if still alive, was being held somewhere in the Middle East by Muslim radicals. When asked by a reporter what Obama's reaction was, Peres replied, "He heard."

The following day the *Jerusalem Post* reported that television evangelist Pat Robertson, the head of the powerful Christian Broadcasting Network—and a longtime advocate for Pollard's release—also sent a letter to President Obama asking for a commutation of Pollard's sentence.

"Pollard's sentence has been totally disproportionate," Robertson noted, "to any concept of what we have of justice."

Following the reporting of Robertson's letter, Yigal Shleifer opined, in the *Jerusalem Report*, that "the rejuvenated campaign on behalf of Pollard is being driven by a new generation of activists who have joined together with a reenergized older generation of supporters and decided to bring his case back into the headlines. Although opposition to Pollard's release still exists in Washington, the passing of the years appears to have muted the opposition significantly, leaving many to believe that clemency for the convicted spy is closer than ever before."

During the evening of May 1 the world was informed that Osama bin Laden, thanks to a bold attack by U.S. Navy Seal Team Six on bin Laden's secret compound thirty-five miles north of Islamabad, Pakistan, was no longer among the living. America rejoiced.

On June 6, after weeks of denials, a tearful U.S. Rep. Anthony Weiner, a congressman from New York and a rising star in the Democratic Party, confessed that he "tweeted" a sexually suggestive photo to a young woman, and also admitted to having "inappropriate" exchanges with other women, both before and after his marriage to an assistant to Hillary Clinton. When I appeared live on CNN, in 2003, to talk about the Pollard case it was Weiner who also appeared, in a taped interview, to argue that Pollard's harsh prison sentence was blatantly unjust.

In mid August, Suzanne Migdall was contacted by a motion picture investor with a multi-million dollar film fund. Suzanne emailed me, "I am following up on this, and will keep you in the loop."

On August 21, an op-ed on Pollard by Alan Dershowitz appeared in the *Jerusalem Post*. It was good to see that, like Don Quixote, Dershowitz was still tilting at that windmill.

In his op-ed Dershowitz noted "several reasons why justice demands that Pollard's sentence be commuted to time served and that he be immediately released."

"The first is a legal and constitutional argument," Dershowitz wrote. "Pollard waived his right to trial by jury in exchange for a promise by the government that it would not seek life imprisonment. The government broke that promise."

The constitutional law professor added: "I know of no other case in American jurisprudence in which a plea bargain has been so blatantly violated and the violation approved by an appellate court."

After delving into a number of facts surrounding the case, Dershowitz concluded: "Pollard's continued imprisonment, in violation of law, equality, justice and compassion, is a stain on America. This stain can be removed if President Obama commutes Pollard's sentence to time served."

Vice President Joe Biden is known for putting his foot in his mouth. This time, though, an inflammatory comment he made was apparently a trial balloon being floated for his boss, the president, to see which way the wind was blowing in the Jewish community in regards to Pollard.

"President Obama was considering clemency, but I told him 'Over my dead body are we going to let him out before his time,'" the *New York Times* reported that Biden said during an October 1 meeting with fifteen rabbis in Boca Raton, Florida.

On October 2, a day after Biden ignited a minor firestorm by his comments on the Pollard case, the *Jerusalem Post* reported that Obama had yet to respond to another request from both Israeli President Shimon Peres and Prime Minister Netanyahu to grant clemency to Pollard.

As Obama was carefully weighing his options, some important Jewish leaders were publicly reacting to Biden's controversial remarks, while Israeli Knesset Speaker Reuven Rifkin also noted his objections. Malcolm Honlein, executive vice chairman of the Conference of Presidents of Major American Jewish Organizations; and Anti-Defamation League Director Abe Foxman were among those who called on Biden to reconsider his views.

With the perception by many that Obama hadn't been overly supportive of Israel, the Pollard issue had to weighing heavily on a beleaguered president, beset by falling public opinion polls, who would probably need the overwhelming support of Jewish voters to carry a swing state like Florida and win the next election. The question was, would Obama, unlike his predecessors—Ronald Reagan, George Herbert Walker Bush, Bill Clinton, and George W. Bush—dare step out on such a precarious limb and finally set Pollard free?

What could hang in the balance, after all, was not only the fate of Jonathan Pollard. What was at stake, quite possibly, was the fate of the Obama presidency itself.

On October 18, Israeli soldier Gilad Schalit was released by his captors in exchange for four hundred and seventy seven Palestinian prisoners—the first step in the release of one thousand and twenty-seven prisoners that Israel agreed to free within two months.

Days later, Libyan dictator Muammar Quaddafi was killed by rebels fighting against his regime—his end similar to that of fellow despot, Saddam Hussein.

On October 27, Barbara Walters appeared on the *ABC Nightly News* to talk about her exclusive interview of Ponzi schemer Bernie Madoff in Butner prison. At he end of the segment Walters said to George Stephanopoulos, "In the next cell is Jonathan Pollard, the convicted spy—you remember him."

On November 22, the anniversary of the Kennedy assassination and the day after the anniversary of Pollard's arrest, it was reported that a number of U.S. Jewish leaders met with Vice President Biden, intent upon changing his mind over pardoning Pollard. In addition, eighteen ex-senators submitted a petition requesting a pardon to the president himself.

"Four drug dealers, a trafficker in stolen goods, a gambler and a turkey made President Obama's Thanksgiving list," Ron Kampeas reported for the Jewish Telegraphic Agency (JTA), "but Israel's best known spy did not."

Notwithstanding, the meeting between Biden and the key Jewish leaders lasted more than an hour in the vice president's office.

On December 11, following Biden's meeting with Jewish leaders over Pollard, then-leading Republican White House hopeful

Newt Gingrich also discussed Pollard in a CNN interview with Wolf Blitzer. In regards to Pollard, Gingrich told Blitzer he was "leaning toward clemency" but hadn't seen all the information to make up his mind.

A strong supporter of Israel, Gingrich then ignited a bit of a firestorm of his own when he was quoted as calling the Palestinians "an invented people," and added he believed in taking an aggressive approach to keep Iran from going nuclear.

Of Pollard, Gingrich said, "I am prepared to say my bias is toward clemency," adding he had a study under way "to compare Pollard's sentence with comparable people who have been handed very long sentences for comparable deeds."

Three days later, Israeli journalist Tzvi Ben Gedalyahu reported a charge by Alan Dershowitz that Bill Clinton might have freed Pollard, in 2000, if Jewish senators had stood up for him. According to Gedalyahu, at the annual Israel Business Forum, Dershowitz revealed that he had talked to Clinton, who, at the time, was approaching the end of his term. "Clinton told me," said Dershowitz, 'How can you expect me to release Jonathan Pollard when your own senators wrote me a letter not to release him'."

I immediately recalled the article John Loftus wrote in 2003 that appeared in *Moment Magazine* in which Loftus argued that the reason Jewish leaders didn't rally to Pollard's side, early on, was because, prior to Pollard's sentencing in March of 1987, Senator Chic Hecht had urged them not to.

And, once again, I also couldn't help but think of the conversation Suzanne Migdall said she had with Hecht when they sat next to each other on that flight to the Bahamas. Hecht, who, in my opinion, was fed faulty information by the CIA, told Suzanne that the case was "a lot worse than you think. It goes so high up, you have no idea."

On April 6, 2012, it was reported that, following a serious decline in his health, Pollard had to be hospitalized a few miles from his prison cell at Butner. Days later, Pollard's wife, Esther, met with former Israeli Prime Minister Shimon Peres in Jerusalem to once again urge Peres to do what he could to set Pollard free. Now the Israeli president, Peres was scheduled to receive America's Presidential Medal of Freedom from President Obama in June.

A few days later the *New York Times* reported that a close personal relationship between Mitt Romney—who had virtually all but locked up the Republican presidential nomination—and Israeli Prime Minister Netanyahu, had existed for over thirty years. Surely, the subject of Pollard had come up in their discussions

"We can almost speak in shorthand," the *Times* quoted Romney as saying about himself and the prime minister. "We have common experiences, and a perspective and underpinning which is similar."

At the same time, speaking as a guest, May 6, on *This Week*, Sen. John McCain, critical of the Obama administration's supposedly chilly relationship with Netanyahu, told host Jake Tapper, "On Israel, the relationship has never been worse."

On June 13, the *Wall Street Journal* reported that while Shimon Peres would be departing the U.S. with the Presidential Medal of Freedom—the nation's highest civilian honor—the Israeli president would, nevertheless, not succeed in persuading the U.S. to let Pollard out of prison.

The Israeli media reported that Peres even brought with him a petition signed by over seventy thousand Israelis seeking Pollard's release. Apparently unmoved, White House spokesman Jay Carney said the request would not be granted.

"Our position regarding Pollard has not changed, and will not change today," Carney stated emphatically. "I would simply remind you that Mr. Pollard was convicted of extremely serious crimes."

Notwithstanding, Peres told Fox News, a day earlier, that "Israelis feel very strongly about [Pollard], and I understand their sentiments. I am not [seeking Pollard's release] as a diplomat, but as a human being."

Then, speaking on Israeli television, Peres said, "I feel like not only a humanistic emissary on the Pollard issue, but also as an emissary of the will of the nation."

At the same time, U.S. congressmen Chris Smith (R-NJ) and Eliot Engel (D-NY) were separately leading a bipartisan effort to free Pollard by seeking signatures to a letter of their own urging President Obama to use his power of clemency to commute Pollard's sentence to time served.

On June 14, Gil Hoffman meanwhile reported in the *Jerusalem Post* that, in spite of Jay Carney's comments, Obama had not exactly "slammed the door" on releasing Pollard—at least according to Peres' diplomatic advisor, Nadav Tamir.

"There was never a real expectation that Pollard would immediately return to Israel aboard the plane of President Shimon Peres," Hoffman wrote in the June 17 edition of the *Jerusalem Post*. "It would have made for a really good movie—but it was never going to happen."

One week later, coming out against clemency for Pollard, Martin Peretz, the former editor-in-chief of *The New Republic*, wrote an op-ed in the *Wall Street Journal* ("The Mendacious Movement to Free a Convicted Spy") in which he argued that "pretending that Jonathan Pollard is a martyr makes a mockery of Israel."

Before the end of the week newspapers around the world were also reporting the passing of Yitzhak Shamir. The ninety-six-year-old Shamir, who reportedly suffered from Alzheimer's disease, served as Israel's prime minister—as did Shimon Peres—when Pollard was spying for the Israelis.

In an op-ed of his own that appeared in the *Wall Street Journal*, on July 5, James Woolsey—who served as CIA director under Bill Clinton—responded to Peretz's commentary. "When I recommended against clemency, Pollard had been in prison less than a decade," Woolsey wrote. "Today, he has been incarcerated for over a quarter of a century under his life sentence."

"There is absolutely no reason for Pollard to be imprisoned for as long as [Aldrich] Ames and [Robert] Hanssen, and substantially longer than spies from other friendly, allied, and neutral countries," Woolsey concluded. "For those hung up for some reason that he's an American Jew, pretend he's a Greek-, or Korean-, or Filipino-American—and free him."

The *Jerusalem Post* reported that after meeting with Prime Minister Netanyahu in Israel, on July 16, Secretary of State Hillary Clinton addressed the Pollard issue with the Israeli media, stating that she did not expect Pollard to be released from prison.

"With respect to Mr. Pollard, he was convicted of espionage, sentenced to life imprisonment, and is serving that sentence," Clinton said. "I do not have any expectation that this will change."

A day earlier, Joseph deGenova, who prosecuted the Pollard case in 1987, reportedly said that President Obama's "animosity toward Israel" would stand in the way of a presidential pardon.

Referring to Hillary Clinton's remarks, a spokesperson for The Committee to Bring Jonathan Pollard Home said the secretary of state's words "represent a resounding slap in the face to President Peres, to Prime Minister Netanyahu, and to the people of Israel….However, Clinton isn't the decision maker, President Obama is."

As the 2012 Olympics began in London, and on the eve of presidential candidate Mitt Romney's visit to Israel—a country that President Obama had not yet visited while commander-in-chief—Edmund Sanders wrote an article that appeared on July 27 in the *Tribune* newspapers. "Though Romney has visited Israel before," Sanders wrote, "he will face challenges and minefields when dealing with the specifics of how he would restart peace talks, prevent Iran from building a nuclear bomb, and respond to Israeli calls for the U.S. to release imprisoned spy Jonathan Pollard, political strategists say."

On the eleventh anniversary of 9/11, an angry mob in Cairo scaled the walls of the U.S. embassy while burning the embassy's American flag in protest of a video that was made in the U.S and allegedly insulted the profit Mohammed.

The violence was far more deadly in Benghazi, Libya, where an armed attack of the U.S. Consulate—orchestrated this time by terrorists sympathetic to al Qaeda—resulted in the deaths of Ambassador Chris Stevens and three other Americans, two of whom were Navy Seals.

The protests soon spread to Sudan, Tunisia, Yemen and Lebanon—then spread throughout the Muslim world.

At the same time, an Israeli minefield was activated in Jerusalem when Prime Minister Netanyahu made it clear to President Obama—who reportedly turned down a request to meet with the prime minister in the U.S. later that month—that by failing to put down a "red line" Iran couldn't step across in its attempts to go nuclear, the U.S. had forfeited its right to stop Israel from taking unilateral military action against Iran.

"The world tells Israel, 'Wait, there's still time', and I say, 'Wait for what? Wait until when?'" Netanyahu told reporters.

On September 24, Iranian President Mahmoud Ahmadinejad spoke before the U.N., and, as he had before, repeated his mantra that Israel "has no roots in history."

Also brushing off threats from Israel to strike Iran's nuclear sites, Ahmadinejad said, "Fundamentally, we do not take seriously the threats of the Zionists. We have all the defensive means at our disposal and we are ready to defend ourselves...."

...

As the clock ticked toward a showdown between Israel and Iran, the 2012 presidential race was headed toward a reckoning of its own. While Barack Obama did go on to win a second term, still, no one could predict with any certainty what the future had in store for our nation; if we would be dragged into another Middle East war; or if Iran's leaders, intent perhaps on genocide, would be committing national suicide instead.

With war clouds looming overhead, what we did know for sure was that for me and my motion picture partner, Suzanne Migdall—as well as for all those who worked tirelessly and, in some cases, anonymously, behind the scenes to try to pry open Jonathan Pollard's prison cell door—it had been a most challenging journey. Nonetheless, we remained hopeful and optimistic that the fruits of our labor would finally result in this beleaguered man's long overdue freedom.

Our quest had always been a simple one: to right this wrong, tell a story that had to be told, make a difference in the world, and, in some small way, enhance both the image and security of Israel.

Pollard also had a dream; a dream to do something that even Moses, the deliverer of the Jews, was never able to accomplish. Jonathan Jay Pollard's dream was to once again set foot in the Promised Land.

And at long last, God willing, he would finally get his chance.

Bainerman, Joel. *The Crimes of a President: New Revelations on the Conspiracy and over-up in the Bush and Reagan Administrations.* New York: S.P.I. Books, 1992

Black, Edwin. *IBM and the Holocaust: The Strategic Alliance Between Nazi Germany and America's Most Powerful Corporation.* New York: Crown Publishers, 2001

Blitzer, Wolf. *Territory of Lies: The Rise, Fall, and Betrayal of Jonathan Jay Pollard.* New York: Harper & Row, 1989

Bodansky, Yossef. *Target America: Terrorism in the U.S. Today.* New York: S.P.I. Books, 1992

_____. *Bin Laden: The Man Who Declared War on America.* Roseville, California: Prima Publishing, 1999, 2001

Brewton, Pete. *The Mafia, CIA and George Bush: The Untold Story of America's Greatest Financial Debacle.* New York: S.P.I. Books, 1992

Cherkashin, Victor and Gregory Feiffer. *Spy Handler, Memoir of a KGB Officer: The True Story of the Man who Recruited Robert Hanssen and Aldrich Ames*. New York: Basic Books, 2005

Clinton, Bill. *My Life*. New York: Knopf, 2004

Cockburn, Andrew and Leslie. *Dangerous Liaison: The Inside Story of the U.S. Israeli Covert Relationship*. New York: HarperCollins, 1991

Coulter, Ann. *Treason*. New York: Three Rivers Press, 2003

Dershowitz, Alan. *The Case for Israel*. New Jersey: John Wiley & Sons, Inc., 2003

_____. *The Case Against Israel's Enemies*. New Jersey: John Wiley & Sons, Inc., 2008

Dyer, Wayne W. *Your Erroneous Zones*. New York: Avon Books, 1976

Early, Pete. *Family of Spies: Inside the John Walker Spy Ring*. New York: Bantam Books, 1988

Emerson, Steven. *American Jihad: The Terrorists Living Among Us*. New York: The Free Press, 2002

Franks, Tommy. *American Soldier*. New York: Regan Books, 2004

Friedman, Alan. *Spider's Web: The Secret History of How the White House Illegally Armed Iraq*. New York: Bantam books, 1993

Friedman, Thomas. *From Beirut to Jerusalem*. New York: Farrar, Straus and Giroux, 1989

Gabriel, Brigitte. *Because They Hate: A Survivor of Islamic Terror Warns America*. New York: St. Martin's Griffin, 2006

Goldenberg, Elliot. *The Hunting Horse: The Truth Behind the Jonathan Pollard Spy Case*. Amherst, New York: Prometheus Books, 2000

_____. *The Spy Who Knew Too Much: The Government Plot to Silence Jonathan Pollard*. New York: S.P.I. Books, 1993

Graham, Bob. *Intelligence Matters: The CIA, the FBI, Saudi Arabia, and the Failure of America's War on Terror*. New York: Random House, 2004

Haig, Alexander M., Jr., with Charles McCarry. *Inner Circle: How America Changed the World: a Memoir*. New York: Warner Books, 1992

Hersh, Seymour M. *The Price of Power: Kissinger in the Nixon White House*. New York: Summit Books, 1983

_____. *The Samson Option: Israel's Nuclear Arsenal and American Foreign Policy*. New York: Random House, 1991

_____. *Chain of Command: The Road from 9-11 to Abu Ghraib*. New York: HarperCollins, 2004

Hoffman, David. *The Oklahoma City Bombing and the Politics of Terror*. Feral House (Internet)

Horowitz, David. *Unholy Alliance: Radical Islam and the American Left*. Washington, D.C.: Regnery, 2004

Keegan, John. *Intelligence in War: The Value and Limitations of What the Military can Learn About the Enemy*. New York: Vintage Books, 2002

Loftus, John, and Mark Aarons. *The Secret War Against the Jews: How Western Espionage Betrayed the Jewish People*. New York: St. Martin's Press, 1994

Lohbeck, Kurt. *Holy War, Unholy Victory: Eyewitness to the CIA's Secret War in Afghanistan*. Washington, D.C.: Regnery, 1993

McCollugh, David. *Truman*. New York: Simon and Schuster, 1992

Meir, Golda. *My Life*. New York: Putnum, 1975

Miller, Judith. *God Has Ninety-Nine Names*. New York: Simon and Schuster, 1996

North, Oliver, with William Novak. *Under Fire: An American Story*. New York: HarperCollins, 1991

Ostrovsky, Victor, and Claire Hoy. *By Way of Deception: The Making and Unmaking of Mossad Officer*. New York: St. Martin's Press, 1990

Posner, Gerald L. *Secrets of the Kingdom: The Inside Story of the Saudi-U.S. Connection*. New York: Random House, 2005

Raviv, Dan. *Every Spy a Prince: The Complete History of Israel's Intelligence Community*. Boston: Houghton Mifflin, 1990

Raviv, Dan, and Yossi Melman. *Friends in Deed: Inside the U.S.-Israel Alliance*. New York: Hyperion, 1994

Richelson, Jeffrey T. *Spying on the Bomb: American Nuclear Intelligence from Nazi Germany to Iran and North Korea*. New York: W.W. Norton, 2006

Ross, Dennis. *The Missing Peace*. New York: Farrar Straus Giroux, 2004

Rushdie, Salman. *The Satanic Verses*. New York: Viking, 1988

Sada, George. *Saddam's Secrets: How an Iraqi General Defied and Survived Saddam Hussein*. Tennessee: Integrity Publishers, 2006

Shaw, Mark. *Miscarriage of Justice: The Jonathan Pollard Story*. St. Paul, Minnesota: Paragon House, 2001

Sick, Gary. *October Surprise: America's Hostages in Iran and the Election of Ronald Reagan*. New York: Random House, Times Books, 1991

Shannon, Elaine and Ann Blackman. *The Spy Next Door: The Extraordinary Secret Life of Robert Phillip Hanssen, the Most Dangerous Double Agent in FBI History*. New York: Grove Press, 2002

Suskind, Ron. The *Price of Loyalty: George W. Bush, the White House, and the Education of Paul O'Neill*. New York: Simon and Schuster, 2004

Taheri, Amir. *Holy Terror: Inside the World of Islamic Terror*. Bethesda, Maryland: Adler & Adler, 1987

Teicher, Howard. Twin *Pillars to Desert Storm: America's Flawed Vision in the Middle East from Nixon to Bush*. New York: William Morrow, 1993

Timmerman, Ken. *The French Betrayal of America*. New York: Crown Forum, 2004

Unger, Craig. *House of Bush House of Saud: The Secret Relationship Between the World's Two Most Powerful Dynasties*. New York: Scribner, 2004

Vise, David A. *The Bureau and the Mole: The Unmasking of Robert Phillip Hanssen*. New York: Grove Press, 2002

Weinberger, Caspar W. *Fighting For Peace: Seven Critical Years in the Pentagon*. New York: Warner Books, 1990

Woodward, Bob. *Veil: The Secret Wars of the CIA, 1981-1987*. New York: Simon and Schuster, 1987

_____. *Bush at War*. New York: Simon and Schuster, 2002

_____ . *Plan of Attack*. New York: Simon and Schuster, 2004

The 9-11 Commission Report. New York, London: W.W. Norton and Company, 2004

CURRENT AND FORTHCOMING TITLES FROM
STRATEGIC MEDIA BOOKS

BUCCANEER
The Provocative Odyssey of Jack
Reed, Adventurer, Drug Smuggler
and Pilot Extraordinaire

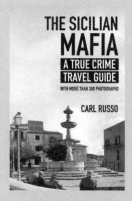

THE SICILIAN MAFIA
A True Crime Travel Guide

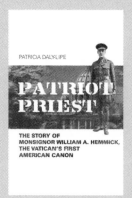

PATRIOT PRIEST
The Story of Monsignor William
A. Hemmick, The Vatican's First
American Canon

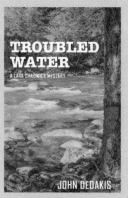

TROUBLED WATER
A Lark Chadwick Mystery

AVAILABLE FROM STRATEGICMEDIABOOKS.COM, AMAZON, AND MAJOR BOOKSTORES NEAR YOU.

WHITE BOY RICK
The true Story of a Detroit Street Legend

LUCKY LUCIANO
Mysterious Tales of a Gangland Legend

AMERICAN GANGSTER REVISITED
The True story of Frank Lucas

COMING IN 2014